Mediavisions

Mediavisions

The Art and Industry
of Mass Communication

Robert Henry Stanley

 PRAEGER

New York
Westport, Connecticut
London

Library of Congress Cataloging-in-Publication Data

Stanley, Robert Henry.
    Mediavisions : the art and industry of mass
communication.

    Bibliography: p.
    Includes index.
    1. Mass media—United States. I. Title.
P92.U5S64 1987   001.51'0973   87-6975
ISBN 0-275-92736-9 (alk. paper)
ISBN 0-275-92737-7 (pbk. : alk. paper)

Library of Congress Catalog Card Number 87-6975
ISBN: 0-275-92736-9
ISBN: 0-275-92737-7 (pbk)

First published in 1987

Praeger Publishers, 521 Fifth Avenue, New York, NY 10175
A division of Greenwood Press, Inc.

Printed in the United States of America

∞

The paper used in this book complies with the Permanent Paper Standard issued by the National Information Standards Organization (Z39.48-1984).

10 9 8 7 6 5 4 3 2 1

For Eija and Katri

Contents

Preface   ix

1 The Rise of Print Culture   1
2 The Hollywood Heritage   43
3 Social Control of Motion Pictures   95
4 Television's Roots in Radio   127
5 On Television   179

Notes   239
Index   251

Preface

We live in an environment permeated by the products of printing, motion pictures, radio, and television. Virtually every city in the United States has at least one newspaper. National magazines appear regularly on newsstands and through mail subscriptions. Paperbacks are plentiful and readily obtainable. Movies are available not only in theatres but on videocassettes as well. Homes and cars are equipped with one or more radios, while transistors bring radio fare to the peripatetic listener, wherever he or she may be. Television programs are especially pervasive and their influence is obviously profound.

How and why the world has become what it is today, and where it might be headed, have a great deal to do with these manifestations of mass communication—that is, of messages directed at and received by large, heterogeneous, geographically dispersed, and anonymous audiences.

This book is designed to provide a critical context for the analysis of both the aesthetics and the agencies of mass communication. Several pertinent questions are considered: How did mass communication evolve into the expressive forms we recognize today? What social processes and dynamics have shaped its subject matter? To what extent does the medium through which mass communication is conveyed affect social relationships and sensibilities? What social, political, economic, and technological factors have given dimension and direction to the industry of mass communication—the so-called mass media? What cultural consequences are traceable to mass media attempts to attract and hold the largest possible audiences? What has been the nature of government and self-regulatory controls over mass communication? How did the oligarchical structure of the American mass media evolve? How are new modes of distribution and exhibition—for example, satellite-to-cable networks and videocassettes—affecting the art and industry of mass communication?

The book is organized chronologically to facilitate analysis of developments in the art and industry of mass communication within the context of concurrent social, political, economic, and technological changes. Each of the book's five chapters has sub-headings to highlight specific subject matter. These sub-headings are also designed to permit reading assignments to be spread out over an entire semester.

The general writing style is informal and narrative. Quotations are used primarily to add flavor to the text and to do justice to ideas that could not be adequately paraphrased. Although the book is intended for students taking introductory or intermediate level courses in mass media and the popular arts, the vocabulary has not been graded for a specific level of comprehension. The language is neither patronizing nor obscure. While there are many words in the text students may not know, the basic concepts considered are readily accessible at the introductory level.

The ideas and information presented in the text owe much to the many writers cited in the footnotes. I am also grateful to my colleagues in the Media Studies Program at Hunter College for creating an environment conductive to critical analysis: James Aronson, Serafina Bathrick, Frank Brown, John Downing, Stuart Ewen, Samuel Fleishman, Arnold Gibbons, James Roman, and Larry Shore. In particular, coteaching with Samuel Fleishman helped to crystalize my thoughts about the art of mass communication. Coauthoring some articles with Ruth Ramsay, a linguistics specialist, helped to sharpen my writing style. Appreciation is also due to Mr. John Beddoe, who did a first-rate job of typing the manuscript. Above all, however, I wish to express my heartfelt thanks to my wife, Eija Ayravainen-Stanley, without whose love and support neither this book nor any of my other writing projects would have been completed. Eija and our daughter Katri, who was born during the period I was working on this book, are a constant source of inspiration.

1

The Rise of Print Culture

The invention and widespread use of printing from movable type—the first of the modern media—dramatically altered the entire fabric of Western culture, making literacy and education possible and ultimately opening the way to mass communication. The publication of books became an integral part of the excitement of the revival of learning in an age of discovery and of intrepid exploration. Printing helped to bring about the transition from the philosophy of the Middle Ages to the new and often perplexing perspectives of the modern era. Without the invention of printing the Industrial Revolution of the nineteenth century and the contemporary electronic revolution may never have occurred.

The relationship between printing and cultural change is of course far too complex to discern any single chain of causes and effects. Causal connections are more like a woven fabric than a chain. Many causal threads cross and recross to form an intricate weave that cannot be readily unraveled. Certain pivotally placed persons play a prominent part in cultural process. So too do the many tools and techniques of technology. Economic relationships are undoubtedly a determining factor. Faced with multiple strands of influence, the most one can do is focus on those seemingly more revealing central threads and recognize the possible distortions implicit in that choice. It is in this spirit that this chapter looks at the printing press as an agent of cultural change.

PRELUDE TO PRINTING

During the medieval period, Europeans were often encouraged to see themselves in a divinely ordained hierarchical structure—a "Great Chain of Being" in which God called each person to occupy an appropriate station in life. Women were expected to be subordinate to men, children to adults, peasants to landlords, apprentices to masters, subjects to kings and kings to the pope. This social order was interpreted by those in the upper reaches of the Roman Catholic Church to be in accord with God's will as revealed in the Bible. At the bottom of this hierarchical order, the most lowly and wretched were presumably to find comfort in the belief that in the kingdom of heaven "the last shall be first."

How many actually shared this image of the world is, of course, impossible to determine with any certainty. Because most of the medieval population were illiterate, there are few records of their inner feelings and beliefs. If their thoughts could, through some magic, be resurrected, very different attitudes might be revealed. For anyone trying to trace the social and psychological landscape of everyday life, the problem of hard evidence is vexatious; in the absence of historical records, descriptions of the inner life of those long gone can only be arrived at by speculation.

Nonetheless, the nonverbal media of the period suggest an environment conducive to belief in the divine ordination of the social pyramid described above. Sculpture, music, painting, and stained-glass windows served to remind recalcitrants not only of the joys of eternal salvation but of the horrors of damnation. Church steeples towering above the pastoral flock were an imposing symbol of the looming presence of the Almighty. Splendid religious pageants rivaled the spectacle of circuses. And elaborate ceremonies of baptism, marriage, and burial enveloped each stage of the life cycle in religious significance. Traditional practices were followed; novelty, change, and independent thought were not sought or encouraged.

The literature of the time also adhered to traditional practices. Throughout much of the millenium following the collapse of the Roman Empire in 476 A.D., manuscript production had been conducted almost exclusively in monasteries. As a result, texts tended to be both religious and orthodox. Although ecclesiastical control of manuscript production was never complete, the scarcity and expense of parchment, which was the principal material used for writing, tended to minimize secular challenges to a spiritual view of the universe. Supplies of papyrus, the tall aquatic plant used as a writing surface, had been cut off by the spread of Islam around the eighth century; papyrus was produced in one limited area in the Nile region of Egypt.

Commerce and its corresponding need for increased communications began to undermine the medieval order of things as early as the eleventh century, when there was increased commercial activity accompanied by a revitalization of city life. The towns and cities that had survived the Germanic invasions at the beginning of the medieval period had become sparsely populated and economically dependent on agriculture. With the expansion of commerce, ancient urban centers grew dramatically in population and in area, and new towns appeared in many places.

It is no mere coincidence that literacy also underwent a revival. Literacy rates increased as commercial transactions necessitated the growing use of contracts, bills of exchange, and business correspondence. There was also an upsurge in lay education, due partly to the increased demand for more literate men capable of handling the growing complexities of commerce. But other factors were also at work. By the middle of the twelfth century, western Europe had found itself awash in new knowledge, recovered from the ancient Greek world by way of the Moslems. In addition to these strong classical influences, fresh and innovative aspects of Islamic and Byzantine culture also had their impact. In response to these developments, great universities were founded: Paris, specializing in theology; Palermo, Salerno and Montpellier in medicine; and Bologna in law. Then others followed, among them Oxford and Cambridge. The growth of commerce and education increased the need for more practical production of writing materials.

THE ADVENT OF PAPER

The introduction of papermaking techniques in Europe served to accelerate the expansion of commerce and education. While paper was invented in China in the second century A.D., its journey across Asia and northern Africa into Europe took well over a thousand years. Techniques for the manufacture of paper were probably first introduced into Europe by the Arabs via Spain, in the twelfth century, and Italy, late in the thirteenth. From Italy, where the imported techniques had been more or less perfected, papermaking spread to France and Germany. By the fifteenth century, it had reached England. Although paper was neither as attractive nor as durable as parchment, it was more practical and less expensive. Consider, for instance, that a typical 150-page manuscript on parchment required preparation of the skins of about a dozen sheep![1]

Ample supplies of paper accommodated the new social needs, making possible a rise in commercial and university manuscript production and the growth of an international book trade. In Paris alone, some 10,000 lay scribes were practicing their craft by the middle of the fifteenth century.[2]

While the written word was no longer exclusively an ecclesiastical domain, it still remained accessible only to a few restricted groups. Paper did nothing to lessen the laborious task of copying each manuscript by hand. Not until the advent of print technology could many of the cultural possibilities of the written word become actualized. "All thought draws life from contacts and exchanges," writes French scholar Fernand Braudel. "Printed books accelerated and swelled the currents which the old manuscript books had kept within narrow channels."[3] Mind could now communicate with mind across time, distance, and the confines of personal experience. The next several centuries witnessed the emergence of a culture increasingly shaped by application of print technology.

THE SPREAD OF PRINTING

The hundred years preceding the invention of printing in the middle of the fifteenth century marked an unusually calamitous time in Europe.[4] The bubonic and pulmonary plagues of the period wiped out a third of the entire population between India and Iceland. England and France waged a war that, with many truces and renewals, lasted over a hundred years. Papal schism and simony were marks of the growing corruption and secularity of the Roman Catholic Church. Increased poverty and misery fanned peasant and proletarian insurrection. Freebooting companies of brigands plundered and pillaged the countryside with impunity. Authority was at a low ebb as the exercise of political power shifted uneasily among the Church, wealthy landowners, and royalty.

By the middle of the fifteenth century, feudalism was in sharp decline, papal authority was on the wane, and the dictates of commerce increasingly shaped the course of human lives and relationships. In various countries, aristocrats were joining forces with an emergent capitalist class to accelerate secular trends and to centralize the functions of government. Innovations in print technology can be seen as both the outcome and the agent of these developments.

One cannot fail to be struck by the speed with which the new techniques for printing spread across Europe. The printing press caught on, as Barbara Tuchman put it, "with unmedieval rapidity."[5] The first work known to have been printed from movable type dates from the early 1450s. This was an indulgence from the press of the German goldsmith Johann Gutenberg at Mainz. It was followed in 1456 by what is generally considered to be the first printed book, the *Vulgate*—the Latin translation of the Bible, made by Saint Jerome at the end of the fourth century A.D. Within just a few years, printing had spread across Germany, reaching Italy in 1464. Printing presses soon appeared in Rome, Milan, Florence, and Naples. Supplies of paper and a stable market for books had undoubtedly attracted many printers to these Italian cities. During the next decade, printing reached France, the Low Countries, Poland, and England in quick succession. William Caxton, a name not unfamiliar to students of English literature, set up his printing press at Westminster in 1476. The 1480s found presses in London, Antwerp, Leipzig, Odense, and Stockholm. Well over two hundred towns and cities had printing presses installed by the end of the century. The new technology of print had spread with a speed comparable to the data processing systems and orbiting satellites of our own time. And not unlike present-day developments, print technology tended to reflect the needs and priorities of the societal forces for whom it was applied.

COMMERCE AND PRINTING

It was the world of commerce and industry that acted as a magnet for the machinery of print. From 1469 on, a large colony of book printers was located in the great trade center of Venice. Many of them gained prominence, such as the brothers Johann and Wendelin of Speyer, who printed one of the first books in Italian—a volume of Petrarch's sonnets. There too, such craftsmen as Nicolaus Jenson, a Frenchman, and the famous Aldus Manutius produced books using a brilliant type-design that went far beyond the primitive typographical efforts of Gutenberg. Manutius, in particular, combined fine typography with an excellent selection of books, including editions of the works from classical antiquity. By the time of his death in 1515, Manutius' enterprise had translated and published just about every known Greek author.

The connection between printing and commerce was nowhere more apparent than in the enterprise established by Anton Koberger around 1470 in the international banking and trade center of Nuremberg. Koberger specialized in theology and scholastic philosophy. Among the works that came from his presses were those of Vincent de Beauvais, Guillaume Durand, and Duns Scotus—and such saintly personages as Aquinas, Jerome, Ambrose, and Augustine. But above all, Koberger was a businessman and manufacturer. As such, his primary concern was to increase the profits from his investments. At the height of his activities, Koberger's enterprise employed 24 presses and 100 men. To cope with expanding business, Koberger often recruited other printers to help in production. He also developed a large commercial network to market his products. For a time, Koberger combined printing, publishing, and bookselling.[6]

Printing from movable type was, in effect, the archetype of mass production—the first mechanization of a complex handicraft. The development of a method of casting replicas of metal type in vast quantity, as S. H. Steinberg explains in *Five Hundred Years of Printing*, "had not only established the main principle of letterpress printing but also introduced to Europe, more than three centuries ahead of its general adoption by industry, the theory of 'interchangeable parts' which is the basis of modern mass-manufacturing technique."[7]

The introduction of the new technology of printing involved more than just the substitution of machinemade products for handmade ones. The early printer, as a pioneer in the techniques of mass production, had to secure financial assistance in order to remain in business. Gutenberg, for instance, had to borrow 800 guilders on two occasions from a Mainz financier to exploit his invention commercially. The lender eventually foreclosed on the inventor, and Gutenberg lost the bulk of his business and type.[8]

Pioneering printers also experienced labor problems, including strikes. The town of Lyon, France, is a case in point. By 1539, it had about 100 presses and a total work force in the print industry of about 1,000. Many of the printing establishments, already in debt to local financiers, found they could only make a profit by reducing wages and expanding the workday. This policy eventually caused the workers to strike. Lyon was not alone. Similar causes had similar effects in Venice, Paris, Geneva, and other commercial centers.[9]

As pioneers in manufacturing and marketing techniques, early printers had much in common with other capitalist entrepreneurs. Books, whatever else they may have been, were also pieces of merchandise manufactured for a profit. Even the production of prayer books was looked upon as a profit-making enterprise. A printer concerned about keeping his firm solvent and staying ahead of his creditors was likely to look at religious works quite differently from a scribe working in a monastery for remission of his sins. "When the profit-seeking printer handled devotional and theological works," writes Elizabeth Eisenstein in her masterful study *The Printing Press as an Agent of Change*, "he was much more likely to assess them in terms of their prospective sales value."[10]

Although profit was the primary motive behind the widespread use of movable metal type for duplicating books and other materials, the printing press—like technological innovations both before and since—had unintended and unanticipated consequences.

PRINTING AND THE MEDIEVAL WORLD VIEW

Prior to the advent of printing, most communication took place primarily in a communal context. Consensus in the community and strong pressures for conformity acted upon the individual, from birth on, to narrow still further the range of acceptable beliefs and behavior. A person was likely to build up his or her mental model of the world from only a handful of sources. There was also likely to be a high degree of social visibility and inspectability, which insured compliance.

In such a setting, people were likely to hold very limited conceptions of time and space. We must recognize that the concepts of time and space are essential components in one's understanding of the world: Without some kind of temporal and spatial frames of reference, life would be chaotic. In large measure, one's comprehension of here and there, now and then, and what was and what will be are shaped by the various means of communication available in the society. Availability of the written word, as Canadian scholar Harold Innis has noted, extends the world of time beyond the range of remembered things and the world of space beyond the range of known places.[11] The early entrepreneurs of printing, by making the written word available on a large scale, helped to redraw the entire framework of time and space within which medieval Europeans experienced their lives. Without anyone having so intended it, the psychological and social landscape of experience started to widen considerably. Over the next several centuries, an entirely new communication and, hence, new cultural environment would emerge.

In the first 50 years of printing—the age of the so-called "incunabula" (literally, cradle period)—some 20,000 or more different books are estimated to have been stamped out by printing presses. Even though, probably, most of these were issued in editions of only 100 up to perhaps 1,000 copies, the total production was still quite impressive. In the sixteenth century as many as 200,000 different editions may have been printed.[12] This rapid increase in book production on a large scale greatly speeded up the flow of information and ideas—including heresies.

The medieval period had witnessed a number of intellectual revivals, most notably the so-called Carolingian Renaissance in the ninth century during the reign of the Frankish ruler Charlemagne. And, as noted earlier, an intellectual quickening in the twelfth century had given rise to and was stimulated by the rediscovery of the classical past. In fifteenth-century Italy, there began an intensification of a secular intellectual spirit in Western European thought, literature, and art, which the preservative powers of print technology would eventually render permanent. "Typographical fixity," to use Eisenstein's term, had finally broken down the cycle of classical texts being discovered, disappearing, and being discovered again. In other words, printing made possible the emergence of an enduring Renaissance by reproducing classical texts in sufficient quantities to ensure their survival. The secularization that took hold in quattrocento Italy involved not only the revival of the Greek and Roman heritage; classical and modern influences blended to achieve a deeper originality of form and content. And printing provided the means of permanently recording these contemporary works, as well.

Print technology provided a means of recording, retrieving, and transmitting information—and all this on a scale hitherto unprecedented in history. Scholars and others who were literate were able to reach more readily through time and across space. Prior to the invention of printing, most scholars had access to a relatively small number of classical texts, and scholarship tended to be geared toward exhaustive commentaries on selected works. Printing facilitated easy and relatively less expensive access to a wider range of texts, stimulating intellectual curiosity about ancient artifacts and languages. Thoughts that had remained dormant for centuries flowered once again in this soil made rich by printers' ink. "Probes into the past were steadily extended," writes Eisenstein. "Texts and languages lost, not merely to the West, but to all men everywhere for thousands of years, were retrieved from the dead, reconstructed and deciphered." Academics, wealthy merchants, and intellectuals of comfortable means were able to collect personal libraries. Scholars sifted, clarified, and developed this heritage. "Once old texts came together within the same study, diverse systems of ideas and special disciplines could be combined," explains Eisenstein. "Increased output directed at relatively stable markets, in short, created conditions that favored, first, new combinations of old ideas and, then the creation of entirely new systems of thought."[13]

A NEW SENSE OF SELF AND SELF-INTEREST

As the age of scribes gave way to that of printers, pride of authorship took on a new significance. Many medieval churchmen regarded pride as the most reprehensible of sins. Monastic practices sought to suppress the individual ego altogether. Since medieval art and literature were intended for the greater glory of the Almighty, writers and artists of the age usually did not affix signatures to their works. Greater secularization served to alter that situation. It is certainly hard to imagine such Renaissance figures as Boccaccio or Machiavelli submerging their personal identities in the collectivity of the group. But the conditions of scribal culture had helped to keep the ego in check. Printing, suggests Marshall McLuhan in *The Gutenberg Galaxy*, helped to set the ego free by providing "the physical means of extending the dimensions of the private author in space and time."[14]

Few writers in the new age of print were more ego-involved than the renegade priest François Rabelais. He is alleged to have asserted, "I intend each and every reader to lay aside his business, to abandon his trade, to relinquish his profession, and to concentrate wholly upon my work."[15] Rabelais was a master of self-promotion. On one occasion he boasted that his *Gargantua*—a robust tale of a completely unrestrained giant who wallows unashamedly in just about every known sensuous and sensual pleasure—had sold more copies in two months than Bibles had in nine years.[16]

The Dutch writer Desiderius Erasmus was conscious of the commercial value of the printed product. He wanted his share of the profits of a growing industry and not only sought out suitable publishers, but stipulated author's fees as well.[17] He became one of the first bona fide best-selling authors of his day. Some 34 editions of 1,000 copies were sold of his first work *Adages*, a collection of wise sayings by Greek and Roman thinkers along with his own commentary. His *Praise of Folly*—in which he satirized pedantry, the dogmatism of theologians, and the ignorance and credulity of the general populace—was also a big seller. The ridicule and scorn with which Erasmus wrote of the abuses and superstitious practices of the Roman Catholic Church eventually earned his books a prominent place on the *Index of Prohibited Books*.

Prior to printing, most literature was read aloud to an audience in a face-to-face situation. Print, as McLuhan puts it, "translated the dialogue of shared discourse into packaged information, a portable commodity."[18] For someone like Socrates, this would have been seen as a deplorable situation. He fretted about the implications of writing, even in his time. "I cannot help feeling," he is alleged by Plato in *Phaedrus* to have said, ". . . that writing is unfortunately like painting; for the creations of the painter have the attitude of life, and yet if you ask them a question, they preserve a solemn silence." Sixteenth-century thinkers had few such reservations. "With print," asserts McLuhan, "the discovery of the vernacular as a PA system was immediate."[19]

The public-address potential of the printing press was not lost on such picaresque personages as Pietro Aretino, who was among the first to use the press as a platform for his own audacious ideas. He was a forerunner of later sensationalist journalists, and—like his contemporary, Rabelais—became famous throughout Europe for the audacity of his publications. A self-styled "Scourge of Princes," Aretino aimed his sharp-edged satire at those in the upper reaches of society and at the social customs and literary pretensions of the time. He was "the first literary realist, the first journalist, the first art critic."[20] His voluminous output of letters, dialogues, poems, comedies, and tragedies included lascivious sonnets as well as religious works.

With the new sense of self fostered by typography came new forms of literary expression. Michel de Montaigne, the sixteenth-century French writer, created the personal essay to describe his reflections and philosophical explorations. By calling his work *Les Essais*, a term he derived from the French verb *essayer* (to try), Montaigne deliberately emphasized the tentative and unsystematic nature of his meditations. Very much that is modern can be found in his stress on the relativity and ambiguity of human affairs.

THE PRESS OF PROTEST

The availability of printed materials and the correspondent growth of literacy may actually have promoted the social fragmentation conducive to Protestantism. "By its very nature," argues Eisenstein, "a reading public was not only more dispersed; it was also more atomistic and individualistic than a hearing one."[21] Reading became a private activity—the very antithesis of communal thought and behavior.

It was in the context of an emerging print culture that a young Wittenberg professor named Martin Luther drew up his set of 95 theses attacking the sale of indulgences, and posted them on the door of the castle church on October 31, 1517. Most significantly, he later had them printed and sent to his friends in a number of cities. Earlier protestations against the policies and practices of medieval Catholicism, by such reformers as John Wycliffe in England and Jan Hus in Bohemia, anticipated much of the thunder of Luther. But it was the printing press in Luther's arsenal that gave his words such explosive proportions.

At first, Luther himself seemed to be unaware of just how potent the weaponry of print could be. In addressing the Pope some six months after the publication of his 95 theses had propelled him into the national spotlight, Luther expressed puzzlement about his newfound fame. "It is a mystery to me," he said, "how my theses . . . were spread to so many places. They were meant exclusively for our little circle here. . . . They were written in such a language that the common people could hardly understand them."[22] In most towns, the "little circle" of learned laymen was likely to gather in the new workshops run by master printers, who often combined their mechanical skills with mercantile and scholarly interests. Scholars, scientists, and intellectuals of the time were on much closer terms with print shops and typographers than is now possible, principally due to today's widespread division of labor and the overall greater industrialization of printing.

It was in the early print shops that the schemes to launch bestsellers were most likely to be hatched. Much of Luther's prodigious production of polemic writings and sermons appeared in print. In two years, some 30 editions of his *Sermon on Indulgences* and 21 editions of his *Sermon on the Right Preparation of the Heart* were turned out. One of Luther's pamphlets sold 4,000 copies in five days. The first edition of his translation of the New Testament, published in 1522, sold 3,000 copies in a few weeks.[23]

Within two years, 14 reprints came out at Wittenberg, and 66 at Augsburg, Basel, Strasbourg, and Leipzig. Luther's Old Testament translation began to appear in 1523 and was equally successful. In the next two decades, both authorized and pirated editions in High and Low German totaled 430, some of which ran to 3,000 copies or more each. These enormous and unprecedented printings did not diminish in the second half of the century. By 1700, the number of copies in print of Luther's translation of the Bible exceeded 2 million. "The scriptures were henceforth in everyone's hands," writes French scholar Lucien Fèbvre, "and the passions roused by religious controversy were such that even those who were illiterate had the text read and explained to them by better educated friends."[24]

Almost overnight, Wittenberg became an important printing center. So too did Geneva, when the Frenchman Jean Caulvin (known to us as John Calvin) settled there to implement his version of Protestantism. In the 1550s, the number of printers and booksellers in Geneva grew from about a half dozen or fewer to some 300 or more. Publishing became the Swiss city's first export industry, as Calvinists zealously sought to propagate their faith. Calvinism became dominant not only in most of Switzerland (Swiss Reformed), but in the Dutch Netherlands (Dutch Reformed), Scotland (Presbyterian), and the German Palatinate as well. It also had a small, albeit vigorous, following in France (the Huguenots), Bohemia, Hungary, and Poland.

EFFORTS AT CENSORSHIP

In early sixteenth-century England, Protestant publications from abroad contributed to a growing disaffection with papal power. But it was Henry VIII's desire for a legitimate male heir, more than any other factor, that led to the establishment of the Anglican Church. Catherine of Aragon, his wife of 18 years, had borne only a daughter, Mary. When it became apparent that his wife would bear no more children, Henry sought papal approval to have his marriage annulled so that he could remarry. (He was to marry six times, in all.) When the pope refused his request, the irate king persuaded a subservient Parliament to make him, not the pope, head of the Church of England. However, Henry VIII was no Protestant. He continued to support the Catholic position on all doctrinal points except that of papal supremacy. Protestants and Roman Catholics alike who refused to acknowledge his spiritual leadership were persecuted with equal severity.

During Henry VIII's reign, an elaborate framework of official state control was constructed to stem the flow of heretical literature. In 1529, a list of prohibited books was instituted under secular authority. On Christmas Day in 1534, Henry VIII issued a proclamation requiring printers to have a royal permit before setting up shop. In 1538, licensing was extended to all books printed in the English language. The importation of printed books was also prohibited.

Such measures, it should be said, were not without economic motive. In granting a royal privilege in 1543 for the printing of all books used in his realm for worship services, for instance Henry made specific reference to the importance of the book trade for the "balance of payment" of the country.[25]

Despite such measures, the Henrician Reformation ultimately resulted in the establishment of an Anglican Church that was more Protestant than Catholic in orientation. During the reign of Henry's young son Edward VI, a *Book of Common Prayer* and 42 articles of faith were drawn up; they were clearly Calvinist in flavor. But Catholicism briefly reemerged to a position of preeminence when Mary Tudor, Catherine of Aragon's daughter, succeeded to the throne. "Bloody Mary," as she was called, had some 300 Protestants burned at the stake. In her effort to restore Catholicism, she chartered the Stationers' Company and limited printing rights to the members of that guild. Comprised of printers, publishers, and dealers in books, the Stationers' Company became the cornerstone of the English licensing system. It was empowered with search, seizure, and even limited judicial functions. However, the rising tide of Protestantism could not be stemmed. Printing presses were too easy to set up and dismantle, and harbor patrols never effectively prevented the importation of heretical materials from the continent. During the long reign of Elizabeth I, the daughter of Henry's second wife, the Anglican Church became decidedly Protestant, although it retained certain Catholic rituals and practices.

A CLASH OF CULTURES

The religious upheaval that first gained substance from the printing presses of Wittenberg did not subside until nearly half of Western Christendom had broken away from the Roman Catholic Church. With area after area becoming Protestant, the Catholic hierarchy launched a major counteroffensive to stem the corrosive effects of printer's ink. A Papal Council convoked at Trent, an imperial city in northern Italy, met on and off for 18 years between 1545 and 1563 to reaffirm and redefine traditional doctrines. Among the council's more significant actions was the inauguration of the *Index of Prohibited Books*, designed to prevent the reading of heretical literature by unauthorized persons. This period also saw an even greater role for ritual and iconography in Catholic communications. Churches were yet more elaborately adorned with paintings, stained glass, and statuary.

In contrast, Protestant reformers in northeastern Europe sought to establish a literate, visually iconoclastic culture. Church murals were whitewashed and replaced with the Ten Commandments; church statues were removed; and stained glass windows were smashed and replaced by clear panes. The furious iconoclasm of Protestantism, writes Lawrence Stone, "was symptomatic of its desire to replace one means of communication with another."[26]

Cultural discord at the close of the Middle Ages may be directly attributed to the fallout from Gutenberg's invention. The image was grappling with the printed word, without realizing the strength of the latter. The old heresy of individualism was becoming the new orthodoxy. By 1641, asserts Stone, "rust was eating into the shackles of the 'Great Chain of Being.'"[27]

Whether Protestantism contributed to the rise of capitalism is still a matter of much controversy. The commercial prosperity of Roman Catholic Italy, southern and western Germany, and the Belgian Netherlands—where the early practitioners of printing sought their fortunes—would seem to belie any clear-cut causal connection. So, too, does the lack of capitalistic activity in Presbyterian Scotland. Nevertheless, the profit-oriented print industry was undeniably bolstered by the new religious faith. "Protestant doctrines," notes Eisenstein, "harnessed an evangelical religion to a new capitalist industry aimed at expanding markets and increased book sales."[28]

The potent mix of Protestantism and printing played a significant part in the linguistic development of modern Europe. Latin, the lingua franca of ecclesiastical authority, had dominated the written word throughout most of the medieval period. As the laity sank into illiteracy following the fall of the Roman Empire, this created a situation of enormous cultural—not to mention ideological—significance. It meant that the language of formal learning, literature, and religion was different from the vernacular—the languages that were spoken by most people. In the age of the so-called "incunabula," Latin still dominated the publishing field. But as the market for published materials spread, articles and books began to be printed in the vernacular of the various regions of Europe. The large output of the printing presses in the emergent Protestant countries was in the vernacular, greatly facilitating literacy among the laity. Various Protestant denominations, ambitious to propagate their respective doctrines, established schools for the general population, where even the son of a cobbler or a peasant might learn to read the Bible and other books in the vernacular.

Comprehensive statistical evidence of the actual numbers of people who could read with any facility is not available. Sir Thomas More's estimate in 1533 that over half the population in England could read an English translation of the Bible is dismissed by Stone as grossly inaccurate. However, Stone feels that, 100 years later, social literacy may have been approaching this figure in certain areas.[29]

CENSORSHIP UNDER PRESSURE

After civil war broke out in England in the 1640s, many in the upper reaches of that society came to see social literacy as a contributing factor in the social disruption. There was a growing realization that literate people, as Stone points out, "are far harder to govern and exploit than illiterate, for the simple reason that it is extremely difficult to make sure that they never develop a taste for subversive literature."[30] The conflict between royalists and parliamentarians, and among competing factions on the parliamentary side, had been augmented by an enormous outpouring of printed materials. The system of state censorship virtually collapsed under the onslaught. The arbitrary and tyrannical Court of the Star Chamber, so named because its meetings were held in a room at the Palace of Westminster that had gilt stars on its ceiling, was abolished in 1641. The effectiveness of the Stationers' Company as the controlling authority in the printing industry was also destroyed.

Among the more eloquent proponents of unlicensed printing in the civil war period was the poet John Milton, whose pamphlet entitled *Areopagitica* was published in 1644 as a contribution to the antiroyalist cause.[31] "And though all winds of doctrine were let loose to play upon the earth, so Truth be in the field, we do injuriously by licensing and prohibiting to misdoubt her strength," he boldly asserted. "Let her and Falsehood grapple; who ever knew Truth put to the worse in a free and open encounter?" But Milton's concept of free expression was quite limited. One need read only a few more pages, after this oft-quoted passage, to see that he would not have tolerated "Popery and open superstition which as it extirpates all religions and civil supremacies, so itself should be extirpated." (However, he would try "to win and regain the weak and mislead.") Nor could he conceive of tolerating that which was impious or absolutely evil, that which was against faith or manners. And blasphemy, atheism and libel were not among "the winds of doctrine" that he would "let loose." Later, Milton himself became an official censor.

Milton was an adherent of the Independents, a radical minority of Puritans—a Calvinist sect that sought to "purify" the Anglican Church of all remaining traces of Roman Catholicism. After the Puritans under Oliver Cromwell came to power, the Anglican Church, the House of Lords, and the monarchy were all legislated out of existence. Cromwell eventually wielded a sovereignty that was far more despotic than any of his royal predecessors. By the time of his death in 1658, many in the country had grown weary of Puritan austerities. Within two years, most of the old institutions were restored. However, many of the issues, which had been so bitterly fought over, remained unresolved. Neither king nor Parliament had established clear supremacy; sharp economic and religious differences still prevailed. The traditional system of censorship based on state licensing, which was reinstituted in 1662, was not finally abandoned until 1694. However, restrictions against reporting the proceedings of Parliament were still maintained. So, too, were controls against treason and "seditious libel."

Seditious libel was a particularly pernicious way of controlling expression. Sedition was so broadly defined that all criticism of those in power could be suppressed. Any publication intended to bring the king into disrepute, to incite disaffection against him or the government, to raise discontent among the people, or to promote feelings of ill will between different classes was categorized as seditious libel. And it made little difference if what was said was true. Indeed, the greater the truth the more serious the libel, since such a charge could cause greater discontent among the people than a false one.

Notwithstanding these restrictions, the abandonment of licensing in 1694 was a major step forward. Books and journals, while still subject to charges of seditious libel, were no longer censored in the sense of being controlled prior to publication.

DEVELOPMENT OF THE ENGLISH PRESS

The lapse of the licensing system clearly marked a watershed in the development of the English press. The newspaper, which had first made its appearance in seventeenth-century Germany, began to emerge as a powerful political and social force in the lives of the English people. By 1710, some 20 newspapers were available in England at least once a week—and in one instance in London, on a daily basis. Such notable writers as Daniel Defoe, Joseph Addison, Richard Steele, and Jonathan Swift were making their mark in journalism at this time. From 1704 to 1713, Defoe edited *The Review*, a newspaper that anticipated many of the techniques later to become associated with the journalist's profession. The high literary quality of this newspaper set the standard for such journalistic enterprises as *The Tatler* (1709-11) and *The Spectator* (1711-12), edited by Steele in association with Addison. The emergence of the newspaper to a position of prominence in England had coincided with the rise of two major political parties, the Tories and the Whigs. Swift was the major political writer for the Tories in their brief reign (1710-14); he produced the *Examiner* (1710), a newspaper in which he exhibited his characteristic satirical wit.

Among the more influential advocates of religious liberty, representative government, and freedom of expression were John Trenchard and Thomas Gordon, who, between 1720 and 1723, wrote in the *Independent Whig* and the London *Journal* under the pen name "Cato." In 1724, their writings were collected and published in four volumes. Libertarian thinkers like Trenchard and Gordon increasingly influenced a substantial minority in and around London. (Such writings were in great demand in the American colonies, as well.)

The proliferation of newspapers alarmed successive parliamentary administrations; and, beginning in 1712, the first of a series of Stamp Acts (press taxes) was imposed. A tax was also placed on every advertisement a publication carried. In addition to raising revenue, such taxes had the express purpose of restricting both the readership and ownership of newspapers. Economic sanctions notwithstanding, however, the press continued to grow in circulation and in strength.

Expanding readership and a rising volume of advertisements enabled publishers to absorb government taxes fairly easily. The sustained growth of London newspapers, which numbered about 89 by 1760, was accompanied by the rise of 30-odd provincial papers in the same period. Magazines also increased steadily between 1730 and 1760, beginning with *Gentlemen's Magazine* in 1730 and continuing with such publications as *London Magazine, Universal Magazine*, and *Town and Country Magazine*. Such magazines served the broadening cultural ambitions of a growing middle class.

The daily and thrice-weekly newspapers functioned increasingly to meet the business needs of this new class with information about foreign markets, shipping, stock prices, and commercial advertisements. As trade expanded, this commercial press gave priority to advertisements—putting them, rather than news items, on the front page.

From the 1730s on, control of the commercial press gradually passed from the hands of printers to those of merchants, tradesmen, and booksellers—members of the new middle class seeking greater economic and political freedom. This issue was made manifest in concern for the plight of John Wilkes, for example, whose imprisonment for writing an article attacking the government became a cause célèbre in the 1760s. The issuance of general warrants to seize evidence in seditious libel cases was declared illegal in 1765, largely as a result of public pressure. After 1771, Parliament (by default) opened its proceedings to the press. The right of juries to decide whether or not a publication had printed sedition was recognized in 1792, with the passage of the Fox Libel Act. A new era in press freedom had been inaugurated.

By the 1830s, the Industrial Revolution in England had given rise to a number of radical working-class newspapers whose circulation ran into the high thousands.[32] Growth of the radical press was bolstered by a large and disparate alliance of English laborers, artisans, and self-employed professionals—groups that were barred by property qualifications from voting for members of Parliament. This coalition rallied around the People's Charter of 1838, a document calling for universal male suffrage, the secret ballot, removal of property qualifications for Parliament and the payment of salaries to its members, annual elections, and equal electoral districts. Circulation of the militant Chartist newspaper, the *Northern Star*, reached more than 50,000 by 1839. Its successor, the *Reynold's News*, secured an even larger circulation within three years of its launching in 1850. Although the Chartist movement itself soon failed, most of its demands were eventually incorporated into the British political system.

The new doctrine of revolutionary socialism had also gained force by 1848, as attacks against authority spread across Europe. But the "spectre of communism," hailed by Karl Marx as haunting that continent, was quickly exorcised. Segments of the radical press in England had given sustenance to socialism through a scathing attack against the whole industrial system—challenging not only the old aristocracy, but the new capitalist class, as well. However, the heyday of radical journalism as a socially disruptive force was short-lived.

Advances in print technology, coupled with rising expenses of staffing and newsgathering, led inexorably to the eclipse of the radical press in the latter half of the nineteenth century. To keep newspapers competitively priced, publishers became increasingly more dependent on advertising. Those without advertiser support invariably operated at a loss. In an effort to attract and hold advertising revenues, publishers aimed for a middle ground in their coverage and interpretation of controversial events.

ADVANCES IN PRINT TECHNOLOGY

The printing press of the 1700s differed little from that used by Johann Gutenberg. A hand press squeezed a flat surface, or "platen," down upon a sheet of paper laid on top of an inked type form, or block. A screw or combination of levers was employed to develop pressure. In 1811, Frederick Koenig of Saxony replaced the platen with a cylinder, beneath which the type form rolled back and forth, picking up ink and fresh paper with each trip. Koenig's first press had a capacity of 800 sheets an hour. Adding a second cylinder made it possible to print both sides of a sheet rapidly, and, by 1814, moving the apparatus by steam power appreciably accelerated the production process. When the *Times* of London installed this model that same year, it was able to turn out sheets at the remarkable rate of 1,100 an hour. Modifications of the cylinder press by David Napier of England in 1824 tripled its output.

Improved papermaking techniques provided another important ingredient in the emergence of the modern press. At its most primitive, paper was made by chopping up old rags in water, then dipping a sievelike tray into the mixture, squeezing the resulting layer, and drying it. Toward the end of the eighteenth century, this process was improved by making it continuous and mechanically operated. Henry and Sealy Fourdrinier subsidized the development of a machine on which it was possible to make a continuous roll of paper. A process to make paper from wood pulp, developed in Germany in the 1840s, further facilitated the production of newspapers and other publications.

THE POPULAR PRESS

Industrialization of papermaking and the introduction of steam-powered iron presses, along with the expansion of canals and railroads, allowed for enormous growth in newspaper circulation during the latter half of the nineteenth century. Sales of the *Times* of London, started by John Walter in the 1780s, reached nearly 60,000 in 1855. England's Sunday newspapers, colorful in content and popular in appeal, sustained the largest increase in sales. By 1855, the leading Sunday journals had sales exceeding 100,000. Moreover, because of their expense, most newspapers were read by more than one person. The availability of newspapers in taverns, coffeehouses, clubs, and the like gave them a readership considerably larger than their actual sales figures would indicate.

Increased circulation and, in particular, advertising revenue had made English newspapers ever more difficult for the government to control. Although empowered to determine guilt in seditious libel cases by the Fox Libel Act of 1792, juries became increasingly reluctant to convict. Libel laws were further weakened with the passage of Lord Campbell's Act of 1843, which made truth a legitimate defense against the charge of seditious libel. In 1853, the advertising tax was removed. Two years later, the system of control based on stamp duty was also abolished.

Abolition of the stamp tax in 1855 encouraged the emergence of the inexpensive metropolitan daily newspaper.[33] The *Daily Telegraph*, launched on the very day the tax was repealed, set the pace in England for this new kind of newspaper. After some initial difficulties, the *Telegraph* was taken over by its chief creditor, Joseph Moses Levy. In a deliberate attempt to attract a larger readership, he reduced the selling price of the newspaper from twopence to a penny—considerably less than most of its rivals. The scope of the newspaper's coverage was also widened, following the practice of the Sunday journals, to include stories of sex and crime. "Extraordinary Discovery of a Man-Woman at Birmingham," and "Furious Assault on a Female" were among the items described on the pages of the *Telegraph* in its early years. The hanging of a woman merited a three-column description. By 1860, the *Telegraph's* circulation had reached 141,000; in the next decade, it climbed to nearly 200,000.

To push sales still higher, the *Telegraph* engaged in daring exploits. For instance, it shared with a New York newspaper the sponsorship of Henry Morton Stanley's trip to Africa in search of Scottish-born English missionary and explorer David Livingston. (Stanley reached Livingston in November 1871, greeting him with the now famous "Dr. Livingston, I presume?") In the next two decades, the newspaper's circulation soared to 300,000.

Circulation of English newspapers grew to unprecedented numbers beginning in the 1890s with the emergence of the halfpenny newspaper. The first and most significant of these cheap papers was the *Daily Mail*, launched by Alfred Harmsworth (later Lord Northcliffe) in 1896. It was billed as "The Busy Man's Daily Journal," and featured short, pithy articles on a broad range of subjects. Coverage of stock exchange prices, politics, sports, and gossip—along with serialized stories and features for women—served to make the *Mail* enormously popular. Its circulation approached the million mark by the end of the century.

As the strength and independence of the English press increased, its role as an intermediary between Parliament and the people became considerable. "The developments in the scale, technology and finance of the press facilitated the growth of newspapers as independent and influential political organs both expressing and guiding public opinion," writes a British media scholar. "Governments and politicians could no longer exert much influence over the press, and proprietors had to respond to the demands of their new paymasters—the public."[34] Put somewhat differently, one might say that government restrictions were replaced by commercial controls.

FOREIGN NEWS AGENCIES

From the second half of the nineteenth century, when Europe had established its control over much of Africa and Asia and began its economic exploitation, the demand for political and commercial information was enormous. Farsighted entrepreneurs established international newsgathering agencies to service the rapidly growing information needs of government and business. Three news agencies—Reuters of England, Wolff of Germany, and Havas of France—divided up the world of news among themselves.

The Havas agency was started in 1835 by Charles Havas, an enterprising French businessman who had survived various regimes, each time benefiting from the special concessions granted his business activities. Out of Havas's pioneering efforts grew an organization of enormous reach and influence. Initially, his principal subscribers were businessmen, financiers, government officials, and the like. The general introduction of the telegraph in the middle of the nineteenth century soon enabled Havas to expand his network of subscribers beyond the boundaries of France.[35]

The success of Havas encouraged two of his former employees—Bernard Wolff and Paul Julius Reuter—to start up their own news agencies. Wolff established an agency in his homeland of Germany, while Reuter (also German-born) attempted to operate a rival service within France. Reuter's French effort failed after a few months and he subsequently turned his attention to London where, despite opposition from the *Times*, he succeeded in establishing his own agency. Based at the hub of the world cable system, Reuter's business expanded steadily, spreading into all parts of the British empire. Soon the three agencies found themselves in competition; and so, beginning in 1856, Reuter, Wolff, and Havas signed a series of agreements mapping out the world into spheres of influence. The rivalry between the European powers affected the fortunes of their respective national news agencies. From 1870 to the beginning of World War I, Reuters—and to a lesser extent Havas—dominated the world flow of news.

The foreign correspondent became a familiar figure on the colonial landscape. Like explorers of an earlier epoch, these overseas reporters were in many ways de facto agents in the expansion of empire. "A generation of explorer-adventurer-reporters grew up, 'gentlemen followers' of colonial wars, half-spies for London and Paris, half-entertainers for the news-reading public whose imagination was fired by accounts of their exploits," writes Anthony Smith.[36] Foreign reporting reflected a Western orientation that was often insensitive to the indigenous culture of overseas territories prior to their domination by the colonial powers. The attitude expressed by the famous explorer-journalist Henry Morton Stanley in a talk given to the Manchester Chamber of Commerce in 1884 provides a striking example of the ethnocentrism. "There are 50 millions of people beyond the gateway of the Congo, and the cotton spinners of Manchester are waiting to clothe them," he asserted. "Birmingham foundries are glowing with the red metal that will presently be made into ironwork for them and the trinkets that shall adorn those dusky bosoms; and the ministers of Christ are zealous to bring, the poor benighted heathen, into the fold."[37] This from one of the more enlightened journalists of the day. European journalists in general were inclined to look at the world from their own cultural perch, with its implicit foundation of white or Western superiority. Their point of departure was not "what is Africa like, or what manner of men and women live there," but rather "how does Africa, and how do Africans, fit into what I already know about the world?" Stanley's information about this vast continent was collected, as Smith points out, "under the inspiration of a socially accepted doctrine of colonialism, in which pursuit of loot, markets and the Christian faith were subsumed into a single quest, which was undoubtedly emotionally uplifting for his audience in imperial England."[38]

Foreign correspondents fed the business community's need for commercial and political information and supplied general readers with dramatic stories and romantic adventure. By definition, news was seen to arise from the exceptional, not the commonplace. There was a growing emphasis on discreet, isolated events. This practice of abstracting only bits and pieces of information about the environment served to obscure the legacy of colonialism and the historical circumstances of industrial development. An emphasis on conflict and civil strife further helped to strengthen the imperial bent of Western journalism. To the late-nineteenth-century newspaper reader, writes Smith, "it seemed that the more distant parts of the globe were permanently subject to violence and drama; the East was constantly ablaze with revolt and carnage, Central America was wracked with picturesque revolution while Africa was the province of romantic jungle explorers."[39]

Such practices prevail even today. Contemporary Western journalists still tend to think of news in terms of aberration rather than normality. The concentration on the exceptional over the commonplace invariably results in a distorted view of the world at large. In less developed countries, in particular, disasters, famines, wars, military coups, and political corruption are the only aspects of life likely to make their way to the pages of Western newspapers.[40]

THE COLONIAL PRESS IN AMERICA

Early colonial administrators in America were well aware of print technology's disruptive potential. In 1671, Sir William Berkeley, who governed Virginia for 38 years, succinctly stated his views, doubtlessly held by many of the Crown's officials: "But I thank God we have not free schools nor printing; and I hope we shall not have [them] these hundred years," he said. "For learning has brought disobedience and heresy and sects into the world; and printing has divulged them and libels against the government."[41]

The early development of a free press is often characterized as a heroic struggle against such tyrannical views; there is much evidence to support this perspective. In the eighteenth century, demands for freedom of the press in America were directed primarily against British colonial rule. Many American rebels certainly found inspiration in the enlightenment ideas of Voltaire, Rousseau, and Locke. John Milton's *Areopagitica* also enjoyed wide circulation in this period. James Alexander of the New York *Weekly Journal* drew on the antimonarchy essays of such radical English writers as John Trenchard and Thomas Gordon in his appeals for freedom from tyranny.

It was the *Journal*'s publisher, John Peter Zenger, who became the center of a celebrated seditious libel case in 1735.[42] The *Journal* had been highly critical of New York's corrupt, inept Governor, Sir William Cosby. Zenger was arrested and charged with "raising sedition." When Zenger went to trial he was represented by the famed Philadelphia lawyer, Andrew Hamilton. Then in his eighties, his white hair falling to his shoulders, the histrionically inclined Hamilton argued eloquently for the cause of liberty. The defendant, asserted Hamilton, could not be found guilty unless what he printed was indeed libelous. To be libelous, said Hamilton, the words themselves must include seditious and malicious falsehoods.

Hamilton compared the power of public officials to a river overflowing its banks: "It is then too impetuous to be stemmed," and would destroy everyone. "It is not the cause of the poor printer, nor of

New York alone, which you are now trying," he told the jury in ringing tones. "No. It may in its consequences affect every freeman that lives under British government on the main of America." In his concluding remarks, Hamilton directed the jury to do its duty by striking a blow for the cause of liberty—the liberty "both of exposing and opposing arbitrary power . . . by speaking and writing—truth." Palpably exhausted, Hamilton limped to his chair. The chief justice charged the jury with a few awkwardly phrased remarks about their obligation not to go beyond the fact of publication, which had already been admitted, leaving the issue of seditious libel to the justices. The jury retired, only to return ten minutes later with a unanimous verdict of "not guilty."

The chief justice did not set the verdict aside, although it was certainly within his power to do so since the jury had gone beyond its mandate in direct contradiction to the law. The idea of a free press was established philosophically, if not operationally. Hamilton won a moral victory. Libel laws were not changed for the next half century but, at least, truth as the best defense against libel was finally enunciated in America.

It should be mentioned, however, that pecuniary motives were also clothed in Hamilton's stirring rhetoric of liberty. The "cause of the poor printer" had been backed by a group of wealthy merchants and landowners seeking a greater share of control in the colony's affairs. Zenger's newspaper had been initially set up by them, as a vehicle for expressing their interests and views.

THE FREE PRESS AND THE CAPITALIST CLASS

The eighteenth-century crusade for freedom, viewed with a more cynical eye, can be seen as an effort to legitimize an emergent capitalist class challenging the royal authorities in order to advance its own economic interests. From this vantage point, the fight for a free press appears more like the calculated product of expediency, rather than the enlightened result of principle. For instance, the wrath of many American newspapers was not evoked against England until its passage of the Stamp Act of 1765. Many considered this legislation, which placed a heavy tax on paper used in publishing, to be highly inimical to the functioning of a profitable press. Newspapers soon began to argue vehemently the revolutionary philosophy. Typical of the militant newspapers was the Boston *Gazette and Country Journal*, to which

Samuel Adams was a frequent contributor. As a propagandist, Adams had few peers. He instilled in his readers fierce hatred against England. Not averse to dipping his quill in the venom of vituperation, Adams gave lurid descriptions of British soldiers beating small boys, violating matrons, and raping young girls. English officials denied these charges, in vain. Bostonians quickly came to bitterly resent the presence of soldiers.

John Dickinson, a colonial journalist, argued outright for the sanctity of property rights and free enterprise. His capitalist viewpoint was expressed in a series of articles, entitled "Letters from a Farmer in Pennsylvania," which were printed in the *Pennsylvania Chronicle* and reprinted in other newspapers throughout the colonies. Although Dickinson was opposed to revolution, he strongly favored home rule for the colonies, and resented English control over foreign trade. Dickinson had nothing but contempt for radicals fomenting revolution; nevertheless, he did more than any other writer, with the exception of Samuel Adams, to bring on the War for Independence.

THE CONTEXT OF FREEDOM

The war had united large property owners, merchants, bankers, and manufacturers—along with small farmers and wage earners—in a common cause. Not all elements of American society, however, were encompassed in the stirring words of the Declaration of Independence: "We hold these Truths to be self-evident, that all Men are created equal, that they are endowed by their creator with certain unalienable rights, that among these are Life, Liberty and the Pursuit of Happiness." The phrase "all men are created equal" meant men and not women. Nor were equality and unalienable rights intended for all men—for living in the rebellious colonies were slaves, indentured servants, and Indians. None of these men, let alone women, were included in the Declaration's claims for freedom. Struggles for freedom and dignity can be better understood when viewed in the historical context of competing classes, alliances, and factions than as abstract universal objectives.

With the end of the war came an end to unity. The noble ideals that invariably form and nurture revolutions too often recede before economic realities, in the aftermath of victory. The new country carried on much as it had before, minus only the control of the British. Having won liberty for themselves, the revolutionaries showed little interest in granting as much to their African slaves. Nor did editors and journalists of the time sound a clarion call for universal suffrage. In the period immediately following the war, American journalism was most undistinguished. The quality of editorship improved, but overt propaganda and partisanship were very much in evidence. The partisan press engaged in extreme vilification and outright lies.

There was a bitter schism between Federalists and the anti-Federalists, between advocacy of a strong central government as against a league of more or less independent states. Proponents of the centralization—who were mainly engaged in commerce, banking, manufacturing, and property management—often seemed intent on gearing America up for a capitalist, industrial future. Advocates of states' rights were made up largely of the agrarian, small farmer class—often augmented by a new urban class of discontented laborers. Land ownership requirements and voting qualifications frequently disenfranchised the city wage earner. But such characterizations are too sharply drawn. Many rich and worldly men opposed centralization, and many poor and obscure persons were for it. Each side included able and enlightened supporters, as well as those with less admirable motives.

In any event, it was mainly men of property and means who, in the summer of 1787, fashioned the Constitution that would replace the rickety Articles of Confederation. Reflecting the financial interests of the men who drafted it, the proposed Constitution was designed to foster economic development and preserve a stable society under the direction of a strong central government. Since state conventions had to ratify the new document before it could become law, movements to amend the Constitution soon began in all the states of the union. Advocates of limitations on central government were bolstered by the French Revolution of 1789, which had set in motion a political transformation far more radical than the American War for Independence.

Opposition to the new Constitution began to dissipate when a series of amendments was added, guaranteeing civil liberties of citizens against incursions by the national government and specifically reserving all unmentioned power to the states.

THE FIRST AMENDMENT

The fountainhead of the law governing freedom of expression is found in the First Amendment to the Constitution, which states in part, "Congress shall make no law . . . abridging the freedom of speech or of the press." It's a rather limited mandate. An earlier version of the amendment, which didn't survive passage in Congress, would have prohibited the states—as well as the federal government—from infringing on the rights of free expression. Leonard Levy, in his *Legacy of Suppression*, argues that the generation who adopted the Constitution, the Bill of Rights, and the early state constitutions did not believe in a broad scope for freedom of expression.[43] Undoubtedly, guarantees of free speech and press meant different things to different people. Certainly, the inherent vagueness of the First Amendment must have significantly contributed to its chances of being adopted.

The First Amendment has never been interpreted to permit totally unbridled expression. At the core of the matter is the delicate balance between freedom to communicate and responsibility for what is communicated. The safeguarding and fructification of free constitutional institutions is the very basis and mainstay upon which freedom of expression rests, and that freedom cannot be held to include the right to destroy such institutions. As early as 1798, Congress approved the Sedition Act, which made it a crime to utter "any false, scandalous and malicious" statements against the Government of the United States, the President, or members of the Congress or "to incite against them the hatred of the good people of the United States." At the time the sedition law was enacted, war with France seemed imminent, and rumors of French espionage and seditious activities were rampant. The law was used, however, in an attempt to suppress all criticism. Twenty-five persons were prosecuted and ten convicted, all in patently unfair trials. When Thomas Jefferson ascended to the presidency in 1801, they were all pardoned. But the episode served as an early reminder of the great difficulties involved in balancing the fundamental freedom of unhindered expression against the danger to society that is sometimes likely to result from that expression.

COMMERCIAL NEWSPAPERS

In the nineteenth century, as the United States expanded its industrial power and its economy, the press changed from a political voice to a vast impersonal institution.

The rapidly expanding economy was creating an enormous demand for information about market conditions and those political vicissitudes affecting the flow of raw materials and manufactured goods. By 1830, there were some 700 or so newspapers in the United States, 65 of them dailies.

Newspaper competition in New York was particularly keen. By 1828, eight morning newspapers competed for advertising and circulation. Five of these were devoted exclusively to commercial affairs. In just the previous year, two new morning newspapers were founded, the *Morning Courier* and the *Journal of Commerce*. The *Courier*, which merged with the New York *Enquirer* in 1829 to become the *Courier and Enquirer*, could boast of a circulation exceeding 4,000 by the early 1830s. In its earliest years, this combined newspaper was edited by the flamboyant James Watson Webb, who constantly engaged in journalistic jousts with his newspaper rivals.

The *Journal of Commerce* had been founded by Arthur Tappan, but it was soon taken over by David Hale and Gerard Hallock. Under their direction, the *Journal* became the *Courier*'s single strongest competitor. Both newspapers, for instance, maintained their own schooners to meet incoming ships, which brought foreign newspapers. The other morning papers in New York belonged to an association organized for the express purpose of sharing such expenses. A three-cornered rivalry emerged, which became so intense that, by 1831, maintenance of newsboats reached a combined cost of $25,000. Advertising revenue helped to defray this expense. In fact, advertisements in the *Courier and Enquirer*, for instance, were often so numerous that supplementary pages had to be printed. Profit was derived primarily from subscription sales. Since the average subscription cost about $8 to $10 a year, large circulations were out of the question. Individual copies could be purchased at the printer's office for 6¢ an issue. But even this price precluded a general readership, since the average worker only earned about 85¢ a day.

THE PENNY PRESS

The forces of economic and political change that were sweeping the nation, however, soon created circumstances conducive to the expansion of newspaper readership. During the 1830s and 1840s, as Michael

Schudson points out in *Discovering the News*, "the country was transformed from a liberal mercantilist republic, still cradled in aristocratic values, family, and deference, to an egalitarian market democracy, where money had new power, the individual new standing, and the pursuit of self-interest new honor."[44]

With the emergence of an expanding market economy and the growing authority of an entrepreneurial, urban middle class came a new, more colorful kind of journalism. Beginning with the publication of the New York *Sun* in 1833 by a 23-year-old job printer, Benjamin H. Day, penny newspapers began to capture a large and ever-widening readership.

The *Sun* was unlike any U.S. newspaper that had gone before.[45] Its emphasis was on local occurrences, particularly those of a sensational nature. For the purchase price of one penny, people could read stories of murder, mishap, and mayhem. The paper was an immediate success; within a few months, its circulation had climbed to 5,000. An important ingredient in its success was marketing. It was the first newspaper in the United States to be hawked on the streets by newsboys, who bought it in bulk from the publisher for 65¢ a hundred. By 1835, when the *Sun* became the first U.S. newspaper to purchase a steam-driven press, its circulation had tripled to more than 15,000 copies a day.

The *Sun*'s success soon spurred imitators. In 1835, James Gordon Bennett launched the New York *Herald* with his own blend of bravado, sensationalism, and capriciousness. Inside of a year, it had a circulation of 20,000.

The penny press quickly spread to other urban areas, as well. In rapid succession, a series of successful newspapers was founded. The Boston *Daily Times* appeared in 1836, and within several weeks of publication could claim a circulation of 8,000. That same year, the Philadelphia *Public Ledger* was launched. Its circulation soon climbed to 20,000, some ten times that of its nearest competition. The Baltimore *Sun*, founded in 1837, saw its circulation jump to over 10,000 within nine months.

These low-priced dailies gave new meaning to McLuhan's notion of the vernacular as a PA system par excellence. Books, theatres, and the temples of religion have all had their day, boasted James Gordon Bennett. "A newspaper can send more souls to Heaven, and save more from Hell, than all the churches and chapels in New York—besides making money at the same time."[46] Like Aretino and Rabelais of an earlier era, Bennett was intoxicated with the realization that the printing press could be a platform from which to address great multitudes of the unseen.

Bennett displayed a particular penchant for provocation. On more than one occasion, he lashed out at his competitors; he even accused some of the six-penny newspaper editors of using their own news and editorial columns to promote their own speculative stock ventures. Such charges prompted James Watson Webb of the *Courier and Enquirer* to assault Bennett, slashing his head with a cane.

Bennett's bravura knew few bounds. "I am going to be married in a few days," he proclaimed in a signed announcement appearing in the *Herald*'s editorial column on June 1, 1840. "The weather is so beautiful—times are so good—the prospects of political and moral reform so auspicious, that I cannot resist the divine instinct of honest nature any longer—so I am going to be married to one of the most splendid women in intellect, in heart, in soul, in property, in person, in manners, that I have yet seen in the course of my interesting pilgrimage through human life."[47]

Some of the penny papers in this period were not even averse to outright fabrication of the news. In the last week of its second year of publication, the New York *Sun* presented a seven-article series that purported to tell of the "Great Astronomical Discoveries, lately made by Sir John Herschel at the Cape of Good Hope." Attributed to the fictitious Edinburgh *Journal of Science*, the articles were actually written by a journalist named Richard Locke. Through a skillful blend of fact and fiction, Locke was able to concoct a very believable tale of life on the moon. The series started with a detailed account of the telescope used for the lunar explorations. Subsequent articles told of the moon's geology, geography, and natural history. The carefully paced narrative culminated with the revelation that the lunar surface was inhabited by batlike men and women who "spent their happy hours in collecting various fruits in the woods, in eating, flying, bathing, and loitering about upon the summits of precipices."[48]

It was a remarkably successful hoax. Other newspapers reprinted the articles, often with favorable comments on the magnitude of the discovery. The story managed to fool not only the average reader, but some members of the scientific community as well. Yale even sent a delegation to New York to investigate the report.

Why was the story so convincing? Why did readers so willingly suspend disbelief? There are some plausible explanations. Locke's use of scientific terminology, along with his continual references to various forms of authority, certainly added an important element of authenticity to the tale. Undoubtedly, the impersonality of the printed word itself also contributed a certain measure of verisimilitude.

But perhaps it might also be significant to question whether or not it mattered to the average person that the story was fabricated. It is reasonable to assume that many people at the time would have been in accordance with diarist Philip Hone when he noted on August 28, 1835, that "if this account is true, it is most enormously wonderful. And if it is fable, the manner of its relation, with all its scientific details, names of persons employed, and the beauty of its glowing description, will give this ingenious history a place with Gulliver's Travels and Robinson Crusoe."[49] Even after rival newspapers revealed the hoax, the *Sun's* circulation continued to climb.

Penny papers of a more sober sort also made their mark. Horace Greeley's serious and high-minded New York *Tribune* first appeared in 1841. Ten years later, Henry Jarvis Raymond and George Jones established the New York *Times*. Under Raymond's editorship, the *Times* soon gained a reputation for sobriety, moderation, and balance.

The appearance of the *Times* marked a new direction in journalism in other ways, as well. Raymond and Jones had begun the paper with a capitalization of $100,000. Just ten years earlier, Greeley had founded the *Tribune* with $2,000. Bennett's initial investment, 16 years before, had been only $500. It was a portent of the big business that journalism was to become. The print technology necessary to produce thousands of papers, combined with the costs of employing a large staff of reporters and managerial personnel, precluded establishment of a newspaper in a major city without substantial capital. Newspapers became not only a national institution; they became institutionalized.

Better printing techniques and faster productive capacity kept pace with rising circulation figures. The development of the web press in 1871, which printed on both sides of the paper fed into it from large rolls, and of the Linotype machine in 1886, which cast rows of type directly from molten metal, allowed for much greater speed and convenience in the production of newspapers. Newsgathering itself was greatly facilitated by the development of telegraph and the establishment of press associations.

DEVELOPMENT OF THE TELEGRAPH

Various systems for employing electricity to send messages had been attempted early in the nineteenth century.[50] In the 1830s, Samuel Morse (a painter turned scientist) perfected the process. Morse adopted a simple key to make and break an electrical circuit, which produced a clicking sound of long or short duration depending on the operator's timing. A pen or stylus marked a motor-driven tape in accordance with the pulse of current in the circuit. Combinations of these "dots and dashes" of sound were developed by Morse into code corresponding to the letters of the alphabet. A frequently used letter such as "e" is represented by a simple dot. The combination for the less frequently occurring "q" is dash–dash–dot–dash. A skilled operator was soon able to send or receive 35 or more words a minute utilizing the code.

After a series of public demonstrations of his electrical marvel in 1838, Morse petitioned Congress for an appropriation to build an experimental line. In 1844, with a government subsidy of $30,000, Morse installed the first operational telegraph line between Baltimore and Washington, D.C.

When Morse sat at a table in the old Supreme Court chamber in Washington and tapped out the dramatic query "What has God wrought?" to his assistant in Baltimore, the bond between communications and transportation had finally been broken. Henceforth, the transmission of communication content by electrical energy was to play an increasingly important part in the social and economic development of the nation and the world.

Almost from the outset, telegraphy was a capitalist enterprise in the United States. In most other countries it was, or became, state owned and operated. Even Britain, birthplace of industrial capitalism, nationalized telegraphy under the Post Office in 1869. Morse had offered his invention to the United States Government; but, when Congress demurred, he and his associates sought private funds. There followed a period of intense rivalry; some 50 telegraph companies sprung up, a few for no other reason than to sell stock. Cutthroat competition was the order of the day. Through an aggressive policy of acquisitions, Western Union eventually emerged out of the confusion in a position of supremacy. By 1866, this company had acquired 50,000 miles of line and was well on its way to becoming a monopoly in the telegraph industry.

Western Union's board members included such tycoons as John Jacob Astor and William H. Vanderbilt. Control of the nation's web of wires was a key to wealth and power. For instance, in 1875 Representative Charles A. Sumner of California charged that information regarding sudden changes in market prices was often withheld from San Francisco until insiders could make a profit. In 1881, Jay Gould—that most rapacious of robber barons—gained control of the giant telegraph company. Gould, who at the time also owned a major New York newspaper, used his privileged access to commercial intelligence ruthlessly. "He scanned the telegraph, or manipulated it, as an open book to the secrets of all the marts," writes Matthew Josephson.[51]

On a number of occasions, Congress tried to break Western Union's monopoly hold over the flow of information—to little avail. More than 70 bills designed to reform the telegraph system were considered by Congress in the decades following the Civil War, but Western Union was able to muster strong opposition. Congressmen in both major political parties who were friendly to Western Union's interests received unlimited supplies of "franks"—forms providing free telegraph service. The franking privilege was a strong inducement for government officials to favor the telegraph company, because it allowed them to keep in touch with constituents, particularly during campaigns.

PRESS ASSOCIATIONS

Western Union's alliance with the major press associations was another source of its influence.[52] By 1848, the mounting expense of carrier pigeons, pony express, railroads, harbor boats to meet incoming ships, and telegraph tolls made cooperation among newspapers an economic necessity. In that year, a number of influential newspapers in New York joined forces to share the costs of procuring national and international news. Each newspaper remained independent but was served by a jointly formed organization that came to be called the Associated Press (AP) of New York. This new association soon achieved a commanding position in the newspaper industry. It employed reporters in all the principal cities in the United States and Canada. Its priority arrangements with the owners of the telegraph wires allowed the organization to sell its dispatches to newspapers outside New York. Subscribers to this service were compelled to foreswear the use of rival agencies.

The preeminent position of the New York group was not seriously challenged until after 1865, with the emergence of the Western Associated Press. Made up of Midwestern dailies, the Western AP began to contest the autocratic control of the New York newspapers. Western customers of the New York AP had become increasingly disgruntled by the service's emphasis on news of interest mainly to the seven charter members. The two press associations finally reached an agreement in 1892 to cooperate with the establishment of a joint executive committee consisting of three New York representatives and two from the West. Each signed contracts with the mighty Western Union, pledging not to use the wires of rival companies. In turn, the giant telegraph company agreed not to enter the newsgathering field (except to sell market reports). The Western newspapers eventually gained dominance of Associated Press; and, as a result of court pressure, the entire association was reorganized in 1900 as a nonprofit cooperative. Members shared the cost of exchanging news and paid the association's news staff, which collated regional coverage and augmented it with additional information. Under the new setup, a member newspaper could still veto service to a local competitor. (This arrangement was maintained until the 1940s, when it was successully challenged in the courts.)

Beginning in 1907, the monopoly hold of the Associated Press was broken by the Scripps newspaper chain's establishment of the United Press Association (UP) as a privately owned enterprise for the gathering and dissemination of news. In addition to supplying its own newspapers, Scripps made the service available to those papers not admitted to the Associated Press. Two years later, the Hearst organization developed a third major news service, the International News Serivce (INS). (United Press and the International News Service merged in 1958, forming United Press International—UPI).

THE JOURNALISM OF PULITZER AND HEARST

During the last third of the nineteenth century, the United States experienced dramatic changes characterized by industrialization, immigration, and urbanization. This was the age of steel mills, oil

refineries, railroad interconnections, expanding factories, and a growing labor force.

Factories needed workers and people were immigrating to the
United States by the millions. Between 1870 and 1900, the population
almost doubled. The influx of people tended to concentrate in the industrial Northeastern states. New York, where the population was fast
approaching 4 million by the beginning of the new century, became a
city of immigrants. There were some 58 cities with a population of
more than half a million by the 1890s.

This expanding industrial society, not unlike the situation in
England, allowed for enormous growth in newspaper circulation. The
first publisher in the United States to reach a truly massive readership
was Joseph Pulitzer, a Hungarian-born immigrant who had learned
the newspaper business in St. Louis.[53] As publisher, editor, and
business manager of the St. Louis *Post-Dispatch*, Pulitzer established a
reputation for combining sensationalism with crusading journalism. In
1883, he bought the New York *World*, a newspaper of some reputation,
which had fallen on hard times. At the time of the Pulitzer purchase,
the *World* had a circulation of perhaps 15,000. Within two years,
circulation had soared to 100,000; and, by 1887, it passed the quarter-
million figure.

The *World's* remarkable success may be attributed to several
factors. Its use of bold headlines and clear illustrations, together with
its emphasis on relatively simple words and sentence structure helped
to attract a broad general readership. Another magnet for readers was
its diverse coverage: stories of sex, scandal, crime, and disaster; extensive political and financial reports; special features for women; a whole
department for sports; crusading editorials. When there was little of
interest to report, the *World* would create its own news.

To keep circulation climbing, the *World* launched a number of
spectacular publicity stunts. In 1885, for instance, the *World* itself
made news when it raised $100,000 from the nickel-and-dime contribu-
tions of readers to build a pedestal for the Statue of Liberty. Among the
World's most remarkable news-producing exploits were those of Nelly
Bly, the by-line name used by Elizabeth Cochrane. She would go to incredible lengths for good copy. On one occasion, she even feigned in-
sanity to get inside the asylum at Blackwell's Island, in order to expose
the conditions there. In 1889, Pulitzer sent Bly around the world to see
if she could beat the travel time of Jules Verne's fictional character
Phineas Fogg. To stimulate reader interest in the exploit, the *World*

offered a free trip to Europe to the person whose guess came closest to the actual time it took Bly to circle the globe. The contest drew nearly a million estimates. Historian Daniel Boorstin would later call this kind of synthetic novelty ''pseudo-events''—happenings that are planned for the express purpose of being reported or reproduced. Pseudo-events—in the form of press conferences, trial balloons, background briefings, and the like—came to play an increasingly important role in U.S. journalism. Since the early twentieth century, noted Boorstin, ''a larger and larger proportion of our experience, of what we read and see and hear, has come to consist of pseudo-events.''[54] Those in a position to create such events tend to set the agenda for national discussion.

Pulitzer's methods were quickly copied by competitors, especially by William Randolph Hearst, who became owner and editor of the New York *Journal* in 1895 and soon outdid the *World* in sensationalism.[55] Scion of a vast fortune, Hearst was determined to build circulation at any cost. Some of his detractors have even accused him of fomenting the Spanish-American War, merely so he could report it. Although such a charge is grossly simplistic, it is not without some degree of truth. Hearst's jingoistic coverage of a Cuban insurgency did much to provoke war hysteria in the United States. Late in 1896, for instance, Hearst sent reporter Richard Harding Davis and artist Frederic Remington to Havana to cover the conflict between Cuban insurgents and Spanish authorities. When Remington requested to be relieved of the assignment because nothing much was happening, Hearst is supposed to have responded: ''Please remain. You furnish the pictures and I'll furnish the war.'' Despite such encouragement, the noted artist left Cuba after a week.

However, Davis stayed on and managed to smuggle out a few dubious tales of Spanish atrocity, culled from rebel sympathizers. In February 1897, he sent out a story about Spanish police boarding a U.S. vessel bound for New York in order to search three young Cuban women who were suspected of carrying insurgent dispatches. The *Journal* featured the story on page one under the five-column headline: ''DOES OUR FLAG PROTECT WOMEN?'' On page two, the text was accompanied by a half-page Remington drawing, imagined from New York, showing one of the women naked and surrounded by policemen searching her clothing.

It was the kind of stuff that built circulation—nearly a million copies of the newspaper were sold. But it was not an accurate depiction of what actually had taken place. The *World*, undoubtedly disgruntled by the growing competition from the *Journal*, sent reporters to interview the Cuban women when they arrived in the United States. The women made it clear that they had been searched by matrons, not by policemen.

Seizing on the opportunity to embarrass its competitor, the *World* exposed the *Journal's* misrepresentation of the facts, under the headline: "THE UNCLOTHED WOMEN SEARCH BY MEN WAS AN INVENTION OF A NEW YORK NEWSPAPER."

Undeterred, Hearst continued to foment war. In 1898, when the battleship Maine exploded in the harbor of Havana, taking the lives of 256 U.S. sailors, the *Journal* offered a $50,000 reward for information leading to the arrest and conviction of the perpetrators. Under the screaming headline: "THE WARSHIP MAINE WAS SPLIT BY AN ENEMY'S SECRET INFERNAL MACHINE," the *Journal* presented a seven-column drawing of the ship anchored over mines, and a diagram showing wires leading from the mines to a Spanish fortress on shore. Such flights of fancy shot the circulation of the *Journal* well past the 1 million mark. Three days after the sinking, the *Journal* proclaimed in bold type: "THE WHOLE COUNTRY THRILLS WITH WAR FEVER."

Hearst was the least scrupulous of all the major newspaper publishers at the time. But his self-proclaimed propensity for "journalism that acts" was not unusual to him. Many other newspapers were reflecting the very same attitude. Large headlines, striking illustrations, and sensationalized stories had become common practice.

NEWSPAPERS OF NOTE

Sobriety and moderation, however, did not disappear entirely from U.S. journalism during this period.[56] The New York *Times*, in particular, demonstrated that a journalistic enterprise could still succeed without resorting to sensationalism. After Henry Jarvis Raymond's death in 1869, the *Times* declined steadily. When Adolphs Ochs purchased the paper in 1896, its circulation had dropped to 9,000. Under the stewardship of Ochs, the *Times* expanded its coverage of financial news, market reports, real estate transactions, and other activities of interest to men of commerce and industry. This business orientation soon found an audience. Within a year, circulation had reached

25,000, and advertising kept pace. In 1898, Ochs dropped the purchase price of the *Times* from 3¢ to a penny—thereby making it accessible to a broader readership. Within three years, circulation had jumped to more than 100,000. While this figure was small compared to the million-plus circulations of the *World* and *Journal*, it was big enough to secure a solid place for the *Times* in U.S. journalism.

A financial news service for private clients, founded in 1882 by Charles H. Dow and Edward T. Jones, evolved later in the decade into the *Wall Street Journal*. Circulation remained small until the 1940s, when the paper broadened its coverage of business and finance to include all events of international and national importance affecting the business community. Eventually, multiple printing plants and domestic satellite relays gave to the newspaper a national readership of well over a million people. The *Christian Science Monitor*, founded by the Christian Science Church of Boston in 1908, also emerged as a nationally read newspaper of distinction. This daily pioneered an interpretative approach to problems and trends in regional, national, and international affairs.

The leading daily in the midwest was the Chicago *Tribune*, which first appeared in 1847. Under the control of Joseph Medill, who with his partners purchased the paper in 1855, it challenged the New York *Herald* in flamboyant personal journalism. It was a vitriolic publication; despite its overt emphasis on moral values, it did not hesitate to use the power of mass circulation to pour invective on those with whom it was in disagreement. But its circulation soared; and then, as now, the Chicago *Tribune* was considered a newspaper with a strong conservative (its critics call it reactionary) point of view. It was antilabor and defended the status quo with vigor and stubbornness. Robert McCormick and Joseph Patterson assumed control of the newspaper in 1914. Under McCormick's direction (until his death in 1955), it became one of the best-written, most forceful dailies in the country.

Other areas outside New York and the Eastern seaboard also had newspapers of distinction. William Rockhill Nelson established the Kansas City *Star* in 1880. This superb publication shunned sensational coverage and showed what a medium of mass communication can accomplish when it determines to drive corruption out of a city by exposing its perpetrators to public view through the instrumentality of the press. Nelson battled politicians and gamblers and campaigned vigorously for improving the quality of life in the rough-and-tumble town of Kansas City. By the time of his death in 1915, the *Star*'s circulation had climbed to 170,000. It remains one of the great newspapers in the United States. In general, though, the newspapers that sprang up in the West and the South were not very impressive. The Denver *Post*, a sober publication today, was launched on sensationalism and a series of stunts and crusades by Harry H. Tammen and Fred G. Bonfils. In San Francisco, the *Chronicle* was an enterprising and exemplary journalistic endeavor until challenged by the emergence of William Randolph Hearst and the San Francisco *Examiner*, a newspaper that typified the overwrought, shocking, and frequently lurid journalism of the period.

For the most part, journalism in the South was undistinguished, although there were a few outstanding newspapers. When Henry W. Grady became part owner and managing editor of the Atlanta *Constitution* in 1880, for example, he helped to develop that publication into one of the best-written, best-edited newspapers in the country. The University of Georgia's School of Journalism, which offers the annual George Foster Peabody Broadcasting Awards, is named after Grady. Another fine newspaper in this generally lackluster area was Henry Patterson's Louisville *Courier-Journal*, which—like the Atlanta *Constitution*—championed the rehabilitation and development of a vigorous South.

ON THE HORIZON

Newspapers provided potential benefits for U.S. society, at least some of which had been realized by the end of the nineteenth century. The advent of the penny press and the rise of mass circulation dailies increased the opportunity for information and entertainment of those who were societally disenfranchised. Information and ideas, available quickly and cheaply to ever greater numbers of people, offered unique possibilities for citizen awareness of, and participation in, the process of government. But the rise of a print-oriented culture was accompanied by perplexing problems: the discontents of urban civilization, the expansion of colonialism, and the breakdown of traditional values and beliefs.

By the waning years of the nineteenth century, new media were already on the horizon that would touch everyday life far more viscerally than had any newspaper or other product of the printed word. Paralleling the emergence of the mass circulation newspaper, there unfolded what Daniel Boorstin has called the ''Graphic Revolution''—the ability to make, preserve, transmit, and disseminate precise images.[57] With the advent of this new cultural machinery, verisimilitude would take on new meaning. Vivid imagery would make everyday reality pale by comparison. Whoever controlled this image-making apparatus might ultimately wield greater power than those who owned banks and factories.

2

The Hollywood Heritage

Few forces have been more influential in shaping the way we see the world than the American movie industry. For more than half a century, the Hollywood ethos has dominated the popular arts of the United States, if not the world. Even today, the influence of the movie industry is thoroughly pervasive and inescapable. Hollywood and its physical and metaphoric environs are a major source of television fare, and the movies still manage to attract lines of customers outside theatre box offices across the country.

This chapter traces the growth of filmmaking from an individual endeavor into a major industry with enormous power, influence, and appeal. The primary focus is on the development, the managerial structure, the production practices, and the artistic creations of the major Hollywood studios, which have dominated the movie industry almost from the outset.

ORIGINS OF MOTION PICTURES

Around the time Johann Gutenberg's printing press was causing a stir in Germany, a new innovation of another sort had become a source of wonder in Italy. Someone had discovered that light passing through a small aperture in one wall of a dark room—a "camera obscura"—projected an image of the outside world onto the opposite wall. The picture was upside down, however.

By the sixteenth century, the camera obscura had become a familiar tool of artists. Placing a lens in the aperture permitted the projection of the outside image onto a small piece of paper. By holding the paper steady, artists were able to trace the perspective of the image with a pen.

Eventually, the lens was put on one side of a box, instead of in the wall. Using mirrors, the image could be thrown onto a glass screen in the box, and seen right side up.

The next step was to preserve the image. In 1727, Johann Heinrich Schulze had shown that certain chemicals, especially silver halides, turn dark when exposed to light. But the combination of chemical and optical principles to produce photography had to await a flash of genius—and for the social and political transformations of the late eighteenth and early nineteenth centuries to stimulate demand.

One of the first attempts to capture the camera image was made in 1802 by Thomas Wedgwood, son of the famous English potter. In 1813, Joseph Nicéphore Nièpce, an amateur French inventor, began to experiment with transferring lithographic drawings by the aid of light. Nièpce made the first negative. While he was perfecting this technique, he heard about similar experiments being made by Louis-Jacques Mandé Daguerre, a Parisian set designer. Daguerre and Nièpce became partners in 1828; but Nièpce died before they could perfect the photographic process together. Daguerre went on alone and, in 1839, produced a workable system of photography—but one in which photographs were not reproducible. Improvements made by William Henry Fox Talbot in England soon made it possible for any number of copies to be made.

As photography improved technologically, the creative possibilities of producing "pictures that moved" were quickly recognized. The interest in picturing motion existed for various reasons—for art's sake, for education, and as a medium for entertainment and profit. By the waning years of the nineteenth century, almost all the technical concepts necessary for the creation of motion pictures were discovered or about to be discovered somewhere in the world.

There were simultaneous efforts in France, Germany, England, and Russia to develop a method of using the static photograph to create the illusion of moving images. A French physiologist, Etienne-Jules Marey, had conceived the idea of an advancing filmstrip, although he had not been able to determine the mechanism for keeping this advance regular. In the United States, the British-born photographer Eadweard Muybridge had been developing a rapid exposure camera.

The real breakthrough was made in Thomas Edison's laboratory in West Orange, New Jersey. By the 1890s, Edison and his talented assistant William Dickson perfected a movie camera called the Kinetograph.[1] Synthesizing the knowledge already developed by others, Edison and Dickson added an important technical innovation—the perforation of the film strip at equidistant intervals, thus controlling the speed of the film advance—and, hence, the motion. But Edison was not interested in a projection apparatus at this time. Dickson devised a viewing mechanism to exhibit the positive prints made from the Kinetograph negatives. Called the Kinetoscope, this device consisted of a large cabinet containing batteries and a motor that turned a strip of film on a spool bank and operated a light. Perforated holes along the margin of the filmstrip caused it to revolve on the sprocketed spools. For viewing, there was an eyepiece and a lens at the front of the cabinet, through which one spectator at a time could peer at the film as it moved in rapid succession along the sprockets. Expanding on the work of Edison, Auguste and Louis Lumière developed a combined camera and projector in 1894, which they named the *Cinématographe*. Early in 1895, the brothers Lumière shot their first film, *Workers Leaving the Lumière Factory*. It was truly literal in concept. They merely turned on the camera to record the events that chanced to occur in front of the lens. The spectacle of "actual moving figures" was presumed to be novel enough to draw the admission price from the pockets of an audience desiring to be entertained.

In the United States, significant advances in motion picture projection were made by Thomas Armat who, working with Francis Jenkins, developed a projector that incorporated the intermittent movement of film, a sprocket providing for a small loop before and after the film gate to relax film tension, and a shutter device designed to give the screen long periods of illumination and relatively short periods of darkness.

Edison's commercial backers offered to finance the manufacture and sale of this projector. It was promoted as the "Edison Vitascope," the wizard's latest invention. The Vitascope had its first public showing on April 23 1896, at the Koster and Bial's Music Hall in New York City. Armat remained discretely in the background, but neither he nor Edison was happy with the arrangement. A year or so later, when Edison devised his own projector, their arrangement was terminated and Armat regained his patent rights.

THE EMERGENCE OF THE MOVIE INDUSTRY

The popular success of motion pictures in the United States was almost immediate. Vaudeville houses soon adopted motion pictures as a standard component of their program schedules. Empty stores, restaurants, and pawn shops—particularly in the densely populated, immigrant, working-class neighborhoods—were converted into money-making movie theatres. For a brief period, the admission charge was a nickel (not an insignificant unit in those days), hence the term "nickelodeon." Within the walls of the small, impoverished halls, immigrant slum dwellers would huddle together on wooden benches to vicariously live the adventures depicted in the two-dimensional, black-and-white images flashed on the silent screen. By 1905, numerous "storefront theatres" were to be found in any good-sized town or city.[2] These establishments offered a chance to escape the travails of the new industrial society.

In order to meet the growing demand for movies, production companies proliferated, springing up in all areas of the country. By late 1908, the competitive battle for audience dollars became so frenzied that the leaders of the industry—that is, those who controlled the patents—moved to combat competition by forming the Motion Picture Patents Company (MPPC).[3] This organization was a complex national monopoly, designed to control all phases of the motion picture industry: production, distribution, and exhibition. Two important motion picture companies were Edison and Biograph, which had grown powerful even in the days when movies were just part of the amusement arcades patronized by factory workers seeking to spend their idle hours. Biograph had been formed by William Dickson in 1895. These two companies controlled the important patents for the industry. Both of them had licensed other firms to use their patents—either involving cameras or projectors, or both.

The competition between Edison and Biograph was very keen, and bid fair to exhaust the resources of both companies. They soon realized the futility of this; and so, as the two major stockholders of the MPPC, they joined forces to organize it—along with Vitagraph and Armat, two other makers of camera and projector equipment. Each of these four manufacturers received enormous royalties for the assignment of their respective patents.

The MPPC's licensees included the U.S. producers Biograph, Edison, Essanay, Kalem, Lubin, Selig, and Vitagraph; the French firm

Pathe Frères; and Kleine Optical, a U.S. importer of foreign films and equipment. Six of the companies were based in New York City, three in Chicago, and one in Philadelphia.

Many of the companies, however, migrated to sunnier climates during the winter months. As early as 1907, director Francis Boggs of the Selig Company in Chicago set up a production unit in Los Angeles to shoot some water scenes in *The Count of Monte Cristo* at the nearby oceanfront in Santa Monica. The move foreshadowed the eventual California base of the industry. Weather would no longer impede the production of films to satisfy a paying audience who were hungry for fantasy.

In an effort to secure its position of control in filmmaking and movie distribution, the MPPC entered into an exclusive agreement with the Eastman Kodak Company, the country's sole manufacturer of raw film stock. The MPPC also organized its own rental exchange, the General Film Company, to distribute films only to exhibitors licensed by the MPPC. But such efforts at monopoly did not go unchallenged. As early as 1911, the threat of serious antitrust prosecution caused the MPPC to abandon its exclusivity arrangement with Kodak.

The most devastating blow to the MPPC came on the economic front. So-called ''independent companies''—that is, outside the trust—gradually gained dominance over all aspects of the movie industry. By 1914, internal dissension, inefficiency, and reluctance to change made the MPPC almost wholly ineffectual; the courts declared it legally dead three years later. Although the MPPC had financial and organizational supremacy over the independents, many members of its hierarchy lacked sensitivity to the mercurially changing tastes of the ever-growing audience for movies.

THE NEW ORDER

Among the independents who successfully challenged the MPPC monopoly was a German haberdasher named Carl Laemmle. He had opened a nickelodeon in 1906, with a modest investment. By 1909—that is, within three years—Laemmle had become the head of a major distribution concern, supplying films to such major film markets as Chicago, Minneapolis, Omaha, and Portland, Oregon. Laemmle went into independent production in 1909, essentially in order to supply his theatres. In one year, he had produced close to 100 films. It is Laemmle who is generally credited with inaugurating the star system. Most companies had intentionally maintained the anonymity of their players, in order to keep salary demands to a minimum. However, movie patrons quickly came to favor certain performers. Laemmle hired a popular player named Florence Lawrence and launched a spectacular publicity campaign to call the public's attention to the fact that she would be appearing exclusively in his productions. The campaign was one of the earliest "publicity buildups" by a film company, and proved profitable enough to be emulated by entertainment media to this day.

Another entrepreneur who proved profitably able to cater to the moviegoing common denominator was Adolph Zukor. An impoverished immigrant from Hungary, Zukor became a prosperous furrier who diversified his interests to include penny arcades, nickelodeons, and—eventually—a chain of movie theatres. Zukor was the first to successfully expand the appeal of the movies beyond the neighborhood and working-class audience, with his presentation of the French-produced *Queen Elizabeth*, featuring the famous stage actress Sarah Bernhardt in the title role. This 1912 film version of Elisabeth's love for Essex was a huge success, despite its plodding staginess. The leading figures of the business and theatrical world, who did not ordinarily attend motion pictures, were out in force for the film's U.S. debut at the Lyceum Theatre in New York City. The lure of movies was spreading.

Zukor was typical of the sharper breed of showmen of those times. He had been dealing with Paramount Pictures Exchange as his distributor, but was not pleased at the constraints and terms imposed by this firm. He proposed a merger; but, when this was turned down by Paramount's management, Zukor maneuvered to buy up Paramount stock. Within a year, he was running that company as well as the production company he had headed since 1912. As the production head of Famous Players Company, Zukor began to collect under contract to this company well-known and popular actors and actresses: James O'Neill, Minnie Maddern Fiske, Geraldine Farrar, and others. With his impressive roster, he was able to raise the price for film rentals sharply, and to impose the requirement that exhibitors accept bad films along with good films—a policy to be known as "block booking."

Another successful independent to achieve a position of power and influence in the movie industry was William Fox. Raised in the tenements of Manhattan's Lower East Side, Fox invested his $1,600 savings in a Brooklyn nickelodeon in 1904. This modest enterprise was ultimately to evolve into a corporate aggregation of staggering proportions. Fox's Brooklyn operation developed into a chain of 15 houses. He then entered the film distribution field, to buy and lease films to his own and other theatres. Fox successfully resisted attempts by the distribution arm of the MPPC—General Film Company—to buy him out; and he instituted a lawsuit against the MPPC, charging it with unlawful conspiracy in restraint of trade in violation of the 1890 Sherman Antitrust Act. It was this suit, which went to trial in 1913, that ultimately resulted in the dissolution of the MPPC by the courts, some five years later. To buttress his position, Fox had created a production company. He purchased the rights to Virginia Cross's novel *Life's Shop Window* for $100. Filming it on Staten Island, he made it into a feature starring Claire Whitney and Stuart Holmes. Soon the production company was turning out a feature every week. In February 1915, Fox and his associates incorporated as the Fox Film Corporation.

The Fox Film Corporation catapulted several players to stardom with an assiduous use of publicity techniques. The company's most famous female star from 1915 to 1919 was the seductive and sinister Theda Bara (née Theodosia Goodman, the daughter of a Cincinnati tailor). Her screen name (an anagram of "Arab death") and her exotic background were fabricated by Fox's publicity department, who presented her to the American public as the child of a French artist by his Arabian mistress, born on the desert sands in the shadow of the Sphinx.

HOLLYWOOD BOUND

In order to accommodate progressively heavier shooting schedules, most motion picture production companies began to center their activities on the West Coast. Southern California weather gave much more latitude in the number of days available for production. Moreover, its natural scenery provided—at no cost—backdrops for African or Saharan desert dramas, for ocean battles, and for Riviera parties in frothy comedies. But sunshine and seacoast were not the only attractions: Los Angeles at the time was the nation's leading open-shop, nonunion city.

There, Hollywood, with all its mythical glamour and glitter became the hub around which most production activity centered, although the majority of the movie companies maintained administrative offices in New York City, close to the center of finance. As the motion picture capital of the world, Hollywood was a magnet for aspiring actors and actresses. Young women, in particular, migrated west in the expectation that they might have that elusive, indefinable quality called personality, for which movie producers were supposedly always searching. In the ten years from 1919 to 1929, up to 50,000 girls are estimated to have been attracted to Los Angeles by visions of stardom and the hope of romance.[4] Most of them were sorely disappointed. But since no one was certain just what made a star—why the camera seemed to like some people and not others—every so often one of these young hopefuls found her way to success. An oil and real estate boom in Los Angeles in the early 1920s added to the myth that, in this promised land, anyone might become rich and famous. "The hordes which flocked to Los Angeles," writes Leo Rosten, "included a generous assortment of the déclassé: hard men and easy women, adventurers, racetrack touts, quacks and cranks of every delicate shape and hue." Moreover, the movie industry attracted its own odd assortment of hoofers, acrobats, bareback riders, sword swallowers, and the like. These were characters, as Rosten put it, "in seach of an offer."[5]

The movie colony itself was a breeding ground for insecurity and self-doubt. Writers, actors and actresses, directors, and almost all the important talent of the movie industry lived under the constant threat of obsolescence. Contracts were drawn and signed for long terms, tying creative workers to a single company for seven years, usually. However, employers renewed the options on the contracts at six-month intervals. At any renewal point, an employee might be dropped—"not renewed." Tension was high, and interest was understandably oriented toward ways to insure that an option would not be dropped.

THE GRIFFITH LEGACY

If the film has a form and rule of its own, it was David Wark Griffith, who first refined and developed that art form.[6] He struck out in fresh ways in the use of the camera—the development of long shots, close-ups, angle shots—and the techniques of editing. He introduced the practice of rehearsing before shooting a scene, and developed a company of players that he directed with both discipline and a desire to explore new ways in film presentation.

The son of a Confederate colonel, Griffith left his rural Kentucky home and worked briefly for a Louisville newspaper. Subsequently, he gravitated to motion pictures, first as an actor, then—quite quickly—

as a director. By the end of 1912, he had made well over 400 films for Biograph. With each film, Griffith increased the complexity and variety of movements within his shots, gradually becoming a master of mise-en-scène—the term for such compositional elements as the choice of setting and lighting, the placement of actors, and the angle and position of the camera. However, he was becoming increasingly dismayed by his employer's adherence to a single reel restriction. Griffith was determined to move from the one-reel film to a longer format, for he saw in the full-length feature the genuine creative potential of the motion picture as an art form.

In the spring of 1911, he had made a two-reel film, *Enoch Arden*, the story of a shipwrecked man who returns home to find his wife remarried; but Biograph released each reel separately. The following year he produced a four-reel biblical epic, *Judith of Bethulia*. It was in this film that Griffith first demonstrated the use of what was later to be called his "montage" style, his remarkable skill at cutting and construction. When Biograph decided to shelve the film temporarily, he broke with the company and eventually embarked on an independent production that would make him world famous.

From a novel entitled *The Clansmen*, Griffith produced one of America's classic films, *The Birth of a Nation*. The dramatic power and reach of this 1915 motion picture constituted a significant milestone in the recognition of the film medium as an art form with a structure and aesthetic of its own. However, Griffith's artistry is undeniably compromised by *The Birth of a Nation's* promulgation of racist propaganda and its glorification of the hooded vigilante riders of the Ku Klux Klan. Pressure from the NAACP resulted in the deletion of several sections of the film. When the film opened in Boston, a crowd of some 3,000 marched to the Massachusetts state capitol, demanding an end to the exhibition. Such responses were testimony to the enormous power of motion pictures. The book on which the film was based, although a popular best-seller, had caused little controversy.

In Griffith's next major film, called *Intolerance*, he intercut a modern story of class hatred and the miscarriage of justice with three stories of intolerance from different historical periods: the overthrow of Belshazzar in Babylon; the crucifixtion of Christ in Judea; and the slaughter of the Huguenots in sixteenth-century France. All four stories progressed simultaneously and the climax was built through the use of shorter and shorter cuts, into a visual symphony of mounting suspense.

Although *Intolerance* was not a commerical success, it remains a towering achievement and, above all, a motion picture from which innumerable directors have learned the art of filmmaking. "Griffith had hit upon a truth with the implications that all motion picture directors since then have been trying to command," writes film historian Lewis Jacobs about the director's work in general. "It is that the primary tools of the screen medium are the camera and the film rather than the actor; that the subject matter must be conceived in terms of the camera's eye and the film cutting; that the unit of the film art is the shot; that manipulation of shots builds the scene; that continuity of scenes build the sequences; and that the progression of sequences composes the totality of the production."[7]

AESTHETIC VISIONS

As motion pictures proceeded toward full features, the aesthetic possibilities of the new medium began to receive more serious attention from cultural critics and intellectuals. In 1915, Vachel Lindsay published *The Art of the Moving Picture* and, in the following year, Hugo Münsterberg's *The Photoplay: A Psychological Study* appeared.

Poet Vachel Lindsay's paean to motion pictures sought to adapt classical aesthetic standards to the new medium.[8] He identified three types of "photoplays" (as movies with pretensions to high art were then called): the photoplay of Action, the photoplay of Intimacy, and the photoplay of Splendor. Each had its antecedent in an older art form. Thus he discussed motion pictures respectively as sculpture-in-motion, painting-in-motion, and architecture-in-motion. But Lindsay clearly saw the potential for a distinct motion picture aesthetic. At the time he wrote, the few films that enjoyed any cultural acclaim were those that mimicked theatrical productions. In a chapter entitled "Thirty Differences between Photoplays and the Stage," he argued cogently for the development of a cinematic art form in its own right. Although he discussed a large number of contemporary motion pictures, it was the future potential of the adolescent art that he emphasized. He called upon the great art museums; departments of English, drama, and art history; and the critical and literary world, in general, to muster their resources in order to establish the theory and practice of the photoplay as a fine art.

Lindsay's contribution is less memorable for its success in formulating a coherent motion picture aesthetic than for its role in bestowing respectability upon the new medium. Recognition of the artistic merit of the motion picture medium received a much bigger boost the following year from Hugo Münsterberg, chairman of Harvard's philosophy department and one of the founders of modern psychology.[9] Münsterberg argued that any appreciation of the aethetic independence of the motion pictures must be predicated on an understanding of their psychological nature. For instance, both depth and movement, he explained, are a mixture of perception and intellect. "They are present yet they are not in the things. We invest the impression with them." For Münsterberg the motion picture medium was endowed with a kind of power the stage could never have, a power that went beyond the mere illusion of depth and movement. Münsterberg was the first to observe that motion pictures obey the "laws of the mind," where a variety of spatial and temporal images can coexist. The close-up objectified the "mental act of attention," thereby giving the motion picture art "a means which far transcend[ed] the power of any theater stage." Flashbacks (he used the term "cutback") paralleled the close-up of objectifying the mental act of remembering. The technique of cutting, in particular, allowed the interests of the inner world of the mind to mold the objective outer world in a way not attainable in other art forms. "Events which are far distant from one another so that we could not be physically present at all of them at the same time are fusing in our field of vision, just as they are brought together in our consciousness." A coherent narrative can be assembled from disparate pieces of time and space, eliding the here and now in favor of a more fragmented vision of experience. Once the basic psychology of the motion picture is comprehended, Münsterberg felt, its unique aesthetic will follow naturally.

Such aesthetic theories had little influence on the emerging movie industry in the United States. The impetus toward film experimentation came from abroad, not Hollywood. In Germany, France, and the Soviet Union, economic considerations did not thwart the desire to push the perimeters of cinema aesthetics.

The flowering of a postwar art in Germany—misanthropic and disillusioned but nevertheless striking and effective—was also evident in films, where there was an effort to probe the emotions and tensions of the postwar generation. This period witnessed the production of a number of sordid, pathological, and expressionistic films, such as *The Cabinet of Dr. Caligari* (1919)—a brilliant and highly stylized treatment of madness and evil. In this film and its successors, theorist Siegfried Kracauer saw evidence of deep psychological dispositions in the German people, which he felt helped to explain the rise of Nazism.[10]

In France, films were influenced by the fashion of surrealism, impressionism, and Dadaism in the ateliers of contemporary artists.[11] René Clair used film to create a pure cinema of visual sensation divorced from conventional narrative. Luis Buñuel, a Spanish director working in France, experimented with surrealist and symbolist themes that did not eschew the most sordid aspects of the human condition.

Intellectuals of every political persuasion saw in celluloid a powerful platform for the initiation of cultural innovation and social change. Sergei Eisenstein, the Russian director, produced vibrantly revolutionary films, which have left an indelible mark on history and cinema alike. In such films as *Potemkin* (1925) and *Ten Days That Shook the World* (1928), Eisenstein demonstrated the power of selective camera work and careful editing to reveal the struggles of a people in the throes of revolutionary change. Most significantly, he abandoned the traditional individual protagonist for a collective one: In these films, the Russian people—the disenfranchised masses—are the true heros. His was a cinema that had little or nothing to do with conventional narrative logic. He saw film editing (or montage, as he called it) as a process that operated according to the dialectic theory of Karl Marx.[12] Each shot (or "montage cell") is a thesis, which, when placed into juxtaposition with another shot of opposing visual content (its antithesis) produces a synthesis (a synthetic idea or impression). Eisenstein theorized widely in books and articles, but it is his films that most brilliantly exemplify the power of montage to jolt an audience into new awareness. His juxtaposition of time and space, his handling of large crowd scenes, his ability to extract every symbolic significance of social contrast, and his use of complex editing techniques gave a new luster to filmmaking and greatly influenced serious students of cinema in this country.

All of these European directors were, to an extent, experimentalists. And all set a pattern of growth and sophistication in the development of motion pictures as an art form—while, in the United States, the Hollywood studios turned out products designed to further the growth of the movies as a medium for mass entertainment.

The Hollywood studios distilled drama packages for the delectation of millions of movie fans. The movie fan magazine became imperative reading for the teenager, and the stars bathed in an ambience of money, glamour, and glory. The movie moguls, intent on achieving what the trade journal *Variety* called "boffo" at the box office, tended to thwart any tendency that directors might have manifested toward sensitivity or creative innovation.

BUSINESS BEHIND THE SCREEN

Behind moviedom's facade of froth and fantasy was the driving motor of big business. By the second decade of the twentieth century, the U.S. movie industry was well on its way to becoming a labyrinth of interlocking directorates and corporate concatenations, whose complexity paralleled the complicated business structures in utilities, chemicals, steel, and transportation.

The 1920s was a period of consolidation in which production, distribution, and exhibition were effectively linked into larger units. Adolph Zukor set the pace. In 1917, his policy of high rental fees and block booking moved several theatre circuits to form their own distribution channel, First National Exhibitor's Circuit. In a further effort to circumvent any association with Zukor's Paramount, First National signed up such major stars as Charlie Chaplin and Mary Pickford. To safeguard his position, Zukor decided to acquire theatres, and obtained a $10 million issue of preferred stock through Kuhn, Loeb, and Company for this purpose.

The Paramount and First National struggle set in motion a race among the major producers to acquire outlets for the exhibition of their products. Exhibitors, in turn, acquired production and distribution companies. Marcus Loew, an enterprising exhibitor who had first made his mark as a furrier, bought a nearly moribund production company called Metro Pictures in 1920 and, four years later, added the Goldwyn Pictures Corporation and the L. B. Mayer Company. The resultant Metro-Goldwyn-Mayer (MGM), Loew's production subsidiary, soon became a leader in the movie industry.

The creation of the vertical structure of production, distribution, and exhibition (which was to characterize the movie industry for so many years) required more capital than companies could generate from their own resources. As the industry expanded, Wall Street financiers began to assume a much more active role. First National was financed through the issuance of preferred stock by Hayden, Stone, and Company. The Du Ponts and the Chase National Bank had sponsored the formation of Goldwyn Pictures. Industrialists such as William C. Durant of General Motors and Harvey Gibbon of the Liberty National Bank became members of the board of directors of Loew's. Laemmle's Universal was backed by Shields and Company for the express purpose of financing expansion into the exhibition. The John F. Dryden-Prudential Insurance Group provided financial underpinning for the Fox Film Corporation. Warner Bros. (which is the official spelling, by the way), a company incorporated in 1923, was financed with securities underwritten by Goldman, Sachs, and Company.[13] Concentration and consolidation of control accelerated, with the introduction of sound to motion pictures.

THE ADVENT OF SOUND

Sound motion pictures were the result of a long prelude of technical achievements and entrepreneurial efforts.[14] As early as 1894, Thomas Edison had attempted to market a combination of his Kinetoscope and phonograph called the Kinetophone. The system lacked adequate amplification and was soon withdrawn from the market. In March 1909, the Motion Picture Patents Company licensed England's Gaumont firm to manufacture and lease "talking pictures." Gaumont's system, called Cronophone, employed two phonographs combined with a motion picture projector. The Cronophone was a failure, both technically and financially.

In the ensuing years, a number of unsuccessful phonograph-linked sound systems appeared on the market. Lee De Forest, a pioneer in the early development of radio, developed a method of photographing sound directly on the film itself. In April 1923, De Forest demonstrated his sound-on-film system, called Phonofilm, at the Rivoli Theatre in New York City. However, various attempts to market the system met with failure. It was left to those with more business acumen to bring about the successful conversion to sound motion pictures.

The big electrical companies were determined to reap the foreordained financial rewards of conversion to sound movies. The J. P. Morgan banking interests controlling AT&T, for example, were well aware of the profit potential of sound films. Research engineers at Western Electric, the manufacturing subsidiary of AT&T, had experimented with both sound-on-film and sound-on-disc recording and reproducing systems for almost a decade. Western Electric's initial efforts to promote its system also met with failure. By the fall of 1924, they had developed a workable sound-on-disc system that synchronized the sound recorded on phonograph records with the movements on the screen.

The major movie companies, already making big profits under the prevailing silent system, were reluctant to invest the many thousands of dollars necessary for the installation and utilization of sound equipment. They quite obviously looked upon the movie industry as a business, first, and an art form, second. And sound, whatever its artistic potential, didn't seem like good business.

However, Warner Bros. soon demonstrated to the solons of the industry that there was money to be made from sound movies. Warners had been experiencing increasing difficulty in securing exhibition outlets for its films with the larger theatre circuits, particularly the Paramount and First National chains, and was therefore looking for a competitive edge. In 1926, Warners joined with Western Electric in forming the Vitaphone Corporation to make sound motion pictures and to market sound reproduction equipment. In order to quickly capitalize on its investment, Warners decided to delay the release of an already completed silent film entitled *Don Juan*, starring John Barrymore, so that a musical score played by the New York Philharmonic could be synchronized with its action. Warners also prepared a supporting program of short musical films that included the talents of Metropolitan Opera tenor Giovanni Martinelli and master violinist Efrem Zimbalist. *Don Juan* and the accompanying short films premiered on August 6, 1926. The program was preceded by a film presentation of Will Hays extolling the wonders of sound motion pictures. Among the enthusiastic audience members who attended this opening night were many of the leaders of the movie industry.

Warners released several other sound films, to favorable audience response. But the big breakthrough came with the October 6, 1927, premier of *The Jazz Singer*, starring Al Jolson. This was the first film with seemingly spontaneous dialogue and ad-libbing. After singing his first song, "Dirty Hands, Dirty Face," Jolson uttered the prophetic words, "Wait a minute. Wait a minute. You ain't heard nothin' yet!" He continued to speak, introducing his next song, "Toot, Toot, Tootsie." Midway through the picture, Jolson engaged in a synchronized dialogue with his screen mother, played by Eugenie Besserer. The dialogue in the natural voice of the performers made an otherwise mediocre movie memorable. The film broke box office records almost everywhere it played.

Warners' financial success provided the incentive for all of the major movie companies to convert to sound. Electrical Research Products, Inc. (ERPI), a special subsidiary set up by Western Electric at the end of 1926 for the development of patents outside the telephone field, managed to terminate its exclusive contract with Warners and began to license all comers. By the middle of 1928, Paramount, First National, Loew's-MGM, United Artists, and Universal had become ERPI licensees. Several smaller companies subsequently fell in line. By the close of 1929, some 90 percent of all the sound motion pictures produced in the United States were made by ERPI licensees.

Radio Corporation of America tried to market a sound-on-film system developed by General Electric. GE used patents that were cross-licensed with those of AT&T's manufacturing subsidiary, Western Electric. For the next few years, GE worked to perfect its sound-on-film Pallophotophone system. In the fall of 1926, David Sarnoff, who was RCA's general manager, was given the task of commercially exploiting GE's sound system. Sarnoff's overtures to major movie companies met initially with some success, but negotiations eventually broke off when RCA failed to produce a marketable system in time to compete with ERPI. Moreover, RCA's sound-on-film system had suffered breakdowns, resulting in costly delays and repair bills.

When it became apparent that the big movie firms were going to prefer the Western Electric-ERPI system, RCA took swift action. In the spring of 1928, it formed a new corporation, RCA Photophone, Inc., with Sarnoff as its president. RCA, GE, and Westinghouse held 50, 30, and 20 percent of the stock, respectively. To provide an initial market for the Photophone sound-on-film system, Sarnoff sought to combine a film-producing company with a chain of theatres.

Late in 1927, RCA bought a substantial block of stock in Film Booking Offices of America (FBO), a small movie company that had studios in California and 35 exchanges throughout the United States. The following year RCA bought controlling interest in Keith-Albee-Orpheum, a vaudeville theatre chain that had fallen on hard times. In October 1928, FBO and the theatre chain were merged with RCA Photophone to create Radio-Keith-Orpheum, a new holding company with assets in excess of $80 million.

CONSOLIDATION

Sound had come to motion pictures only months before the Great Depression enveloped the United States. The concentration of capital necessary for the conversion to sound, coupled with the economic crisis of the 1930s, eventually resulted in reorganization of the movie industry into fewer and fewer entities.

The outcome of this reorganization was an industry with eight major companies. The "Big Five" (those that were vertically integrated—that is, the companies that controlled all three facets of the movie business: production, distribution, and exhibition), were Warner Bros., RKO, Twentieth Century-Fox, Paramount, and Loew's-MGM. The "Little Three" were Universal, Columbia, and United Artists. Of these, Universal and Columbia were producer-distributors while United Artists was solely a distributor. Together, these eight companies produced or distributed 95 percent of all motion pictures shown during this period in the United States.[15]

Bitter battles and litigation marked the trail of this concentration and consolidation of the movie industry. The case of William Fox is an example of this infighting.[16]

Fox's production activities had shown slow but unbroken progress, and he gradually expanded his theatre holdings. He also pioneered in sound films, purchasing the patent rights to a sound-on-film system that was developed and promoted under the name Movietone. To safeguard this system, he purchased the U.S. rights to Tri-Ergon, a European system using an ingenious flywheel mechanism to prevent variations in the speed of the film as it moved through the sound reproduction equipment.

In 1929, Fox secured control of Loew's and Gaumont, a British company operating about 300 theatres in the British Isles. But this incredible amalgamation required financing; and Halsey, Stuart, and Company (an investment banking firm aligned with ERPI and the telephone interests) extended the necessary assistance in the form of short-term loans. With the first tremors of the October 1929 stock market crash, the Fox pyramid began to crumble. When Fox tried to renew his loans, the bankers forced him to relinquish control of his company. Finding himself in an untenable position, Fox reluctantly sold his holdings to General Theatre Equipment, a company closely allied with Halsey, Stuart, and Company.

William Fox was hardly left destitute; he received $18 million for his shares and was retained as a special advisor at $500,000 per year for the succeeding five years. However, he was determined to regain supremacy in the movie industry. Fox subsequently threw millions of dollars into litigation, contending that subsidiaries of AT&T and RCA had pirated the flywheel devise of his Tri-Ergon sound system. In March 1935, the U.S. Supreme Court, reversing a lower court decision, ruled in favor of the giant electronics corporations. Had Fox's suit been successful, he would have collected immense sums in damages and license fees.

The amount of capital necessary for the conversion to sound further strengthened the hold of the financiers. Yet the precise implications of high finance's involvement in the movie industry are not easy to determine. In a 1937 study, *Money behind the Screen*, two British writers tried to document, through the use of charts and detailed financial data, how the Eastern banking interests (particularly the Morgan and Rockefeller groups) had seized control of the actual production of motion pictures. "Whether the movies will regain their former financial succcess," they concluded, "ultimately depends on whether the Morgans and the Rockefellers will find it in their interest in the increasing change of American life to provide the masses with the type of pictures that alone will induce them to flock to their cinemas."[17] While this study provided a useful analysis of potential sources of control over movie content, it said nothing about how such control might work in practice. Nor did it give any indication why high finance should want to make movies that "the masses" would find unappealing. In any case, by the 1930s moviemaking had developed into such a complex of production managers, technicians, and bureaucratic layers that mere ownership of the "means of production" no longer constituted the key to power. The decisions of high finance in the movie industry were much more likely to be shaped and, arguably, controlled by the studio managers brought in to coordinate day-to-day production activities. And there is little reason to doubt that, for financier and studio chieftain alike, the principal objective was profit—as much profit as possible. Of course, the path to profit was in the production of motion pictures with a broad appeal.

When Hollywood became another bastion of big business, the men of Wall Street did attempt to play a direct role in running some of the studios. The result of these outsiders' intervention, as Joseph Kennedy (presidential father-to-be) pointed out in his 1936 study of Paramount, was gross mismanagement and ineffeciency at all levels.[18] He found that shooting schedules were being ignored; expensive scenarios were being discarded; costly stars were being alienated; negative costs were exceeding their budgets by $7 million annually; and the planning of the next year's production schedule was in seemingly hopeless disarray. On the basis of Kennedy's recommendations, Barney Balaban, a theatre operator who was sensitive to audience tastes, was brought in as president. Adolph Zukor, who had managed to maintain the nominal post of board chairman, was returned to a position of power as head of production. The lesson was not lost on other companies. By the end of the 1930s, all of the major studios were back under the control of men experienced in the entertainment business.

THE STUDIO SYSTEM

The Hollywood studio system reached its zenith in the 1930s and early 1940s.[19] During that period, the denizens of "cardboard city" left an indelible impression on the U.S. cultural landscape. The neighborhood movie house attracted Americans in far larger numbers than either the legitimate theatre or the library. Millions attended movies at least twice a week, regardless of what appeared on the screen.

Studio heads maneuvered the intricate balance of integrating the demands from the New York office for a steady supply of easily salable films made at the lowest possible cost, with pressures from the moviemakers themselves for productions that were often costly and sometimes controversial.

METRO-GOLDWYN-MAYER

MGM was the biggest, most prosperous, and most prolific of the studios in the 1930s and early 1940s.[20] Its trademark was Leo the Lion, with his head enhaloed by a scroll proclaiming the Latin *Ars Gratia Artis* ("Art for Art's Sake"). But the studio operated like a well-oiled machine, with each aspect of production functioning effectively in an interlocking structure. With its roster of competent directors; stable of major stars and featured players; large cadre of screenwriters, lighting experts, set designers, and outstanding cameramen, the studio was able to turn out an average of one feature every nine days.

At its height, MGM could boast of 29 sound stages, and a 100-acre back lot, with a park that could be photographed as anything from a football field to the gardens at Versailles. Some 3,000 or so craftsmen, technicians, and laborers were on the payroll. The studio's extensive research library could provide a writer or producer with such esoteric information as the appropriate number of stars in a U.S. flag flying over a Western outpost in the 1880s.

The set designer was Cedric Gibbons, whose work ranged from the intricate and detailed backgrounds for *Dinner at Eight* (1933) to the replica of an old sailing ship used in *Mutiny on the Bounty* (1935). His set designs won him 11 Academy Awards between 1929 and 1956. The costumer was Gilbert Adrian, whose influence can be seen in everything from elaborate period pieces such as *Marie Antoinette* (1938) to the hats, vests, and capes worn by the Munchkins in *The Wizard of Oz* (1939). The wardrobe department under his supervision employed over 170 milliners, seamstresses, tailors, and the like. Dresses routinely cost from $500 to $1,500.

The studio's stable of talented actors and actresses was unparalleled in Hollywood history. ("More stars than there are in Heaven," as the MGM publicity slogan had it). In 1935, MGM had some 253 players under contract. Its star performers included Lionel Barrymore, Joan Crawford, Clark Gable, Greta Garbo, Helen Hayes, Myrna Loy, William Powell, Norma Shearer, and Spencer Tracy. The salient importance and profitability of the studio's star players can be seen in the case of Clark Gable. When David O. Selznick prepared to make *Gone with the Wind* (1939), he decided that he wanted Gable for the role of Rhett Butler. MGM archon Louis B. Mayer agreed to lend the star only on the condition that the studio be given the distribution rights to the film and half the profits.

MGM had the biggest and most expensive group of screenwriters in the movie industry. In 1939, the studio had 80 writers on the payroll, among them F. Scott Fitzgerald, Ben Hecht, Anita Loos, and Herman Mankiewicz. Sometimes as many as a dozen writers would work on the same script. "Writers were assigned in relays, rather as though they were pieces of sandpaper to be used up and replaced," explains Aljean Harmetz. "Scripts resembled nothing so much as a seven-layer cake, and it often took an archaeological expedition to discover who was responsible for which layer."[21]

The studio had an able cadre of contract directors, but most of them were of the kind about whom learned treatises are written. Clarence Brown, known for his tactfulness, directed the highly styled Greta Garbo films: *Anna Christie* (1930), *Anna Karenina* (1935), and *Conquest* (1937). Sam Wood, a specialist in light comedy, handled many of the Marx Brothers pictures (their best work was done at Paramount in the early 1930s). The prolific W. S. Van Dyke, celebrated for making his movies fast, turned out the highly successful "Thin Man" series starring William Powell and Myrna Loy, as well as the Jeanette MacDonald-Nelson Eddy musicals. Sidney Franklin was responsible for the studio's theatrical and literary adaptations, such as *The Guardsman* (1931), *The Barretts of Wimpole Street* (1934), and *The Good Earth* (1937).

Victor Fleming, the "man's director" par excellence, was the provider of such adventure films as *Red Dust* (1932), *Treasure Island* (1934), and *Captains Courageous* (1937). The latter film, about a boy who learns to love seafaring on a fishing ship, was made on a sound stage in front of a large screen, with neither a boat nor an ocean anywhere in sight.

The question is often raised among film aficionados, "Whose vision does a studio-produced motion picture reflect?" In France in the 1950s, some of the writers for the magazine *Cahier du cinéma* thought they detected traces of "personal style" in certain Hollywood films.[22] This became known as the *politique des auteurs*, the "position of being for authors." The idea was that some American directors had somehow managed to make personal statements despite the restrictions imposed upon them by the studio system. Since the early 1960s, it has been fashionable in the United States to regard the studio director as the *auteur* of his films.[23] At MGM, most of the directors were artisans rather than *auteurs*, and they were not averse to following orders. When a studio turns out some 40 or more pictures a year, there must be tight supervision and a factory production line approach. Very few directors attempted to buck the studio system, even though many undoubtedly had the talent to impress personal visions on their films.

MGM's only *auteur* of sorts was production chief Irving Thalberg, second in command of the studio under Louis B. Mayer. Most MGM pictures of the early 1930s bore the imprint of Thalberg. (He was the model for Monroe Stahr in F. Scott Fitzgerald's *The Last Tycoon*.) His influence was felt at the subtle level of lighting and camera angles. He was especially adept at the editing of films. It is arguably editing, more than any other factor, which determines the final pace, tone, and character of any film. In making the average feature, about 200,000 feet of film was shot. Generally, this footage was cut down to less than 8-10,000 feet. Thalberg's supervision of the editing process gave him almost total control of the studio's output. But the complexity of sound production soon made his method of control untenable. In 1933, Mayer reorganized the studio into separate, relatively autonomous production units. Individual producers were given full responsibility for their own productions. Very few directors cut their own films. In most instances, the final product reflected a collective vision.

WARNER BROS. PICTURES

The emphasis at Warners was on maximum economy of means.[24]

Discipline and order took priority over temperament and talent. Costly retakes were generally avoided and production schedules were rigidly followed. Its strict code of production efficiency was imposed on technicians, directors, and stars alike.

Hastily made, fast-paced, action-filled, topical melodramas helped to sustain the studio during the early years of the Depression. Its 1930 production of *Little Caesar*, starring Edward G. Robinson as a small-time hood who rises to the top of the underworld, began a controversial cycle of films in which the gangster is the central figure. The following year, in *The Public Enemy*, James Cagney achieved stardom as a ruthless, albeit not always unsympathetic, hoodlum. While most of Warners' crime films lacked subtlety or depth, and the characters were more caricatured than realistic, they were attractively cast and surged with a definite vigor and excitement. The most acclaimed of the studio's early crime films was *I Am a Fugitive from a Chain Gang* (1932), which starred Paul Muni as an innocent man brutally victimized by the criminal justice system of an unnamed state.

Humphrey Bogart joined the studio's roster of tough guys in 1936, with his chilling characterization of snarling gangster Duke Mantee in the screen version of Robert E. Sherwood's *The Petrified Forest*. Some of the scenes may seem stiff and awkward to today's audiences. But the film admirably succeeds in recreating the arid heat of the Arizona desert and the seedy atmosphere of the cheap roadside lunchroom in which the drama takes place. There are also solid performances by Bette Davis and Leslie Howard.

Low-budget musicals with an emphasis on backstage life were another Warners staple. *Forty-second Street* (1933), *The Gold Diggers of 1933*, *Footlight Parade* (1933), *Dames* (1934), and a plethora of similar films used to full advantage the singing and dancing of such able young performers as Ruby Keeler, Ginger Rogers, and Dick Powell. The musicals were greatly enhanced by Busby Berkeley's elaborate, daring and lascivious (for that period), kaleidoscopic production numbers. His characteristic penchant for dance routines of lavishly gowned women in long shots against sylvan fountains became a standard presentation and, ultimately, an object of satire.

In 1935, Warners initiated a series of romantic adventure films with the release of *Captain Blood*, starring Errol Flynn as the swashbuckling, dashing Peter Blood. Flynn went on to play essentially the same role in several highly successful Warners films, the most notable of which was *The Adventures of Robin Hood* (1938). The studio spared little expense in telling the tale of the legendary English outlaw who robbed from the rich to give to the poor. A woodland area in Chico, California (nearly 600 miles north of Hollywood), was temporarily transformed into Sherwood Forest. Most of the film's principals and 300 extra players, members of the crew, wardrobe, hairdressing, makeup, and technical personnel were on location in Chico for six weeks. At the studio facilities in Burbank, the setting for a banquet in Nottingham Castle was carefully reconstructed—complete with roast oxen, sides of venison, gas flares, musical pipes, and hooded falcons. The entire picture took some four months to shoot, at a cost in excess of $2 million.

The end result stands as one of the supreme examples of creative teamwork in the Hollywood style. Cinematographers Tony Gaudio and Sol Polito achieved extraordinary photographic effects, using the fairly new three-color Technicolor process. Muted greens and browns and vivid touches of scarlet give the film the look of a Renaissance painting. Erich Wolfgang Korngold devised an intricate musical score to complement the characters and situations depicted on the screen. Milo Anderson was responsible for the authentic appearance of the costumes. The magnificent sets were the creation of art director Carl Jules Weyl. Seton I. Miller and Norman Reilly Raine wrote the suspenseful script. The fast-paced action scenes owed much to the skillful editing of Ralph Dawson. Michael Curtiz maintained a tight grip on the directorial reins.

Curtiz was the most prolific of the studio's directors, turning out some 43 mystery, melodrama, and adventure films between 1930 and 1939. William Dieterle directed a series of prestigious biographical films, which included *The Story of Louis Pasteur* (1936), *White Angel* (1936—a biography of Florence Nightingale), *The Life of Emile Zola* (1937), *Jaurez* (1939), and *Dr. Erhlich's Magic Bullet* (1940). Mervyn LeRoy's credits included mostly musicals and action melodramas. The incomparable Howard Hawks handled comedies and romantic melodrama, but he was at his best with strong action stories featuring tough masculine figures in peril. Hawks is often proclaimed as the first and best of U.S. *auteurs*, but Warner's rigid organization and tight production schedules didn't permit even directors of his caliber to pursue personal visions.

Most of Warners' films adhered to that narrative mode that has come to be characterized as "classical Hollywood cinema."[25] Its salient features include a clear cause-effect connection of events; character traits as the causal agents; sharply delineated character conflict; understated direction; continuity editing; and a high degree of plot closure at the end. These familiar filmmaking practices work together especially well in the studio's 1941 screen adaptation of Dashiell Hammett's detective thriller *The Maltese Falcon*.

The story's events focus on the activities of a wry, cynical private eye—the now legendary Sam Spade (perfectly embodied by Humphrey Bogart)—as he investigates the murder of his partner and searches for the mysterious, priceless, and finally elusive gem-encrusted golden falcon. The colorful characters he encounters in his pursuit include: Gutman (Sydney Greenstreet), a greedy "fat man" with a mirthless laugh and a propensity for pomposity ("I tell you right out, sir, I'm a man who likes talking to a man who likes to talk!"); Joel Cairo (Peter Lorre), a man of many passports and uncertain sexual identity; and Wilmer (Elisha Cook, Jr.), a "gunsel" with a cold, demented look in his eyes.

Spade treats these comic opera villains with scorn and distrust. He also maintains emotional distance from the principal female character in the case, the alluring and deceitful Brigid O'Shaughnessy (Mary Astor). Spade is a man motivated by his own peculiar code of honor and decency. When he realizes that O'Shaughnessy murdered his partner, he is determined to have her pay for the crime. Repressing his desire to protect and save her, he turns her over to the police. The scene ends with a shot of her tearstained face as the bars of the elevator door close across it, foreshadowing the bars of the prison cell that awaits her.

This film marked the directorial debut of John Huston, who also wrote the tightly constructed screenplay. His sedate directorial style provides an illustrative example of the conventions that operated in the movie industry to conceal any trace of a motion picture's status as a manufactured product. Virtually every shot in the film is a tightly knit composition. Light, focus, camera angle, framing, set design and staging, costuming, and camera distance all worked to keep the principal object of narrative interest in the foreground and center of the screen at any given moment. The inherently disruptive effect of editing was minimized by maintaining spatial and temporal continuity from shot to shot. Separate shots were matched through continuing action, connecting glances, common sounds, and other such devices. All shot sequences were taken from the same side of an imaginary 180° axis to ensure constant screen direction and some common space from shot to shot. Only occasional oblique angles and quiet chiaroscuro (light and dark shading) reveal the director's hand, and these serve primarily to highlight the oddness of the characters. Huston's invisible style succeeded so well, in fact, that observing its workings requires considerable concentration.

PARAMOUNT

Paramount was the most "European" of the U.S. studios. This is attributable, in large part, to the fact that so many of its craftsmen, technicians, and directors had developed their skills while working for Germany's UFA (*Universum Film Aktiengesellschaft*) studio conglomerate. The influence of German theories of lighting and camerawork pervades much of Paramount's output during the 1920s and 1930s. Its German art director, Hans Dreier, and cinematographers, Karl Struss and Theodor Sparkuhl, created extravagantly ornate pictorial compositions.

The director whose work best represented the studio's style was Josef von Sternberg. His most notable sound films featured Berlin-born actress Marlene Dietrich as the archetypal femme fatale, a woman who attracts men at the cost of suffering to them and sometimes to herself. The most acclaimed of the von Sternberg-Dietrich films was *The Blue Angel* (1930), a joint Paramount-UFA production, filmed in Berlin simultaneously in English and German-language versions. "This technically superb picture," writes Lewis Jacobs, "had all the qualities Sternberg was to overemphasize in his later efforts: luminous chiaroscuro of a deep, low tone, remarkable camera angles and composition, elaborate background details, a smooth and easy blending of sequences through dissolves, and music and song which moved with the images."[26] Von Sternberg and Dietrich made six more films together, each more elaborate than the last. *Morocco* (1930), *Dishonored* (1931), *Shanghai Express* (1932), *Blonde Venus* (1932), *The Scarlet Empress* (1934), and *The Devil Is a Woman* (1935) are all distinguished more by complex mise-en-scène than plot or character.

Another director who brought a touch of continental elegance to Paramount's output was Ernst Lubitsch. His specialties were musicals and sophisticated sex comedies with an emphasis on witty dialogue and clever visual innuendo. Utilizing the talents of Maurice Chevalier and Jeannette MacDonald, he turned out such charming trifles as *One Hour with You*

(1932) and *The Merry Widow* (1934). His highly successful comedies of manner included *Trouble in Paradise* (1932) and *Design for Living* (1933). By 1935, he had become Paramount's production chief. Among the studio's other notable directors was Armenian-born Rouben Mamoulian, who had worked in both opera and legitimate theatre before turning his talents to filmmaking. He was a master of technical innovation. In such films as *Applause* (1929), *Dr. Jekyll and Mr. Hyde* (1932), and *Love Me Tonight* (1932), he experimented with overlapping dialogue, sound flashbacks, and synthetic sound. He also directed *Becky Sharp* (1935), the first feature to be shot in the three-color Technicolor process.

Veteran producer-director Cecil B. De Mille provided Paramount with a number of profitable sex-and-violence-soaked spectacles during the 1930s. These included *The Sign of the Cross* (1932)—which featured Claudette Colbert as Queen Poppaea swimming in a bathtub filled with asses' milk—and *Cleopatra* (1934)—a sexual extravaganza complete with royal barges, elaborate costumes, and an inexhaustible supply of slave girls. The ludicrous dialogue in these films often turned the drama into unwitting comedy. De Mille fared little better in his treatment of U.S. history. *The Plainsman* (1937), *The Buccaneer* (1938), and *Union Pacific* (1939) are resplendent with massacres, fights, train wrecks, trite dialogue, and below-par acting by most of the players.

The zany satire of the Marx Brothers and the bawdy sex comedies of Mae West were also among Paramount's releases. Its top male star was Gary Cooper, who was used in everything from light comedy to continental intrigue to lavish spectacle. In 1937, the studio employed 12 producers, 65 writers, 15 directors, and 80 contract players.

TWENTIETH CENTURY-FOX

The Fox studio produced a number of big-budget films, but its most distinctive product was cheaply made series. Among its most profitable pictures in this category were the saccharine sagas featuring child-star Shirley Temple. During her years of preadolescence, Miss Temple is reported to have earned over $20 million for the studio. The low-budget bucolic comedies of cracker-barrel philosopher Will Rogers (who died in a plane crash in 1935) and the popular "Charlie Chan" series (starring Swedish-born Warner Oland as the redoubtable Oriental sleuth) also helped to fill the company's coffers. Oland made 17

Chan films before his death in 1938. Sidney Toler, a Missourian of Scottish descent, succeeded Oland in the role of Chan and made 11 more films in the series for the Fox studio.

In 1935, Fox merged with Twentieth Century Pictures, a company formed by Darryl Zanuck in 1933 to produce films for United Artists. Under Zanuck's stewardship, the newly formed Twentieth Century-Fox turned out pictures that, with rare exception, were bland and predictable. During the mid-1930s, Fox's production budget was about $20 million for 53 features, an average of about $375,000 each.[27] Some 29 of the pictures were produced under Zanuck, for about $500,000 each. The other 24 were "B" pictures (inexpensive formula films designed to fill out double bills). These were produced by veteran Sol Wurtzel at an aggregate cost of about $5 million, some $200,000 for each feature.

The studio's leading male performer was Tyrone Power, whose first important screen appearance was in the 1936 production, *Lloyds of London*. This film made Power, who was only 23 at the time, a major star. During the next several years, he played opposite most of the studio's female stars, including Alice Faye, Sonja Henie, Linda Darnell, and Betty Grable, among others. Few of the "Fox girls," as they were called, were known for their acting talents. Grable, of course, became the prototype of all the "pinup girls" during World War II.

The great John Ford was the studio's major director during the 1930s. His films included *The Prisoner of Shark Island* (1935), *Young Mr. Lincoln* (1939), and *Drums along the Mohawk* (1939). At the close of the decade, Ford directed the film version of John Steinbeck's novel *The Grapes of Wrath*, about the social injustices endured by migrant workers in the United States. Ford's direction combined with Nunnally Johnson's screenplay, Gregg Toland's photography, Alfred Newman's music, and the performances of Henry Fonda and Jane Darwell to make this one of the most poignant and beautiful pictures to come out of Hollywood.

Several of Ford's films have been identified with the Left, but he seemed more interested in exploring human relationships under the pressure of extreme stress than in dealing with political or ideological issues. In *How Green Was My Valley* (1941), for instance, he succeeded admirably in presenting a dramatic depiction of class stratification as well as insight into the daily lives of ordinary workers. However, as at least one observer has noted, the central purpose of this film "was neither to illuminate the plight of the Welsh miners nor to champion the cause of the labor movement but instead to commend the virtues of family solidarity and social tradition at the expense of personal desire."[28]

RKO RADIO PICTURES

The productions of a particular studio during the 1930s can often be identified by the contract players who appeared, the types of stories shot, the directorial techniques employed, and even by such things as lighting methods, set designs, and costumes. However, the range of RKO's styles was so large, so miscellaneous, that this studio's overall output has no recognizable image.

During the Depression years, RKO's trademark of the blinking radio tower atop a spinning globe introduced some of Hollywood's most unique and memorable motion pictures. Among the studio's most impressive pictures from that period is the monster thriller *King Kong* (1933), which was codirected by Merian Cooper and Ernest Schoedsach. Willis O'Brien was responsible for the film's remarkable special effects.

A great deal of inventive talent went into producing the models and trick photography that make the movie so memorable. The miniature figures used in the animation sequences were all constructed by Marcel Delgado, who had first worked with O'Brien on one of the first full-length features to use animated models, *The Lost World* (1925). To construct the figure of Kong, who stood 18 inches high and weighed almost ten pounds, Delgado used a metal skeleton covered with cotton. He then applied liquified latex rubber to the model and covered it with rabbit fur. Some of the models of the prehistoric animals were fitted with rubber bladders to give them a realistic-looking breathing effect. Appropriately scaled models of the human performers were also made. A full-sized foot, hand, and bust of Kong were built for close-up shots. Kong's bust had a 6½-foot-wide face, 1-foot-long ears, and a 36-foot-wide chest. Six men huddled inside the bust to operate the 86 motors powering the facial and head movements.

The animation of Kong and the other models was achieved through the use of stop-motion photography. After each slight movement, the model was photographed, the camera stopped, and the model was reset. Live actors were combined with the animated models through the use of "rear screen projection." For example, there is a

scene in the film in which Kong removes some of female-lead Fay
Wray's clothing. To achieve this effect, Miss Wray was filmed by
herself while invisible wires pulled away her clothes. This footage was
then projected on the back of a translucent screen, and the movements
of Kong in front of the screen were animated to correspond with the
disrobing. This sequence alone is said to have taken 23 hours to film.
The entire film took 55 weeks to produce, at a cost of $650,000. (The
inferior 1976 remake of *King Kong*, by Dino De Laurentiis, cost a
reported $22 million to produce. Some $2 million was spent just to construct a 40-foot-high mechanical ape.)

RKO's *Flying Down to Rio* (1933) introduced the combined dancing talents of Fred Astaire and Ginger Rogers. The talented dance
team soon received top billing in such popular RKO releases as *The
Gay Divorcée* (1934), *Top Hat* (1935), *Swing Time* (1936), and *Shall We
Dance* (1937). In all, there were nine RKO films featuring Astaire and
Rogers. Mark Sandrich directed several of these films, but it was
Astaire who controlled every phase of the development of a dance
number. "He forced camerawork, cutting, synchronization and scor-
ing to ever higher standards of sensitivity and precision," writes Arlene
Croce.[29] Some of the dance routines required as many as 40 takes.

RKO was the studio where creative talent often enjoyed the
greatest freedom. Early on, the RKO management had initiated a
policy of attracting independent producers to the lot to make a specific
number of features relatively free from managerial supervision. In effect, each production unit operated as a semiautonomous satrapy.

There's a certain irony in the situation that prevailed at RKO,
since that studio—perhaps more than any other—was closely
associated with the men of Wall Street. The Rockefellers, for instance,
maintained a substantial interest in RKO through direct holdings in
the movie company's stock by Rockefeller Center, Inc. In 1938,
Nelson Rockefeller was responsible for bringing in George Schaefer as
the studio's corporate president, with a mandate to turn out high-
quality pictures. Schaefer's enlightened production policy resulted in
such distinctive features as *Gunga Din* (1939), *The Hunchback of Notre
Dame* (1939), and the incomparable *Citizen Kane* (1941).

Of all the films made under the RKO imprint, *Citizen Kane* has enjoyed the greatest critical acclaim. Many critics regard it as the most
original, creative motion picture ever made. *Citizen Kane* was produced
and directed by Orson Welles, who also appeared in the title role. The
script for the film was written by Welles and Herman Mankiewicz.

The story tells of newspaper magnate Charles Foster Kane, dying lonely and bitter in his castle, Xanadu. The editor of a newsreel (a parody of *The March of Time*, which will be discussed later in this chapter) prepares a film biography of the dead millionaire and decides to unravel the meaning of the last word Kane uttered before his death—"Rosebud." A reporter is dispatched to discover the significance of this word by interviewing the people who knew Kane well during various phases of his life. Through flashbacks, each person paints a detailed—albeit biased—picture of Kane, but not one can explain the meaning of his last utterance. In the final shot of the film, the audience finds out the material referent of the word, but its abstract significance remains a mystery.

Welles's directorial techniques provide a dramatic contrast to those of classic Hollywood cinema.[30] An iconoclast of the conventional wisdom, he employed extreme low-angle shots, stark contrasts of light and dark, and vast in-depth perspectives to reveal complex psychological and social relationships. His cinematic imagination is especially evident in the film's effective use of long takes and rapid cuts to create rhythm and mood. He also made remarkable use of music, disembodied voices, overlapping dialogue, and other such techniques that he had first honed in radio programming. Few films have had greater influence on the art of filmmaking.

THE LITTLE THREE

Columbia Pictures specialized in low-budget features. It grew out of a company formed in 1920 by Joe Brandt and Harry and Jack Cohn with backing from banker A. H. Giannini. Harry Cohn became both president and production chief, the only movie mogul to hold both positions simultaneously. The studio moved to the front ranks of the industry in 1934 with its production of *It Happened One Night*, starring Clark Gable (on loan from MGM) and Claudette Colbert (exercising a Paramount contractual option that permitted her to make one outside picture a year). This film was directed by Frank Capra, who was largely responsible for keeping the studio solvent during the 1930s. Capra's craftsmanship comes through clearly in the deftly edited close-ups of the witty banter between Gable and Colbert. The film was received with favor by both the critics and the public.

In the triumphant aftermath of the film's success, the studio signed

Capra to a six-picture contract at $100,000 a picture plus 25 percent of the profits. During the next several years, Capra filled Columbia's coffers with the receipts from such social-minded pictures as *Mr. Deeds Goes to Town* (1936), *Lost Horizon* (1937), *You Can't Take It with You* (1938), and *Mr. Smith Goes to Washington* (1939).

Capra's films have often been criticized for their sentimentality and populist ideology. But they are really far more complex and ambiguous than many critics may be willing to concede. Though Capra (and his screenwriter Robert Riskin) seemed to commemorate the virtue of the common man and to condemn the greed and cunning of the wealthy, his films reveal a belief in the stupidity of the average citizen and in the danger of mass democracy. "Unlike actual Populists in the American past, he was not making a critique of the American social and economic system, did not even want a redistribution of wealth and power," writes Robert Sklar. "He simply wanted more neighborly and responsible people to be at the top of the social and economic hierarchy."[31]

In addition to the high-budget Capra films (*Lost Horizon* cost $2 million to produce), Columbia also churned out a larger number of "B" pictures. The studio had several series of feature films during the late 1930s and 1940s. Among the most successful of these were *Blondie*, starring Penny Singleton and Arthur Lake; *Boston Blackie*, starring Chester Morris; and *Lone Wolf*, with Warren William portraying the gentleman thief created by Louis Joseph Vance. Some 70 percent of the features produced by Columbia each year fell into the low-budget, second-feature category.

Universal Pictures, which had remained under the control of pioneer movie mogul Carl Laemmle until 1936, had been a leading studio in the 1920s, but by the 1930s it had slipped into a second-place position. Nevertheless, the studio did produce a number of significant films during the decade, including *All Quiet on the Western Front* (1930), *Showboat* (1936), and *Destry Rides Again* (1939).

The studio's major creative efforts were in the horror-fantasy genre. Films such as *Dracula* (1931), *Frankenstein* (1931), and *The Invisible Man* (1933) raised provocative questions about the possibilities and perils of human creativity. The true villain of these films, as Richard Pells has pointed out, was not so much "the vampire, the phantom, or the walking dead" but rather the "scientist who, whether motivated by innocence or megalomania, dedicated his career to the unfettered pursuit of knowledge regardless of its consequences." Thus, these films were essentially conservative in nature. They cautioned audiences "that some mysteries were better left unsolved, that to pass beyond the boundaries of human custom and social tradition was to invite madness and desolation."[32]

Most of Universal's tales of fear were not great commercial successes. In the latter part of the decade, the studio managed to stay afloat primarily through the release of such profitable pictures as *Three Smart Girls* (1936), *100 Men and a Girl* (1937), and *Mad about Music* (1938)—all featuring a talented teenager named Deanna Durbin.

United Artists (UA) was not a production studio per se, but a distributor for the films of independent producers. It was founded by Charlie Chaplin, Mary Pickford, Douglas Fairbanks, and D.W. Griffith in 1919 to distribute their own films.[33] Among the most prominent producers who released their films through this company during the 1930s were Samuel Goldwyn, David O. Selznick, and Walt Disney.

The logo "Samuel Goldwyn Presents" became synonymous with solid pieces of popular art and served to introduce much new talent to the industry. The taste and attention to detail that he brought to his productions became known in Hollywood as "the Goldwyn touch." Goldwyn's most impressive work was in association with director William Wyler and included such prestigious pictures as *Dodsworth* (1936), *Dead End* (1937), and *Wuthering Heights* (1939). Under the UA banner, the prolific Goldwyn produced 21 pictures from 1935 to 1940. Most of these were successful both with the critics and at the box office.

David O. Selznick set up Selznick-International in 1935 to produce technicolor features. Investors in this company included A.H. Giannini of the Bank of America, Wall Street financier Robert Lehman, and Cornelius Vanderbilt Whitney—all of whom were on the board of directors. But as his many memos make clear, Selznick maintained control over every department of his studio operation.[34] Indeed, his meticulous attention to detail often bordered on the obsessive. Taking as his studio motto "In a tradition of quality," Selznick turned out such lavish productions as *Little Lord Fauntleroy* (1936), *A Star is Born* (1937), *The Prisoner of Zenda* (1937), and *The Adventures of Tom Sawyer* (1938).

While producing for United Artists, Selznick secured the screen rights to Margaret Mitchell's Civil War epic, *Gone with the Wind*. However, he delayed filming the story until after his UA contract had expired. Among the reasons for the delay was Selznick's desire to secure Clark Gable on a loanout from MGM to play the pivotal role of Rhett Butler. As noted earlier, Louis B. Mayer (who was Selznick's father-in-law, at the time) agreed to lend his prize star only on the condition that MGM be given the distribution rights to the film and half the profits. MGM eventually gained sole ownership of the film, which continued to make money for the studio for the next four decades. (*Gone with the Wind* was technically renovated in 1967 for large-screen, 70-mm projection, with enhanced color and stereophonic sound.)

Walt Disney began distributing his animated cartoons through United Artists in 1932. Disney had been under contract to Columbia, but he was dissatisfied with the low production advances he received and was especially offended by that studio's practice of block booking his works with what he regarded as inferior cartoons. His arrangement with UA called for the production of 18 Mickey Mouse cartoons and 13 Silly Symphonies for the 1932–33 season. The latter were based on musical themes rather than some central character, and used movement, color, sound effects, and musical synchronization to full advantage. *Flowers and Trees* (1932), an idyll in which plants are animated to the music of Mendelssohn and Schubert, got as many bookings as the most popular Mickey Mouse cartoon and won for Disney the first of many Oscars.

In 1933, the art of animation took another big step forward with the production of Disney's Silly Symphony short, *The Three Little Pigs*. This cartoon creation, which cost $22,000 and grossed $250,000, won for Disney his second Oscar from the Academy of Motion Picture Arts and Sciences. The upbeat theme song "Who's Afraid of the Big Bad Wolf?" became a nationwide hit, and added to his profits and prestige. Disney himself, of course, didn't draw the cartoons or do the synchronization and musical themes. Under his guidance, scores of artists toiled to turn out the thousands of separate drawings needed for each film short.[35]

When Disney's contract with UA expired in 1937, he switched to RKO where he produced his first feature-length cartoon, the phenomenally successful *Snow White and the Seven Dwarfs* (1937). One of the principal reasons for the prescient Disney's departure from UA was the company's refusal to allow him to keep the television rights to his cartoons.

The degree of managerial control differed from studio to studio. But in general, creative personnel were required to toil on the short tether measured by the requirements of business, not the free rein of artistic expression. Producers were assigned a director, a story, a star or two along with supporting cast, a crew, a budget, and a time limit. Writers, directors, players, and technicians were all expected to be at the studio early in the morning and often stayed well into the night. If a contract player refused to accept a role, he was likely to be suspended for months without recompense. Everyone involved in the production process was relentlessly shuffled about from project to project. The typical studio head was likely to see himself, in the words of the old Hollywood quip, as "Czar of all the rushes."

NEWSREELS

For the most part, the major studios eschewed controversy. The vicissitudes of the 1930s were rarely reflected in the subject matter of feature films. Glimpses of those turbulent times did appear on movie screens in the form of the newsreel.[36] The newsreel was a standard part of the theatre program, running for about ten to fourteen minutes.

Fox Movietone was the largest of the newsreel organizations. It had such an extensive staff that, unlike other newsreels, Fox Movietone did not have to buy footage from other companies, free-lancers, or foreign concerns. Its format was modeled after the separate divisions of a newspaper: There was a feature-events section (the main announcer for these was Lowell Thomas), a women's fashion section, a sports event, and some other general interest topic (such as a musical event, or flamingos in Florida, or a theatrical celebrity with an unusual story to tell). The rigidity of the format meant that much of the material was not time sensitive, and was not so much news as feature interest. This formula was retained well into the 1940s, despite the rapid parade of news events that was sweeping Europe, Africa, and Asia.

Hearst's Metrotone News, which MGM distributed, was often the center of censure and contention. The Hearst press had, over many years, come to be labeled as yellow and tabloid journalism. Hearst's connection with the outbreak of the Spanish-American War had never been completely expunged from the public memory, and there is reason to believe that Hearst's generally tarnished journalistic reputation was a handicap to his Metrotone News. In 1935, after demonstrations both inside and outside movie theatres became common and after several audience boycotts of these newsreels, the company's name was altered to "News of the Day," and references to Hearst's affiliation with the company were omitted. However, the stature of the company was not elevated, although it did not cease operations until 1967. Probably the most important technician employed by Metrotone-News of the Day was Wong Hai-sheng, a photographer-cameraman. His film footage captured some of the most moving and important moments of current history for his contemporary audiences. His shot of a little baby, smeared with blood and crying helplessly and uncomprehendingly amid the ruins of bombed South Station in Canton, China was seen by millions and millions of people around the world. Whether accidental or arranged, it was a masterful bit of portraiture, and, as propaganda, made the vision by "Newsreel Wong" one that the world adopted as embodying the horrors of civilian casualties of war.

Pathe News, the RKO release, was far more sports-oriented than any other newsreel, having its own sports department. In addition to the sports emphasis, it had the obligatory humorous interludes, as well as short sequences on domestic news. In 1935 and thereafter, Pathe News was vocally represented by Harry von Zell. Pathe tried more than most newsreel companies to get "exclusive" news. For example, the Pathe coverage of the infancy and development of the Dionne quintuplets was extensive as well as exclusive, for some time.

Paramount's news policy was determined by a board of editors, rather than one man's point of view; and Paramount News claimed several very prestigious "scoops." It was the first newsreel film company that managed to obtain footage of German propaganda films from the German Office of Propaganda. Paramount News was also the first to show footage from the USSR; and it had the exclusive rights to Admiral Byrd's expedition to the Antarctic. Eventually, the cameramen for the South Polar expedition were accorded an Academy Award for their film footage—most of which was used by Paramount's parent company, Paramount Films, in a feature-length film.

Universal was the newsreel industry's low-budget operation. Using no in-the-field sound recording, Universal dubbed in sound effects and music to back up the narration read by their chief announcer, Graham MacNamee. Such thrift enabled Universal to hold its own with the bigger figures in the news field. Like the bigger newsreels, Universal began each segment with whatever was their most important news of the moment, and then moved down the stories in descending order of importance.

Although they were more a product of show business than journalism, newsreels occasionally presented events of great magnitude.

Among the covered events were the burning of the Hindenburg, the assassination of Alexander I of Yugoslavia, the Lindbergh kidnapping and subsequent trial of Bruno Hauptmann, and the bombing of the battleship Panay.

The Lindbergh-Hauptmann case was a cause célèbre for a number of reasons, not the least of which was the nationality of the accused kidnapper. Hauptmann, an unemployed tradesman, was of German origin. Propaganda residue from World War I still existed; the epithet of "kraut" was used by many when speaking of the accused.

The Depression had exacerbated ethnic suspicions, since competition for jobs was keen and there were strong feelings that "100 percent Americans" should get jobs first. In addition to all the foregoing, the baby that Hauptmann was accused of kidnapping and murdering was the child of one of the country's hero figures, the man who had made the first solo flight across the Atlantic—the "Lone Eagle," Charles Lindbergh.

Newsreel coverage of the case was unremitting; pictures of the family members, the detectives, the cop on the beat, the neighbors, the porch of the house, the doctors, and endless scenes of the property of the Lindberghs (Mrs. Lindbergh was the former Anne Morrow, daughter of a U.S. ambassador, and wealthy in her own right) appeared in virtually every newsreel for months before the trial, in an attempt to keep public interest at a peak. Many of the techniques that were later to become standard newsreel practice first appeared during this case. When the trial itself was held, cameras were brought into the court before and after the daily proceedings, to record the reactions of witnesses. A death row interview with Hauptmann was wangled by one newsreel (Paramount News), and shots of the electric chair were shown on movie screens in every hamlet and metropolis across the country.

The spring of 1935 produced a new hybrid: *The March of Time*. This film form was a cross between a newsreel and a documentary film; it was produced once a month, at a cost of $50,000 to $75,000 per issue. Unlike the regular newsreels, *The March of Time* ran about 20 minutes and used a full panoply of feature-film techniques and technology. There were well-constructed scripts; on occasion, actors were employed to impersonate political figures who could not or would not appear; music was carefully arranged and, on occasion, composed;

and, in 1938, the format was adapted to encompass only a single theme within each production. There was no attempt at pseudo-objectivity; on the contrary, there was open partisanship and involvement with the issues presented by *The March of Time*. The intent was to maintain a controversial and stimulating vehicle to arouse an audience that had come to regard news in the movies as soporific. The mixed reception that was given to treatments by *The March of Time* did not ruffle its producer, Louis de Rochemont, at all. He wanted the productions to be topics of conversation, debate, and argument. The bland pablum that was usually served up as news was not the way to build a following; but vigor, shock, pictorial forthrightness, and confrontation brought the public back again and again to see what was the latest mission, cause célèbre, or outrage. Segments dealt with breadlines and poverty, with demagogic politicians and bureaucrats, with unemployment, and with the shadows of war, among other pressures of the day.

In January 1938, the first single-topic issue of *The March of Time* was released. It was probably the most controversial release this organization ever put out, not because of the single-topic format—but because the subject was "Inside Nazi Germany, 1938." The isolationist outcry that arose over this film's distribution echoed even in the halls of Congress. Movie exhibitors were most unwilling to show pictures that touched on European or Asian politics. Many regarded the exhibition of such a film as giving Hitler a forum for addressing the U.S. public. But the film was a strong indictment of Hitler and his policy; and *The March of Time* was, by now, firmly ensconced in the programs of thousands of movie houses.

THE IMAGE ARSENAL

The diversionary feature-film fare of the major studios had helped to mitigate the harsh realities of the 1930s. By the end of the decade, however, movies began to assume a new role and significance. As the ominous shadow of war enveloped all of Asia and Europe in its darkness, Hollywood marshaled its talents and production resources to combat the enemy on the propaganda front. With the diminishing of the foreign market for U.S. films (due to Hitler's advances and the fortunes of war), industry leaders allowed their anti-Nazi sentiments to come to the fore. Of course, the primary aim of production continued to be profit.

Warners raised a storm of controversy with its 1939 release, *Confessions of a Nazi Spy*. The film was based on material drawn from the actual trial of 18 spies for Nazi Germany and served as an exposé of the German-American Bund, which was an organization that ostensibly provided a cultural outlet for German-Americans but actually carried out Nazi propaganda and spy activities predominantly on the east coast of the United States. The German consulate filed an official complaint, charging that the film was part of a U.S. conspiracy. Fritz Kuhn, *gauleiter* of the German-American Bund, even threatened to sue Warners for $5 million. German diplomatic forces openly worked for suppression of the film in the United States as well as abroad. As a result of this campaign, the film was banned in 18 Latin American and European nations.

A number of anti-Nazi films appeared before the attack on Pearl Harbor precipitated U.S. entry into World War II. *Foreign Correspondent* (1940) featured Joel McCrea as a naive U.S. journalist who eventually uncovers a fifth-column plot against England. The film concludes with a fervent appeal by reporter McCrea for the United States to arm itself. "The lights are going out in Europe," he warns. "Ring yourself around with steel, America." *Escape* (1940) described the efforts of a young man to rescue his mother from a Nazi prison. *Four Sons* (1940) gave an anguished account of the Nazi occupation of Czechoslovakia. In *The Man I Married* (1940), the fanaticism of the Third Reich is seen through the eyes of an American woman. *The Mortal Storm* (1940) chronicled the vicissitudes of a German middle-class family in a small university town at the time of Hitler's seizure of power.

One of the most provocative pictures of the period was *The Great Dictator*—an October 1940 release—in which Charlie Chaplin played a dual role, appearing both as a timid Jewish barber and as Adenoid Hynkel, the ranting, posturing dictator of Tomania. The film alternates between incidents in the life of the little barber and episodes in the career of the hysterical dictator. Their lives come together at the end of the film, when the barber, mistaken for Hynkel, takes the dictator's place before the microphones and delivers a fiery, impassioned plea for peace and understanding.

Chaplin enjoyed a degree of creative autonomy that was unique in the movie industry.[37] As early as 1915, his rare gift of mime and seemingly limitless imagination earned him $1,250 a week—an especially impressive figure when one considers that income tax at the time was negligible and the dollar was worth at least four or five times its current value. Within a year, his salary had soared to an incredible $10,000 a week plus an annual bonus of $150,000. By 1919, he owned a substantial share of the newly formed United Artists and had total control of his own productions. In *A Woman of Paris* (1923), his first UA release, he often made from 50 to 200 takes to achieve the nuances of detail and action so characteristic of his work. He also had the luxury of an exceedingly slow production pace. In the years between *A Woman of Paris* and *The Great Dictator*, Chaplin had made just four films: *The Gold Rush* (1925), *The Circus* (1928), *City Lights* (1931), and *Modern Times* (1936). Production costs on *The Great Dictator* ran over $2 million and more than half a million feet of film were shot. Chaplin spent months on retakes, editing, and musical scoring. The result was a brilliant seriocomic representation of the Hitler mythology.

Throughout the production of the film, not only those sympathetic to Nazism but also well-meaning pacifists cautioned Chaplin against offending Hitler. UA's business office was advised by the movie industry's self-regulatory agency that the film would run into censorship problems. Through it all, Chaplin persevered. "If they won't give theatres to show my picture," he asserted, "I'll show it myself. In tents. I'll charge 10 cents straight. I'd like to do that anyway, so that everyone can go see it."[38] Despite bomb threats and boycotts, UA was able to secure a substantial number of bookings. The film eventually grossed nearly $5 million worldwide, earning Chaplin not only acclaim but also a profit of about $1.5 million. (Chaplin later wrote that, had he been aware of the actual horrors of the Nazi concentration camps, he could not have made the picture.)[39]

The anti-Nazi films of the pre-Pearl Harbor period drew the ire of isolationist organizations like the America First Committee. Two of its senatorial supporters, Republican Gerald Nye of North Dakota and Democrat Burton Wheeler of Montana, introduced a resolution calling for an investigation of what they alleged was motion picture propaganda designed to promote U.S. entry into the European war. In one speech, Nye warned that motion pictures had become "the most gigantic engines of propaganda to rouse war fever in America and plunge the nation to her destruction." He went on to list the heads of the movie companies, many of whom bore Jewish names, and said that "in each of these companies there are a number of production directors, many of whom have come from Russia, Hungary, Germany, and the Balkan countries. . . . Go to Hollywood. It is a raging volcano of war fever. The place swarms with refugees."[40]

During September 1941, the Senate Subcommittee on War Propaganda conducted hearings to investigate the charges that Hollywood was promulgating propaganda designed to promote U.S. participation in the European war. The movie industry was represented by no less an eminence than Wendall Wilkie, the defeated but enormously popular Republican presidential candidate in 1940. In presenting the industry's case, Wilke resolutely embraced the principle that movies are entitled to the same freedom from government restraint enjoyed by the press. Several studio executives appeared as witnesses and forcefully denied the propaganda charges. Darryl F. Zanuck was the most telling, asserting that most Hollywood pictures were powerful sales vehicles for "the American way of life, not only to America but to the entire world."[41] The hearings were temporarily discontinued in October and then, following the attack on Pearl Harbor, dropped entirely.

Shortly after U.S. entry into the war, President Franklin D. Roosevelt established the Office of War Information (OWI), which incorporated the information activities of a number of prewar agencies.[42] The agency was headed by Elmer Davis who, prior to his appointment, had been a news analyst and commentator for the Columbia Broadcasting System. Under the direction of Lowell Mellett (a former Scripps-Howard editor), the OWI included a motion picture bureau whose primary function was to serve as a liaison between the movie industry and the government. Among other services, the bureau supplied filmmakers with the special information needed for the production of various war-related movies.

The motion picture bureau did try to exert a direct influence on motion picture content, but Mellett's request to see scripts prior to production met with strong opposition. The position of many in Hollywood was expressed by producer Walter Wanger who said, in an article published in the spring of 1943, "Censorship before utterance is abhorrent to Americans, who believe that autocracy can have no deadlier weapon than the blue pencil."[43] (Wanger, it should be mentioned, did not use this occasion to point out that the movie industry had its own privately instituted, privately enforced, censorship code.)

Although the motion picture bureau's functions were purely advisory, the government did have the power to invoke certain sanctions against recalcitrant moviemakers, through other wartime agencies. The Office of Censorship, established by executive order soon after Pearl Harbor, could bar the export of films it felt hurt the war effort.

Studios remained free to make any picture they wanted without consulting the government, but cooperation was fostered by the knowledge that a film might be doomed to domestic exhibition exclusively. The majority of the major studios eventually acceded to the motion picture bureau's request for scripts prior to production. According to one account, from mid-1943 until the end of the war, "OWI exerted an influence over an American mass medium never equalled before or since by a government agency."[44]

The movie industry as a whole was more than willing to work with the government in most matters concerning the war. In mid-1940, the leaders of the motion picture industry had formed the Motion Picture Committee Cooperating for National Defense. The purpose was to distribute, transport, and exhibit government-made films dealing with national defense. The major studios assisted the government in producing a diversity of shorts. After the attack on Pearl Harbor, the Committee changed its name to War Activities Committee-Motion Picture Industry and expanded its membership to include exhibitors and theatre owners. Some 16,000 movie houses were committed to the exhibition of government propaganda shorts, which were released every other week. On alternating weeks, the major studios provided a series of short subjects on various themes under the heading *America Speaks*. Among the more effective films in this series was MGM's two-reel production *Mr. Blabbermouth*, which stressed the danger of careless talk in wartime. Paramount's *Letter from Bataan* highlighted the need for conserving food and materials. Columbia's *Men Working Together* began with a war poster coming to life, and continued by portraying the unity of purpose between the men on the battlefront and those on the home-front production lines. The studios produced the *America Speaks* series without any charge to the government. At the height of the war, some 50 percent of the screen time available for shorts went to the government war effort.[45]

Propaganda shorts of all sorts were presented to the general public. Walt Disney's Donald Duck, for instance, was enlisted by the Treasury Department to remind the U.S. public of the new tax law of 1942, which brought millions of people onto the tax rolls for the first time. In *The New Spirit*, an eight-minute Disney-produced short, Donald Duck is shown listening to the radio, with the American flag literally waving in the pupils of his eyes. In a fervor of patriotism, he beseeches the radio to tell him how to aid the war effort. At first, the answer ("By paying your taxes") enrages the web-footed patriot; but, when he is informed of the power his taxes have to purchase armaments ("Taxes to beat the Axis"), he gladly sets about calculating his income tax. The film short was seen by an estimated 26 million people—37 percent of whom reported, in a Gallup poll, that it had an effect on their willingness to pay taxes.[46]

Throughout the war years, the Disney animation apparatus remained in high gear, turning out dozens of propaganda films.[47] In Disney's 1942 film *Donald Duck in Nutzi Land*, the goose-stepping regimentation of Nazism is depicted when the irascible Donald Duck dreams that he is working in a German munitions factory. Awakening from this nightmare, he sees the shadow of an outstretched arm and starts to respond with a "Heil", but realizes that it is actually the shadow of the arm of a miniature Statue of Liberty. The film concludes with Donald's heartfelt thankfulness that, in fact, he lives in the United States and is safe at home. This animated short made the Fuehrer a figure of ridicule throughout the nation. The song (by Oliver Wallace, a Disney Studio composer) used in the film was recorded by Spike Jones. It became such an instant hit—due both to clever orchestration and its irreverent attitude—that the song title "Der Fuehrer's Face" was given to the cartoon, as well.

Among the other films produced by Disney's propaganda arsenal was *Education for Death* (1943), which focuses on the education of a German lad called Hans, as he grew from young school age to an adult soldier. There are moments of humor in the animated film, but the tone is far more ominous than anything Disney had done for general release, up until that time. Young Hans is carefully trained in Nazi doctrine and—when necessary—retrained, when he shows signs of gentleness of nature. In *Reason and Emotion* (1943), the brain is presented allegorically as an automobile. The driver is Reason; the passenger chained in the backseat is Emotion who, when he occasionally gets into control, wreaks great damage. The two traits live together in the minds of all humans, the film implies. However, in the mind of the moronic Nazi soldier, Emotion reigns supreme—with Reason the helpless victim.

Disney's most ambitious wartime propaganda film was *Victory through Air Power* (1943), which was based on Major Alexander de Seversky's 1942 book of the same title. Through animation, graphs and maps, and live-action shots, the 65-minute film presents the same message as the book—that is, that air power is the means by which the war could and should be won. The film's clever visual vernacular includes a portrayal of the Japanese nation as an octopus gripping the Pacific in its tentacles, with war scenes and graphs of enemy action—using predominantly red and black to indicate violence. In a closing scene that depicts the bombing of Tokyo from the air, the screen is filled with symbolic lightning bolts; and, as the "octopus" draws in upon itself and dies, the viewer is drawn back from the scene to a broader, more distinct view. To the strains of "America, the Beautiful," an American eagle atop a flagpole is seen, coated in the golden rays of a new dawn. Next in focus is the American flag waving bravely, which then becomes the background for the final title shot, "Victory through Air Power."

A large quantity of newsreel footage (estimated variously at from 70 to 80 percent) dealt mainly with war topics. As the war escalated, newsreel footage was supplied in considerable amounts by the U.S. Army Signal Corps, the Navy, and by other military personnel who had been trained by *The March of Time*. Pictures of devastation and carnage became steadily more explicit, and the earlier attitude of theatre owners about displaying them changed considerably. At the outset, theatre owners often proclaimed to potential customers "No war-filled scenes shown here," and Radio City Music Hall (as well as some other exhibitors) excised the more gruesome sections out of movie newsreels in order to protect the sensitivities of their "family audiences." However, the messages of the government addressed to a nation at war were incorporated into newsreels in other ways. Celebrities at War Bond Rallies, recipes for a rationed housewife, Boy Scout scrap collection drives, and scenes of USO canteens and wartime weddings were standard fare for all the newsreels. Once the United States was in the war, the general tone was one of concerted effort and national unity.

The March of Time managed to maintain some of its cutting edge. It devoted the bulk of its production to topics dealing with the war, with topics dealing with the home front as runner-up. There were issues on many of the important countries—important because of their positions vis-à-vis the war. These showed the people, the way of life, the political leaders, and the policies of each country. The issue on "Inside Fascist Spain" pointed out the repression of any kind of opposition, and reminded the audience that political prisoners in Spain were incarcerated for demanding rights that every American thinks are human rights. The murder of many of these political prisoners for such insurrectionist activities as demanding a 40-hour week, or free elections, was a reminder of the issues at stake in the war with the Axis powers. "One Day at War—The Soviet Union, 1943" was an edited creation using Soviet footage, and drew together the events that might have represented a day's activities in that country: home-front labor and volunteerism, defense and civil defense procedures, personal vignettes, and so on. Home-front films showed celebrities entertaining at the USO, the rise of war industry on the west coast, and other matters reporting the behaviors of a nation at war.

A number of Hollywood directors contributed their talents to the nation's propaganda arsenal. Frank Capra, who became a lieutenant colonel in the U.S. Army Signal Corps, produced a series of documentary films for the government under the rubric "Why We Fight." These 50-minute films were intended to indoctrinate new recruits with information about the enemy, their allies, and the reasons for their being sent into battle. In all, seven films were produced. The first installment in the series, *Prelude to War*, was released for viewing by civilian audiences. In this film, the Axis leaders—Tojo, Hitler, and Mussolini, were depicted as evil personified. Viewers were urged to "remember these three faces" and, "if you ever meet them, don't hesitate!" The advantages of the American way of life and of democratic principles were supported with references ranging from Lafayette, the Declaration of Independence, and Lincoln to Moses, Confucius, and Jesus.[48]

During the war years, Hollywood continued to turn out propagandistic feature films. But attempts to influence were almost always incidental to the entertainment. Out of every ten features released by the movie industry between the end of December 1941 and August 1945, roughly three had any content that related to World War II.[49] There were films about why we were fighting, who our allies were and what they were like in war, and who and what our enemies were. There were also films about the home front, explaining or depicting some of the changes in life-style due to the war. Another category of films concerned war production and the occupations related to the war effort. There was also a spate of films about U.S. fighting forces, and their victories.

Although burdened by labor and material shortages and compelled to tolerate an occasional outburst of congressional scorn, the big studios nevertheless prospered during the war years. Throughout this period, Hollywood's production of new features was only slightly below the peacetime level, and official estimates showed weekly attendance at a stable 85 million.

Industry leaders looked to the future with seemingly justified optimism. Some estimates put average weekly attendance in 1946 at an all-time high of 90 million. Profits soared to a record $120 million. But there were ominous signs on the horizon. A diversity of activities began to lure people away from movie theatres. Bowling and miniature golf were becoming popular pastimes. Automobiles—in scarce supply during the war—became readily available. However, the most foreboding factor, was the specter of television, which was winning a prominent place in U.S. homes.

HOLLYWOOD IN TRANSITION

Television burst onto the American scene like a delayed time bomb. Simple informational statistics reveal—more than any rhetorical utterance—just how pervasive and ubiquitous television became in the postwar years.[50] By the mid-1950s, some 600 television stations were sprinkled across the United States. Annual set manufacture had climbed from 6,000 in 1946 to over 7.7 million a decade later. Fully 65 percent of all U.S. homes were equipped with at least one television set by 1955. That year the average home had the set on about five hours a day. Within a few more years, television would permeate almost every household in the nation. Popular programs soon attracted 40, 50, and sometimes 60 million or more viewers.

The same period witnessed a precipitous decline in movie attendance. Despite a sharp rise in the population of the United States in the decade following World War II—from 141 million people to 167 million—the estimated average number of movie tickets sold weekly fell from 90 million in 1946 to less than 47 million ten years later.

An atmosphere of disquiet and anxiety pervaded Hollywood in the postwar period, as the big studios underwent retrenchment and reorganization. In the fall of 1947, the giant MGM cut its studio staff by 25 percent. Other movie firms soon adopted similar cost-cutting measures. Employment in the various craft unions fell from 22,100 in 1946 to 13,500 in 1949. Production schedules were slashed and long-term contracts with producers, directors, writers, and actors were allowed to lapse.

Added to its economic woes, the movie industry also faced legal problems.[51] In July 1938, the U.S. Justice Department had begun litigation against Paramount, Warner Bros., RKO, Twentieth Century-Fox, and Loew's-MGM for combining and conspiring to unreasonably restrain trade and to monopolize the production, distribution, and exhibition of motion pictures. Universal, Columbia, and United Artists were charged with combining and conspiring with the other five companies, for the same purpose. When war seemed imminent in 1940, a "consent decree" (a legal maneuver in which an accused corporation admits nothing but promises not to do it again) was issued, permitting the studios to retain their exhibition outlets with minor restrictions. But the case was reactivated in 1944 and concluded in May 1948, when the U.S. Supreme Court ruled that the vertical integration of the major companies violated federal antitrust laws. The high court remanded the question of theatre ownership to the federal district court in New York. In 1949, the district court decided that separation of production and distribution from exhibition was the appropriate remedy.

The five vertically integrated companies—beginning with RKO and continuing with Paramount, Warner Bros., Twentieth Century-Fox, and Loew's-MGM—signed a consent decree that broke the corporate chains linking production and distribution to exhibition. The consent decree called for the divestiture of specific theatres, as well as the divorcement of theatre circuits. Since RKO and Paramount (which did wait for the district court's inevitable edict) were the first two companies to sign consent decrees, they obtained a major concession. In due course, the new production and distribution companies were permitted to acquire theatres, while the new theatre companies were eventually permitted to produce films—so long as the reintegration did not impair competition.

The old Paramount company was dissolved and its assets were transferred to two new companies: Paramount Pictures Corporation and United Paramount Theatres. In 1953, the latter company merged with the American Broadcasting Company.

The other three integrated companies—Warner Bros., Twentieth Century-Fox, and Loew's-MGM—attempted to forestall divorcement through a series of appeals, but eventually they acceded to the government's demands. The last of the big studios to undergo divorcement was Loew's-MGM, whose split was not finally completed until 1959.

CHANGING PATTERNS OF PRODUCTION

Production activity became more dispersed in the 1950s, but the *Paramount* case did little to prevent the development of new concentrations of control. The major theatre chains were able to continue their dominance over exhibition, even though they were required to divest some of their holdings. Distribution, the key to controlling independent production, continued to be dominated by the *Paramount* defendants.

United Artists, which had evolved in the early 1950s into a company run by lawyers, moved to the front ranks of the movie industry soon after it embarked on a policy of financing the motion pictures of actors and directors, as well as independent producers—foreshadowing the commercial practices prevalent today. John Wayne, Burt Lancaster, Gregory Peck, and Robert Mitchum—among others—joined UA's roster of actor-producers.

Actors, writers, and producers in the top income bracket were attracted to independent production by the less onerous levy on capital gains and corporate profit. High taxes had swallowed up so much of their salaries that there seemed to be little incentive to remain an employee. Under the extant tax structure, an independent producer could earn income as a percentage of profits rather than as a salary, reducing his effective tax rate from 90 to 60 percent.

Many with creative talent were additionally attracted into the UA fold by the asssurance that they could make their pictures wherever and however they wished. UA provided some measure of financing, assisted in such particulars as leasing studio space and drawing contracts, and guaranteed promotion and distribution. United Artists' policy of trusting talent to make their own films with a minimum of front-office interference, encouraged directors like Otto Preminger, Billy Wilder, Joseph Mankiewicz, and William Wyler to release their films under the UA banner.

Most of the major companies followed UA's lead. MGM, for instance, began to sign with independent producers and stars under short-term contracts for a limited number of pictures. The studio arranged for financing, and the producing agent invested enough of his own money in the project to qualify for the lower corporate-profits taxation. Generally, the deal called for the producer to receive a percentage of the aggregate earnings from the entire package. The studio head was now relegated to determining which packages of directors, stars, and writers to put under short-term contract. Contract negotiations were—and are—a highly individual matter of bargain and barter. But under its standard contract, MGM (like most of the major studios) generally shared 50 percent of a picture's profit with the independent producer. MGM added up to 25 percent onto the initial production cost (the amount depending on whether or not studio space or equipment was used) to cover the operation of its production facilities.

Of course, independent producers only maintained a degree of independence if their pictures proved profitable. Moreover, as a condition for a release commitment, a major distributor usually insisted that a producer rent its equipment, technical services, and studio space. Also, the distributor often demanded the right of final approval on the director, writers, actors, and anyone else rendering service on the film. The distributor, who generally received 30 percent of the gross income, was much more likely to show a profit than the producer. Only about one film in four showed any profit for the independent producer. (The general rule of thumb in the movie business is that a film will begin to show a profit after its gross income from distribution reaches 2½ times its "negative cost"—the total cost of making the film.) The distributor, however, had already enjoyed a substantial income from its studio rental charges and its distribution fee.

While over half of the feature films released by the major movie companies in the late 1950s were made by independent producers, it was moviedom's aristocracy who still determined the character and quality of these productions. Those who sought financing outside the studio nexus ran the risk of not being able to get their films distributed. In the final analysis, most independent producers experienced very little independence or autonomy, and the rewards often did not justify the risks incurred or the creative energy expended.

THE NEW HOLLYWOOD

The Big Five and the Little Three who loomed so large in the 1930s and 1940s have all become or been absorbed by conglomerates—those corporate configurations that operate in a number of different and often unrelated markets. The erratic earnings record of the major movie studios, dating from the advent of television, made them particularly susceptible to mergers and corporate takeovers.

RKO was swallowed up in 1955 by General Tire and Rubber, a corporation whose far-flung interests have included tiremaking, chemicals, plastics, rockets, guided-missile controls, and submarines. The studio continued to make movies, turning out a total of 13 features in 1956. But most of the ones that were released did not do well at the box office. Early the following year, the new management shut down RKO's entire domestic distribution organization and arranged for Universal to handle the remainder of the studio's already completed films. In 1958, Desilu—a television corporation developed by two former RKO contract players, Desi Arnaz and Lucille Ball—purchased RKO's sprawling studio facilities. RKO's tenure as a theatrical movie company had come to an end.

Controlling interest in Universal Pictures was bought by Decca Records in the early 1950s. In 1959, the record company sold the 423-acre Universal studio lot (but not the production and distribution operation) to Revue Productions, the television subsidiary of MCA Inc. (which was the largest talent agency in the nation, at the time). In 1961, under pressure from the Justice Department, MCA was forced to decide between being an agent and being an employer of talent, since this dual role clearly constituted a conflict of interest. MCA moved to divest itself of its talent agency. The television business had become so lucrative that, by 1962, MCA was able to absorb both Universal Pictures and the controlling company, Decca Records. MCA diversified its activities over the years—acquiring such companies as Spencer Gifts, a national mail order and retail gift operation; Columbia Savings and Loan of Colorado; and G. P. Putnam's Sons, a leading publisher of hardcover and paperback books. Its other income-producing enterprises include the Universal Studio Tour, which has become one of the nation's most profitable tourist attractions.

Several of the major studios were assimilated into complex corporate enterprises during the 1960s. In 1966, Paramount became part of Gulf + Western Industries, a firm involved in everything from auto parts, candy, tobacco, musical instruments, and lingerie to zinc mines, oil drilling, nuclear power plants, rocket engineering, and jet and missile parts. (Paramount, in turn, moved into big-time television production the following year through the purchase of Desilu Productions for $17 million.) United Artists was acquired in 1967 by Transamerica, a giant corporation with interests in insurance and other financial services. (UA had previously gained control of a large inventory of feature films, including some 700 pre-1948 Warner releases.) Early in 1967, Warner Bros. merged with Seven Arts Productions, a Canadian distributor of films to television. The new corporation was called Warner Bros.-Seven Arts Ltd. Two years later, this enterprise was merged into Kinney National, a service-industry conglomerate with interests in funeral parlors, rent-a-car agencies, parking lots, and building maintenance companies. In July 1971, Kinney's growing entertainment holdings were transferred into a separate, superordinate sister company called Warner Communications. The interests of this media colossus now span broadcasting, books, magazines, movies, records, and cable television.

Movie studios were a tempting takeover target because of their ownership of film libraries, real estate assets, and musical and literary copyrights. In the 1960s, control of MGM was sought by Philip Levin (a wealthy builder and real estate developer), then by Time Inc. and Edgar Bronfman of the Seagram liquor empire, and was finally gained by Kirk Kerkorian (a Las Vegas–based financier and casino owner). The new management that Kerkorian put in place virtually liquidated the studio. Fifteen imminent film projects were brusquely canceled. The company's 46-year-old collection of props, costumes, and other musty memorabilia were turned over to an auction house. (Judy Garland's *Wizard of Oz* slippers fetched $15,000.) MGM-owned land in Culver City—as well as theatres in Australia South Africa, and England—were sold. In the fall of 1973, MGM announced that it would only make six to eight ''special'' movies a year. At the same time, the studio withdrew from film distribution, assigning its domestic distribution rights to United Artists for ten years and its foreign distribution rights to Cinema International, a joint venture of Paramount and Universal. The once-proud lion, although prosperous in his old age, found himself presiding over roulette wheels, crap tables, and slot machines. In 1981, Kerkorian bought control of United Artists, which had been debilitated by the box office failure of its $40 million *Heaven's Gate* (1980)—writer-director Michael Cimino's now-notorious spectacle about the plight of immigrant settlers in nineteenth-century Wyoming.[52] The two studios were later merged to form MGM/UA Entertainment. This entity, which possessed one of the largest film libraries in the industry, was sold in 1985 to Atlanta-based entrepreneur Ted Turner of the Turner Broadcasting Systems.

Columbia Pictures and Twentieth Century-Fox managed to make it through the 1970s with their corporate identities relatively intact, although each endured a period of bitter internecine strife.[53] In 1982, Columbia was acquired by Coca-Cola, the giant soft-drink company. Three years later, the Fox studio (briefly owned outright by oil man Marvin Davis) was absorbed into tabloid-press lord Rupert Murdock's News Corporation, a powerful media conglomerate with worldwide interests.

Although the despotic moguls of old have either died off or been deposed by conglomerates, financiers, lawyers, and computers, the institution of Hollywood has changed far less than is commonly assumed.

Moviedom is still a magnet that attracts hope. The ability to make money is still the principal yardstick of success. And a surplus of ego and anxiety is still endemic to all phases of production. More than a place, as David McClintock notes, "Hollywood is a state of mind. And all the same elemental forces that drove it in the twenties and thirties still drive it today. In addition to the pleasures of power, there are money, fame, sex, a stake in creating American popular culture, and an opportunity to have a great deal of fun in the pursuit of these pleasures."[54]

3

Social Control of
Motion Pictures

In primitive cultures people often believed that behind the immediate physical reality of things lay spirits, that apparently inanimate objects had life within them. To our modern sensibility, such notions may seem unsophisticated and naive. And yet, for many of us, the photographic image is thought to offer direct access to the real.[1]

This power of photography to represent objects and people as we might recognize them in everyday encounters imbues motion pictures with a seemingly living force, which words on a printed page can never provide. But everything we see in a motion picture has gone through a complicated creative process involving lighting, lenses, film stock, camera movement, and so forth. Even the filming of actualities—that is to say, news, sports, speeches, and the like—involves apparatuses and procedures that are highly manipulative in nature.

The photographic verisimilitude of motion pictures (and television) is achieved within a highly prescribed series of conventions, many of which were developed in the heyday of Hollywood. Some of these conventions are linked specifically to the manufacture of the image and its reproduction; some have to do with the aesthetics of composition and editing; others have developed out of the fundamental task of storytelling.

On top of this, motion picture conventions reflect the often single-minded pursuit of profits by the front office and the stockholders, and the factorylike atmosphere prevalent in many of the studios. "The bureaucrats and accountants," as David Robinson puts it, "eager to overcome the unpredictable and intractable element in the creation of films, began to codify certain principles of commercial production that still prevail in the industry: the attempt to exploit proven success with formula pictures and cycles of any particular genre which temporarily sells, at the expense of other and perhaps unorthodox product; the quest for predictable sales values—star names, best-selling success titles, costly and showy production values—which have little to do with art.''[2] The standardized assembly-line techniques developed to accomplish this codification of production further conventionalized the entire operation and output.

Perhaps almost as influential in forging the widely accepted practices and procedures that prevailed in Hollywood was the constant pressure from institutions of social control outside the industry—civic, political, and religious groups—for motion picture censorship. The development and nature of public demands for censorship and the private constraints instituted to accommodate them are the focus of this chapter.

EARLY ATTEMPTS AT CONTENT CONTROL

One of the first demands for censorship came as early as 1895, when the showing of an innocuous short film—provocatively promoted as *Dolorita in the Passion Dance*—at a Kinetoscope parlor in Atlantic City offended moral-minded sensibility; the film was promptly removed. The following year a Vitascope presentation of a prolonged kiss between Mary Irwin and John C. Rice, from their Broadway hit *The Widow Jones*, produced a flurry of moral concern. ''Such things call for police interference,'' protested one irate observer.[3] In New York City, a showing of the short film *Orange Blossoms*, which featured a young bride disrobing on her wedding night—so deftly as to reveal very little flesh—was closed in 1897 by court order.

But there was more at stake than just sexual permissiveness. Many of the early films also attacked authority. Edwin Porter's tale of banditry and retribution, *The Great Train Robbery* (1903), captivated audiences with its variety of scene and locale, its close-ups of the bandit firing at the camera, and its combination of suspense and movement. Yet along with its innovative techniques, the plot showed lawmen who were just as ruthless as the criminals. Porter's film *The Kleptomaniac* (1905) depicted the parallels of crimes committed by two women—one wealthy, the other poor. The wealthy woman was pardoned as a victim of kleptomania, while the poor woman who stole bread to feed her hungry family was sentenced as a criminal. The link to social injustice, which was a common experience among many in the audiences, could not have been totally ignored by those watching the films. Such injustices magnified on the screen served to build credibility in and loyalty for the movies, and must have certainly carried a potent cultural charge.

Alarmed by the force of movies, legislators began to enact laws designed to control the content of the new medium. The first municipal censorship ordinance was passed in Chicago in 1907. It not only empowered the superintendent of police to issue permits for the exhibition of motion pictures, but also invested him with the right to withhold or deny such permission for films deemed immoral or obscene. Standards for judgment were determined by the personal predilections of the local authorities. Beginning in 1911, state censorship boards began to appear. The first state to pass a censorship law was Pennsylvania; Ohio and Kansas followed in 1913; Maryland in 1916; New York in 1921; Virginia in 1922.

In an effort to counteract bad publicity and to prevent the closing of outlets showing their films, the members of the Motion Picture Patents Company (MPPC) joined forces in March 1909 with Dr. Charles Sprague Smith of the People's Institute of New York, an institution for adult education, which recognized the value of movies as a medium of mass communication.

The result was the formation of what soon came to be called the National Board of Review of Motion Pictures, the first national system of voluntary censorship. It was created in response to an immediate threat against the fledgling movie industry. In December of the previous year, Mayor George B. McClellan of New York City, under pressure from local church and civic leaders, had ordered all movie houses in the city closed. The stated purpose for closing the movie houses was to inspect the dwellings for safety hazards, but the mayor announced that he would issue new licenses only on the condition that exhibitors agreed, in writing, to remain closed on Sundays. The mayor also threatened to revoke the licenses of exhibitors who showed films that tended to degrade or injure the morals of the community. Exhibitors successfully petitioned the courts for injunctions allowing theatres to open, but further confrontations were inevitable.

The industry-supported National Board of Review soon came under fire for its allegedly liberal policies and its opposition to official censorship. Many began to question whether the review board's function was to oversee or to overlook. Moreover, it should be recalled that the board's chief industry supporter, the MPPC, proved unable to survive—despite its apparent monopolistic power.

Pressure groups attempting to bring motion pictures under legal control received new impetus in 1915 when the U.S. Supreme Court, in the *Mutual* case, unanimously upheld Ohio's censorship law. The nine justices ruled that "the exhibition of motion pictures is a business pure and simple, originated and conducted for profit, like other spectacles, not to be regarded, . . . as part of the press of the country or as organs of public opinion."[4] This was the principle that, for nearly four decades, relegated motion pictures to the status of sideshow, rather than as a medium for artistic expression and the dissemination of ideas. Even after the high court held, in 1925, that liberties protected by the First Amendment applied substantively to state actions through the due process clause of the Fourteenth Amendment, motion pictures remained outside the pale of constitutional protection.

The absence of constitutional safeguards compelled moviemakers to tread cautiously, manifesting a marked solicitude for the institutions of social control. State and municipal censors, exercising the many potentialities of their power, grew increasingly hostile to any display of cinematic eccentricity. Congress, too, considered legislation for regulating the content of motion pictures. In 1915, Representative Dudley M. Hughes of Georgia, chairman of the House Education Committee, introduced a bill to establish a five-member Federal Motion Picture Commission, which would examine, censor, and license all films prior to their interstate shipment. The cost of the Commission was to be borne by the movie industry.[5]

THE RISE OF SELF-REGULATION

Although the bill was defeated, its very existence alerted industry leaders to the need for a strong national organization to avert federal censorship. In the summer of 1916, the leading producers and distributors formed the National Association of the Motion Picture Industry.[6] The members of this organization sponsored a constitutional amendment putting movies under the protection of the First Amendment, but it was defeated in Congressional committee.

This defeat led industry leaders to institute their own regulatory measures. In March 1921, moviedom's reigning powers (under the aegis of the National Association of the Motion Picture Industry) adopted a 13-point code to serve as a yardstick for the production and exhibition of motion pictures. Subject matter proscribed by the code included: exploitive use of sex; white slavery; illicit love; nakedness or scanty attire; prolonged expression of passionate love; vice; the presentation of gambling or drunkenness in an attractive light; the depreciation of governmental authority or religion; undue bloodshed and violence; the display of vulgar or improper gestures and attitudes; and the use of salacious advertising matter. The membership of the association agreed to adhere to this unusual industrial agreement; but, since the 13-point code lacked any mechanism for effective enforcement, it had little impact on motion picture content.

By the early 1920s, agitation over the content of motion pictures had swelled to unprecedented proportions. In 1921 alone, nearly 100 censorship bills were introduced, in 37 states. In the period following World War I, there had been a general relaxation of moral standards. This was the age of jazz, speakeasies, and sexual promiscuity. In many ways, motion pictures mirrored this new social milieu. Innuendoes of illicit passion, seduction, divorce, and the use of narcotics and alcohol all made their way to the screen.

Director Cecil B. De Mille set the style with such suggestive titles as *Old Wives for New* (1918), *Don't Change Your Husband* (1919), *Male and Female* (1919), *Why Change Your Wife* (1920), *Forbidden Fruit* (1921), and *The Affairs of Anatol* (1921). In such films, De Mille provided audiences with a voyeuristic view of the imagined indulgences of the rich and sophisticated. But these domestic melodramas, while often sexually provocative, were really cautionary tales in which straying wives and husbands were invariably reconciled in the final reel.

The offscreen escapades of some of the players and other studio personnel proved to be far more damaging to moviedom than any cinematic representation of sex and sin. One of the first hints of scandal came in 1920 when Mary Pickford, "America's Sweetheart," established residence in Nevada and secured a divorce from her husband, actor Owen Moore. A short time later, she and Douglas Fairbanks were married in California. The attorney general in Nevada made newspaper headlines when he filed suit to set aside Pickford's divorce decree because of alleged "collusion, fraud and untruthful testimony." The Nevada Supreme Court eventually upheld the divorce, but Pickford's fall from grace provided fuel for the legislative locomotive of professional reformers.

That same year, the suspicious suicide of the screen star Olive Thomas, who was the wife of Jack Pickford, Mary Pickford's brother and himself a movie idol, added to the impression that Hollywood was a synonym for something unsavory. Attacks against the movie industry intensified late in the summer of 1921, when popular comedian Roscoe "Fatty" Arbuckle (who had shortly before signed a three-year, $3-million contract with Paramount) became implicated in the death of a minor screen actress named Virginia Rappe. Testimony placed Arbuckle alone with the young woman in the locked bedroom of a San Francisco hotel. Screams were reported to have been heard through the door. Arbuckle was indicted for manslaughter and tried three times (the first two trials resulted in hung juries). Newspapers across the country gave the case front-page coverage. Although Arbuckle was eventually acquitted, his acting career was destroyed.

Other scandals erupted as well. The murder of William Desmond Taylor, a director with Famous Players-Lasky, provided headlines for months. Taylor had been shot to death at his home on the night of February 1, 1922. At the scene of the crime was found evidence that linked the director romantically with actress Mary Miles Minter. Comedienne Mabel Normand, another of Taylor's alleged amours, was known to have been one of the last people to see him alive. The mystery became more intriguing when it was revealed that Taylor may have also been involved with Minter's mother. The murder was never solved; and, although Normand and Minter were eventually cleared of suspicion, their careers were ruined by the scandal.

The image of Hollywood as the new Babylon did not sit well with the industry's leadership. While the Arbuckle case was being tried on the front pages of newspapers throughout the country, industry leaders sought the services of Will Hays, an ultraconservative Republican who was postmaster general in the Harding administration, to head a new self-regulatory trade organization designed to supercede previous, less effective attempts at unity.

Early in 1922, in a letter signed by moviedom's most powerful monarchs—including Adolph Zukor, William Fox, Samuel Goldwyn, and Carl Laemmle—Hays was offered a three-year contract at an annual salary of $100,000 to command the hastily organized Motion Picture Producers and Distributors of America (MPPDA). Under its bylaws, Hays—who was formally appointed as president, chairman of the board of directors, and chairman of the executive committee—had the power of veto over all decisions by the board of directors; a two-thirds vote by the board was required to override his veto.

Hays proved to be an astute choice. In Massachusetts, the legislature had passed a censorship bill in 1920; but it was vetoed by the state's governor, Calvin Coolidge. A similar bill was passed the following year, however, and motion picture exhibitors in the state managed to collect enough petitions to force a referendum on the censorship legislation in the November elections of 1922. Since this was the first test of the general public's attitude about movie censorship, Hays decided to launch a fierce campaign—under the banner of free speech—to defeat the legislation. The result of the referendum was a resounding victory for Hays; the censorship bill was defeated by a margin of almost 3 to 1. By the end of the year, the pressure for censorship seemed to abate.

The MPPDA's first tentative attempt at formal self-regulation came in July 1924, when its board of directors passed a resolution requiring that a synopsis of all plays, novels, and stories be submitted for approval before filming. To enforce compliance, Colonel Jason Joy (one of Hays's aides) was sent to Hollywood in December 1926 to set up a Studio Relations Committee within the Association of Motion Picture Producers (AMPP). This organization was the West Coast affiliate of the MPPDA, and was established in 1924 to handle management-labor negotiations. Under the AMPP's aegis, the producers created a jointly owned, subsidiary firm called the Central Casting Corporation to regulate the employment of extras. The exclusive right of this corporation to furnish extras to the major companies eliminated the frequently futile attempts of aspiring movie players to gain employment by lining up outside studio gates. Central Casting soon became one of the largest placement agencies in the country.

Colonel Joy worked with the AMPP's members on a voluntary basis, advising them of the prevailing political winds. Guidelines for production were formalized in 1927, when a study conducted by an MPPDA committee on the specific rejections and deletions made by state censorship boards resulted in the codification of two lists of admonitions, known as the "Don'ts" and "Be Carefuls." The "Don'ts" contained 11 items that could not be shown on the screen. Included were: profanity, by either title or lip; licentious or suggestive nudity; illegal drug traffic; any inference of sexual perversion; white slavery; miscegenation (which, at the time, was against the law in several southern states); sex hygiene and venereal diseases; childbirth; children's sex organs; ridicule of the clergy; and willful offense to any nation, race, or creed. The "Be Carefuls" concerned such things as: use of the flag; international relations; arson; firearms; theft; robbery;

brutality; murder techniques; methods of smuggling; hangings or executions; sympathy for criminals; sedition; cruelty to children or animals; the sale of women; rape or attempted rape; seduction; the institution of marriage; the use of drugs; and excessive or lustful kissing.

The newly adopted self-regulatory rules for screen conduct were touted by the Hays Office (as the MPPDA came to be called) as an indication of the industry's ability to responsibly police itself. To many observers, however, the strength of the evidence was insufficient to support such a claim. As in earlier attempts at self-regulation, the "Dont's" and "Be Carefuls" were broad and general in character and lacked a mechanism whereby they could be enforced with any real authority.

With the general introduction of sound in 1929, criticism of movie content increased in intensity. To ward off the attacks of reformers and censorship advocates, more substantial self-regulatory fortifications were needed.

A NEW CODE OF CONDUCT

In 1930, the industry leadership revamped and expanded its self-imposed code of conduct, to compensate for the changes in motion picture production resulting from the use of sound. The new guidelines, officially called the Motion Picture Production Code, detailed the various offenses that could not be committed against middle-class morality. For example, the audience was never to be enticed into sympathizing with the advocates of crime, wrongdoing, evil, or sin. No aspect of the law—divine, natural, or human—was ever to be ridiculed. Vulgarity, obscenity, and profanity were verboten. The sanctity of marriage and the home was to be upheld. Sexual relationships, even within marriage, were to be downplayed; and illicit sex of any sort was to be punished, in the end.

Once again, however, the enforcement mechanism for the new code proved to be weak. The members of the AMPP agreed to submit every film they produced to the Studio Relations Committee before it was sent to the laboratory for printing. If a film violated the code's canons of morality, it could not be released until the necessary changes were made. But the decisions of the Studio Relations Committee could be overruled by an appeals board composed of three members selected on a rotation basis from the AMPP's Production Committee. The members of the rotating panel of producers were often reluctant to condemn rival productions, since they knew that their own films might come under the scrutiny of the panel.

Evasions of the code's moral prescriptions multiplied, as the full impact of the Depression struck Hollywood. Films such as *Bachelor Apartment* (1931), *Breach of Promise* (1932), and *Beauty for Sale* (1932) featured illicit love affairs, risqué situations, and off-color dialogue. A number of female stars portrayed sympathetic prostitutes or kept women, among them Tallulah Bankhead in *Faithless* (1932), Jean Harlow in *Red Dust* (1932), and Irene Dunne in *Back Street* (1932). Press and pulpit alike denounced such films, finding little compensatory value in the fact that these "fallen women" were often punished with Old Testament severity for their transgressions.

Screen depictions of the gangster as "tragic hero"—to adopt Robert Warshow's phrase[7]—in films such as *Scarface—Shame of the Nation* (1932) also gave credence to the belief that the code was little more than a defensive strategem intended to avert government censorship. This violent and cynical portrayal of a Chicago mobster was banned by a number of censorship boards, in spite of the MPPDA's issuance of a seal of approval.

Perhaps it was the pictures of Mae West, more than anything else, that most offended the reform-minded. Her mockery of morality in such vehicles as *Night after Night* (1932), *She Done Him Wrong* (1933), and *I'm No Angel* (1933) made West one of the principal targets of the growing army of reformers. "In word and gesture Mae West was the living mockery of all the Code's pieties," notes Alexander Walker in *The Celluloid Sacrifice*. "But Hollywood made her welcome for one excellent reason: her films were enormous moneymakers."[8]

HOLLYWOOD UNDER ATTACK

Still, as the reform movement gained momentum, the major producers became ever more sensitive to the demands for stricter screen censorship. By 1934, reform-minded Catholic, Protestant, and Jewish organizations were insisting that, unless the industry started adhering to its own mandate, they would seek federal censorship. A committee of Roman Catholic bishops organized a Legion of Decency in an effort to bring the moviemakers to redemption. In such cities as Philadelphia, there was a call for all Catholics to boycott movie theatres. The big studios, in an effort to prevent organized protest, decided to repent. Joseph Breen, a devout Catholic and father of six children, was put in charge of administering the Code's prohibitions and admonitions. The members of the MPPDA agreed not to release any film without a certificate of approval signed by Breen, in his capacity as head of the newly formed Production Code Administration (PCA). The MPPDA also passed a resolution empowering the PCA to impose a $25,000 fine against any members who sold, distributed, or exhibited a film not bearing the seal of approval.

The PCA closely followed productions from script to preview. Looking to avoid trouble, producers often consulted with Breen's staff on story material even before a property was purchased. Operating under a self-imposed set of taboos, the PCA soon became more restrictive than many of the state and municipal censors.[9]

PCA prohibitions sometimes bordered on the absurd. For instance, the PCA objected to a scene in *The Merry Widow* (1934) in which Maurice Chevalier took Jeanette MacDonald in his arms, carried her across a room (kissing her as he did so), and placed her on a sofa. The PCA agreed to give the film a certificate of approval only on the condition that MacDonald keep both feet on the floor as she was placed on the sofa.

Yet, the decisions of the PCA were not always restrictive enough to suit the Catholic Church. Early in 1936, the Church began its own review and classification of motion pictures. The task of assigning moral ratings was undertaken by the International Federation of Catholic Alumnae. Films were placed in one of four categories: A-1, morally unobjectionable for general patronage; A-2, morally unobjectionable for adults; B, morally objectionable in part for all; C, condemned.

Studios often went to ridiculous extremes to avoid receiving a "condemned" rating. MGM's 1941 release of *Two-Faced Woman*, a comedy of errors in which Greta Garbo played identical twins, was branded with a "C" even though the PCA had given it a certificate of approval. The basic plot line centered around a plain wife's attempts to entice an indifferent husband by impersonating her own glamorous twin sister. To win Catholic approval, MGM agreed to shoot a completely new scene, in which the husband receives a telephone call apprising him of the masquerade. The rest of the film is senselessly played as though he didn't know that the sexy sister he was pursuing was really his wife.

Catholic concerns about motion picture content were not limited to sex and sin. The Knights of Columbus and other pro-Franco Catholic groups actively boycotted and picketed theatres showing *Blockade* (1938), a mildly proloyalist film dealing with the Spanish Civil War. As a result of Catholic pressure, the film was banned in several cities.

Expostulations against movies came from many quarters. Director Frank Capra, in his autobiography, tells of the controversy surrounding the release of *Mr. Smith Goes to Washington* in October 1939, a few weeks after war had broken out in Europe.[10] In this film, James Stewart played an idealistic—albeit painfully naive—short-term senator who finds Washington rife with graft and corruption. In the film's climax, Stewart makes an emotional appeal to the conscience of not only his fellow senators but also the public at large. The big studios, fearful of punitive legislation from Congress, were rumored to have offered Columbia (the company that released *Mr. Smith*) $2 million to withdraw the film from circulation. Joseph Kennedy, then ambassador to Great Britain and himself a former movie magnate, wrote a letter to Harry Cohen, the president of Columbia, urging him to withdraw the film from European distribution and exhibition. Kennedy was apparently fearful that *Mr. Smith* might do harm to the prestige of the United States abroad.

The plight of *Citizen Kane* provides another indication of the kind of pressures to which motion picture production was subjected.[11] This 1941 RKO release loosely paralleled the career of press magnate William Randolph Hearst. Many movie theatres, fearing retaliation from the Hearst newspapers, refused to book it. Even the Rockefeller-controlled Radio City Music Hall, where most of RKO's major features premiered, declined to present the picture. Louella Parsons, Hearst's syndicated movie columnist, had reportedly threatened Nelson Rockefeller with a family exposé in the Hearst papers, if the film appeared at the Music Hall. *Citizen Kane* raised such a cinematic storm that, on behalf of several industry leaders, MGM's Louis B. Mayer even offered to pay RKO in excess of $800,000 to destroy the negative and all the prints.

George Schaefer, RKO's corporate president at the time, showed uncharacteristic resoluteness for a movie executive. Determined to release the film nationwide, he threatened the major theatre chains with a suit charging conspiracy. Warners gave in and booked the film, and the others soon followed.

Hearst was so outraged over the film that, for a while, he banned publicity for all RKO features, in his newspapers. The Hearst papers also dropped an announced serialization of the novel *Kitty Foyle*, originally to be timed with the release of the RKO film version. Rumors also began to circulate in the movie industry that those doing business with Schaefer and RKO could expect the same kind of treatment. A smear campaign among RKO stockholders suggested that the studio wasn't prospering because Schaefer was antisemitic and, therefore, couldn't get along with Jewish film executives. As RKO's stock began to drop in price, Floyd Odlum of the Atlas Corporation, who was already a major shareholder and an outspoken opponent of Schaefer's policies, bought controlling interest in the movie company. By mid-1942, Schaefer was finished at RKO. Within two weeks of his departure, Orson Welles and his Mercury Theatre Company were summarily ordered off the lot. Other Schaefer-inspired production units suffered much the same fate.

CHALLENGES TO THE PRODUCTION CODE

The power of the Production Code Administration began to diminish during the 1940s. For instance, the threat of a $25,000 levy for exhibiting a film without PCA approval was removed in 1942, because it was thought to be in violation of the antitrust laws—although this change had little immediate impact, since the fine for recalcitrant producers and distributors remained in effect.

The first serious challenge to the movie industry's code of good conduct came from Howard Hughes, who had produced and directed a film called *The Outlaw*. This fictional account of the legendary bandit Billy the Kid featured a robustly proportioned 19-year-old named Jane Russell in the leading female role. Throughout the film, Hughes focused a great deal of cinematic attention on her breasts. There were countless shots of Russell bending over while wearing a loose-fitting blouse. As Murray Schumach (onetime industry reporter for the New York *Times*) wrote in his book on movie censorship, *The Face on the Cutting Room Floor*, this film "marked the beginning of 'mammary madness,' a Hollywood fixation that has still not abated."[12]

After screening the film in the spring of 1941, the Code Authority determined that more than 100 cuts would have to be made before it could grant its seal of approval. Hughes appealed the PCA's ruling, and was granted a hearing before the board of directors of the parent association in New York City. At the hearing, Hughes' publicity director Russell Birdwell displayed stills of such stars of Jean Harlow, Norma Shearer, Marlene Dietrich, Rita Hayworth, and Betty Grable. A mathematician—using calipers—demonstrated that, proportionately, the amount of anatomical exposure in the objectionable shots of Jane Russell was no greater than that shown in the stills from the PCA-approved movies of the other women. The argument apparently worked; Hughes had to make only a few cuts, and a seal of approval was soon granted.

By the time Hughes was ready to release *The Outlaw*, Twentieth Century-Fox—the studio scheduled to distribute the film—had canceled its agreement. So he decided to market the film himself. He rented the Geary Theatre in San Francisco, a legitimate house that normally presented plays rather than motion pictures. The film's premiere in February 1943 was accompanied by a major advertising and publicity campaign. Pictures of Jane Russell in provocative poses were plastered on large billboards throughout the San Francisco Bay area. *The Outlaw* played to record-breaking crowds for ten straight weeks. Hughes then withdrew the film and concerned himself with the war effort.

At the war's end, Hughes again made plans to release the film. Early in 1946, United Artists, which at the time was not a member of the recently renamed Motion Picture Association of America (MPAA), distributed *The Outlaw* nationwide. Once again, Hughes launched a massive advertising campaign. Newspapers, magazines, billboards, and even skywriting proclaimed the attributes of Jane Russell. An airplane wrote the words "The Outlaw" in the sky over Pasadena, and then made two enormous circles with a dot in the middle of each. Newspaper advertisements for the movie asked such provocative questions as: "How would you like to tussle with Russell?" and "What are the two reasons for Jane Russell's rise to stardom?" Some advertisements contained the false and misleading statement: "Exactly as filmed—not a scene cut." Much of the material used in the publicity campaign had not been submitted to the Code Authority for approval, or had been rejected after being submitted.

In what was then an unprecedented action, the Motion Picture Association moved to withdraw its previously issued seal of approval. The Hughes Tool Company, owner of Hughes Productions, filed suit against the MPAA in the U.S. District Court in the Southern District of New York—charging violation of the antitrust laws, restraint of trade, and contravention of the First Amendment guarantee of free expression. The Hughes complaint requested damages totaling $6 million.

In April 1946, the suit was brought before the district court, which issued a temporary restraining order prohibiting the MPAA from revoking its certificate of approval. In June, the district court vacated the restraining order and denied Hughes's motion to enjoin the MPAA from voiding its certificate of approval until the case was tried on its merits. In rendering his decision, Judge John Bright outlined the events leading up to the MPAA's revocation of its seal of approval. He found no evidence that the policies of the trade association tended to reduce or destroy competition in the production, distribution, or exhibition of motion pictures. Nor did he find that the MPAA's practices were aimed or designed to achieve such an effect. With regard to Hughes's meretricious advertising activities, Judge Bright held that "the industry can suffer as much from indecent advertising as from indecent pictures. Once a picture has been approved the public may properly assume that the advertisement and promotional matter of the picture are likewise approved. The blame for improper, salacious or false advertising is placed as much at the door of the defendant as of the producer."[13] Hughes appealed this decision to the U. S. Circuit Court of Appeals for the Second Circuit, but his request for a stay was again denied. On September 6, 1946, Hughes Productions was ordered to return the certificate of approval for *The Outlaw* and to remove the MPAA's seal from all prints of the motion picture.

Since the MPAA's $25,000 fine no longer applied to exhibition, a number of theatres were willing to show *The Outlaw* even though it lacked a certificate of approval. However, many state and municipal censorship boards insisted upon alterations and deletions before the picture was permitted to be shown. A Maryland judge upheld a complete ban on the picture, and noted that Jane Russell's breasts "hung over the picture like a thunderstorm spread out over a summer landscape."[14] Hughes's widely publicized difficulties with the censors had a salutary effect on the box office. By 1948, United Artists was able to secure enough play dates to enable the film to earn over $3 million.

The financial success of *The Outlaw* undoubtedly weakened the self-regulatory mechanisms that had developed in the 1930s, particularly since the film also carried a "condemned" rating from the Roman Catholic Church. United Artists again defied the self-imposed restrictions of the movie industry in 1953, when it decided to release Otto Preminger's *The Moon Is Blue* even though the film had been denied a seal of approval by the MPAA's Production Code Administration. This innocuous comedy—essentially a lighthearted look at seduction and adultery—had also been condemned by the National Legion of Decency. The prevailing belief that defiance of the dictates of the Catholic Church and the Code Authority spelled economic disaster for a motion picture was completely shattered when *The Moon is Blue* also reaped a box office bonanza. By the end of 1953, the film (made on a budget of $450,000) had played in some 4,200 theatres and earned over $3 million.

Since United Artists had not been a member of the MPAA at the time *The Moon is Blue* was released, the Code Authority could not impose its $25,000 fine against the intractable company. The opportunity to fine a full-fledged MPAA member came in late 1953, when RKO (now controlled by Howard Hughes) decided to release *The French Line* (starring Jane Russell), a three-dimensional film that had been refused the seal of approval. The sequence that the PCA found most offensive occurred during the picture's finale when Miss Russell—wearing a one-piece, black-satin tights outfit with three large leaf-shaped pieces cut from the midriff area—did a provocative bump-and-grind dance while singing the song "Lookin' for Trouble." When *The French Line* made its debut in St. Louis, the archbishop of that city forbade all Catholics to attend the movie, under pain of mortal sin. The PCA imposed a $25,000 fine against RKO for releasing the film without a seal. The offending film was withdrawn, slightly reedited, and released nationwide in mid-1954. Advertisements for the picture proclaimed, "Jane Russell in 3-D . . . it'll knock *both* your eyes out!" Late in 1955, the PCA and RKO finally reached a compromise, after some of the objectionable material was cut. The film received the seal of approval, and the unpaid fine was rescinded.

The notoriety caused by RKO's unauthorized release of *The French Line* doubtlessly put another dent in the PCA's enforcement machinery. A more crushing blow came in early 1956 when United Artists, without code authority approval, released Otto Preminger's *The Man with the Golden Arm*, an adaptation of the Nelson Algren novel on drug addiction. United Artists, which had rejoined the MPAA, withdrew once again, in protest over the association's refusal to reverse the PCA's decision. Geoffrey Shurlock, who had succeeded an ailing Joseph Breen as head of the PCA in the autumn of 1954, later conceded that the film should have received approval. But at the time, he had little choice—since the Production Code specifically prohibited "scenes which show the use of illegal drugs, or their effects, in detail." The case against the outmoded Code was strengthened when the Legion of Decency failed to condemn the picture, even though it had been released without the PCA's imprimatur.

As calls for modernization of the Code began to escalate, the MPAA's board of directors decided to set up a four-member review committee under the direction of Eric Johnston, who had succeeded Will Hays as head of the association. The task of the committee was to study the entire Production Code with an eye toward possible revisions.

A NEW CATHOLIC CAMPAIGN

The Catholic Church, meanwhile, had launched a major campaign against what it regarded as a growing tendency on the part of the Code Authority to allow greater explicitness in the filmic treatment of sexual matters.

The Catholic campaign against the "rising tide of moral laxity in films" intensified in the winter of 1956 when the PCA approved Warner Bros.' release of Elia Kazan's *Baby Doll*. Based on two short plays by Tennessee Williams, the film starred Carroll Baker as a child-wife who, although nearly 20 years old, sleeps in a crib, sucks her thumb, and has yet to consummate her marriage with her middle-aged husband. The film was promptly condemned by the Legion of Decency on the ground that its subject matter was "morally repellent both in theme and treatment." The Legion further charged that "carnal suggestiveness" pervaded the film's action, dialogue, and costuming.[15] Cardinal Spellman of the Archdiocese of New York singled out the picture for special condemnation. On Sunday, December 16, 1956, the outraged prelate mounted the pulpit at Saint Patrick's Cathedral to denounce the film and enjoin Catholics to stay away from it "under the pain of sin."[16] Cardinal Spellman's stinging denunciation sparked a Catholic crusade against *Baby Doll* throughout the country. In several cities, Catholic organizations set up picket lines at theatres showing the film. In some dioceses, bishops imposed a general economic boycott against theatres where *Baby Doll* was playing. Exhibitors even received bomb threats.

Although Catholic condemnation of *Baby Doll* unquestionably reduced the film's national exposure (the film secured only an estimated 25 percent of its potential bookings), the resultant controversy provided ammunition for those who were critical of the Church's encroachment on motion picture content. Reverend James Pike, then Dean of New York's Protestant Episcopal Cathedral of St. John the Divine, took strong issue with Cardinal Spellman's condemnation of the film. "Those who do not want the sexual aspect of life included in the portrayal of real-life situations," said Reverend Pike, "had better burn their Bibles as well as abstain from the movies."[17] Critics of the Catholic use of general boycotts included the American Civil Liberties Union, who called this type of action "contrary to the spirit of free expression in the First Amendment. It can threaten a theatre's existence, and may deny to other groups within the community a chance to see films of their choice."[18]

The fragile link between the Catholic Church and the movie industry had remained intact as long as profits were high. With the general decline in theatre attendance during the 1950s, Hollywood's disaffection with the dictates of the Legion of Decency intensified. However, the leadership of the Catholic Church was not easily deterred from its efforts to organize actions against those films it regarded as objectionable. Nevertheless, the *Baby Doll* incident had marked a turning point in the Legion of Decency's influence on motion picture content. Beginning in 1958, the Catholic Church's grip on the movie industry was gradually weakened. In an apparent attempt to accommodate the increasing independence and sophistication of U.S. Catholics, the Legion expanded its movie classification system in late 1957 and again in 1963, to allow for greater flexibility in the assignment of ratings. In 1966, the Legion of Decency was renamed the National Catholic Office of Motion Pictures in a further attempt to emphasize the organization's more adaptive approach to motion pictures.

CURTAILMENT OF CENSORSHIP

Beginning in 1952, the censorship power of state and municipal officials was also significantly curtailed, when the U.S. Supreme Court brought motion pictures within the pale of constitutional protection.

The case to come before the high court that year involved Roberto Rossellini's award-winning film, *The Miracle*, which told of a peasant woman seduced by a bearded stranger whom she believes to be Saint Joseph. Later she conceives a male child whom she imagines is Jesus Christ.

The motion picture division of the New York State Education Department, which had been vested since 1927 with the full authority to preview all movies shown in the state, licensed the Italian-made film—first without English subtitles and then with subtitles, in 1949 and 1950 respectively. In December 1950, *The Miracle* opened at New York's Paris Theatre with two French films, as part of a trilogy called *The Ways of Love*. Within a few weeks, however, the city commissioner of licenses declared that *The Miracle* was "officially and personally blasphemous," and he threatened to suspend the theatre's license.

Francis Cardinal Spellman, Archbishop of New York, also found the film objectionable, and enjoined Catholics throughout the country not to patronize theatres where it was scheduled to be shown. Following the Cardinal's denunciation, hundreds of members of the Catholic War Veterans picketed the Paris Theatre. The theatre also received bomb threats and had to be evacuated by the police on several occasions.

As opposition to *The Miracle* mounted, the chancellor of the New York Board of Regents, which oversees the education department, requested three board members to review the motion picture division's approval of the film. When this special three-member committee found some basis for the claim that the film was sacrilegious, and therefore in violation of state law, Joseph Burstyn, the U.S. distributor of *The Miracle*, was directed to show cause why his license should not be rescinded. He appeared before the committee and challenged its authority to revoke a license once it had been granted. After viewing the film, and assessing the merits of briefs and exhibits filed by interested persons and organizations, the full board unanimously agreed that *The Miracle* was indeed sacrilegious and decided to revoke Burstyn's license. He, in turn, appealed the board's decision in the courts. The Appellate Division of the New York Supreme Court and the New York Court of Appeals both upheld the action of the Board of Regents.

In late May 1952, a unanimous U. S. Supreme Court, in reversing the lower court decision, ruled that the state had no legitimate interest in protecting the various religions from distasteful views sufficient to justify prior restraint.[19] More importantly, the high court held that motion pictures were a significant medium for the communication of ideas and, as such, they were within the free speech and free press guarantees of the First and Fourteenth Amendments. However, the broader issue of the constitutionality of licensing per se was left unresolved.

Subsequent Supreme Court decisions during the 1950s continued to erode the powers of the censors. Finally, in 1961, the high court handed down a ruling on the constitutional status of licensing itself. The case involved *Don Juan*, a film version of Mozart's opera *Don Giovanni*. The film's distributor, Times Film Corporation, had apparently decided to challenge the city of Chicago's censorship law. After paying the license fee, the distributor refused to submit the film to Chicago's superintendent of police for previewing. When the city refused to grant a license for exhibition, Times appealed the decision in the federal courts, charging that Chicago's licensing system and all prior restraint of motion pictures was unconstitutional. Both the district court and court of appeals dismissed the complaint.

In a 5-to-4 decision, the U. S. Supreme Court upheld the city's power to license films and ruled that prior censorship of films was not unconstitutional.[20] Motion pictures, said the majority of the court, are not "necessarily subject to the precise rules governing any other particular method of expression. Each method . . . tends to present its own peculiar problems." Taking care to limit the scope of its ruling, the court cautioned that no "unreasonable strictures on individual liberty" should result from prior restraint. In a heated dissent, Chief Justice Earl Warren cited historical examples of the abuses of prior restraint and concluded that the majority's decision "officially unleashes the censor and permits him to roam at will, limited only by an ordinance which contains some standards that, although concededly not before us in this case, are patently imprecise."

In the 1965 *Freedman* case, the high court dealt for the first time with the procedures of licensing. The justices unanimously reversed the conviction of Ronald Freedman, a Baltimore theatre manager, for exhibiting the film *Revenge at Daybreak* without a license.[21] Although the court recognized the exercise of licensing power, it held that Maryland did not provide adequate procedural safeguards "against undue inhibition of expression." Moreover, the court shifted the burden of proof to the censors and required swift judicial review of licensing decisions in future cases.

OBSCENITY AT ISSUE

With most forms of prior restraint in a state of doubtful legality, those seeking to control motion picture content increasingly turned to the nation's obscenity laws.

Both state and federal jurisdictions have consistently maintained that obscene material is not protected by the First and Fourteenth Amendments. However, beginning in 1957, the U. S. Supreme Court, in attempting to define obscenity and to set standards for applying that definition, increased the diversity of subject matter covered by the constitutional shield, oftentimes to topics previously thought to be obscene.

The high court handed down its first major decision on obscenity in the 1957 *Roth* case, which involved mailing of allegedly obscene circulars and advertising matter.[22] Although the court ruled in a 5-to-4 decision that "obscentiy is not within the area of constitutionally protected speech and press," it qualified its judgment by stating that "sex and obscenity are not synonymous." Obscene material, stated the court, deals with sex in a manner "appealing to the prurient interest." The court rejected the British *Hicklin* test of obscenity, which allowed material to be judged merely by the effect of an isolated excerpt upon particularly susceptible persons, and sanctioned the test that had been evolving in the federal and state courts: "whether to the average person, applying contemporary community standards, the dominant theme of the work taken as a whole appeals to the prurient interest." Under the protection of the Constitution, the court included "all ideas having even the slightest redeeming social importance." Although the *Roth* case dealt specifically with printed matter, its impact was felt on all media of expression.

The high court continued to refine its definition of obscenity throughout the 1960s. In 1964, the court applied its obscenity standards directly to the motion picture medium, in the *Jacobellis* case.[23] Nico Jacobellis, a theatre manager in Cleveland Heights, Ohio, had been convicted on two counts of possessing and exhibiting an obscene film, *The Lovers*. This French film, which contained a short but explicit love scene, had already been shown in a number of cities in the United States, including Columbus and Toledo, Ohio. At least two critics of major importance rated it among the ten best films of the year in which it was produced. In a 6-to-3 decision, the Supreme Court ruled that the film was not obscene within the standards enunciated in the *Roth* case, since it was not "utterly without redeeming social importance." Justice William Brennan, writing the judgment for the court, stated that "material dealing with sex in a manner that advocates ideas . . . or has literary or scientific or artistic value or any other forms of social importance may not be branded as obscenity and denied constitutional protection." Justice Brennan, whose opinion was joined by only one other justice, held without qualification that a national standard should be used in applying the test for obscenity. In particular, he saw the inherent danger in localized standards—that is, inhibition of expression—since sellers and exhibitors might be reluctant to risk criminal conviction by testing the variations of taste among different locales. The four other prevailing justices concurred separately without addressing themselves to the issue of national versus local standards.

Two years later, the Supreme Court further clarified its definition of obscenity in the *Memoirs* case.[24] The Superior Court of Suffolk County, Massachusetts, had found the book *Memoirs of a Woman of Pleasure*—more commonly known as "Fanny Hill"—to be obscene. This decision was upheld by the Supreme Court of Massachusetts. The U. S. Supreme Court, however, ruled that the Massachusetts courts had failed to consider the "redeeming social value" of the work. Justice William Brennan, in his opinion of the court in which Chief Justice Earl Warren and Justice Abe Fortas joined, stated that the test for obscenity requires the coalescence of three elements. It must be established "that (a) the dominant theme of the material taken as a whole appeals to a prurient interest in sex; (b) the material is patently offensive because it affronts contemporary community standards relating to the description or representation of sexual matters; (c) the material is utterly without redeeming social value." Each of the three criteria, said Justice Brennan, must be applied independently. One cannot be weighed against or canceled by another. It should be noted that Justice Brennan substituted the word "value" for "importance." Although seemingly a fine distinction, social value is a broader, more general test, which suggests value of any degree—important or unimportant. The social value criterion appeared to permit minimal standards for determination of literary, scientific, or artistic worth. Although Justices William Douglas, Hugo Black, and Potter Stewart, offered separate opinions in concurring with the reversal, the "social value" criterion seemed to have the support of a majority of the court.

CHANGES IN THE PRODUCTION CODE

The greater legal freedom accorded to motion pictures, coupled with the threat of television and the court-imposed dismantling of the vertical structures of distribution and exhibition, eventually resulted in a major overhaul of the industry's self-regulatory mechanisms.

From its inception in 1930, the Motion Picture Production Code had undergone only minor changes. Late in 1956, as an aftermath of *The Man with the Golden Arm* controversy, MPAA president Eric Johnston announced significant revisions in the Production Code. The Code was simplified and its language was made more precise. Certain of its provisions were rearranged into more logical order; and new provisions were added, to deal with topics not previously treated. The MPAA also modified the Code to allow greater latitude in the treatment of such topics as drug addiction, miscegenation, prostitution, and abortion. At the same time, new restrictions were placed on mercy killing, blasphemy, and the details of physical violence. Although the changes in the Code were not dramatic, they permitted a certain flexibility of interpretation.

In the fall of 1957, the right to reverse a PCA ruling was vested in a newly created appeals committee, the Production Code Review Board. This marked a significant departure from past practice, since the new review board included exhibitors and independent producers as well as representatives from the major production-distribution companies. Four years later, interpretation of the Code's provision that forbade "sexual perversion or any reference to it" was broadened by the board of directors of the MPAA to permit the release of such films as William Wyler's *The Children's Hour* (which dealt with lesbianism) and Otto Preminger's *Advice and Consent* (which had a homosexual theme).

Despite the substantive and procedural changes in the administration of the Production Code, PCA rulings still continued to be out of harmony with the changing temper of the times. United Artists' 1959 release, *Happy Anniversary*, was initially denied code approval because of its cavalier treatment of a prenuptial tryst. In the film, David Niven and Mitzi Gaynor portrayed a long-married couple who recall a sexual liaison prior to their wedding. United Artists, which had once again rejoined the MPAA, appealed the Code Authority's adverse ruling to the Production Code Review Board, but announced in advance that it would release the picture regardless of the outcome. A clumsy compromise was reached when it was agreed that an off-camera soliloquy would be added to the film's sound track, in which the Niven character repented by saying: "I was wrong. I never should have taken Alice to that hotel room before we were married. What could I have been thinking of?" Such absurd applications of the Production Code only served to subject the Code Authority to further derision.

FROM SELF-REGULATION TO ADVISORY RATINGS

Critics of the Code's outdated manners and morals called increasingly for a classification system restricting certain films to adults. It was hoped that such a system would allow for the treatment of more mature and sophisticated themes in motion pictures. Even religious and civic groups began to rally for an MPAA classification system. Once again, United Artists took the lead when it promoted its 1960 release, *Elmer Gantry*, as intended for "adults only." Based on a 1927 novel by Sinclair Lewis, the film starred Burt Lancaster as a charlatan evangelist. The trade publication *Variety* reported that, because United Artists had released *Elmer Gantry* with an advisory, the film received a "B" rating from the Legion of Decency; without the "adults only" admonition, it would surely have been condemned.[25] Although *Elmer Gantry* received critical acclaim, the film was not a box office success. UA executives attributed the film's disappointing returns to its restricted audience designation.

After careful consideration, the board of directors of the MPAA decided against replacing the Production Code with a formalized classification system. Instead, Eric Johnston proposed increased circulation and publicity for the *Green Sheet*, a publication of film ratings.[26] This monthly publication first appeared in 1933 and was distributed by the MPAA-supported Film Board of National Organizations. The ten organizations represented in this amalgam included the American Library Association, the Daughters of the American Revolution, the American Jewish Committee, the National Congress of Parents and Teachers, and the Protestant Motion Picture Council. The editor of the *Green Sheet* (whose office was located in the New York headquarters of the MPAA) prepared, for each film considered, a complete rating based on reviews submitted by representatives of the member organizations. Until 1963, only PCA-approved films were rated. Beginning that year, coverage was expanded to include nationally distributed—albeit unapproved—films. Films were rated in the *Green Sheet* according to their suitability for five age designations: adults, mature young people, young people, general audience, and children. Although the *Green Sheet* (last published in December 1969) was disseminated to newspapers, schools, libraries, and churches, it had minimal impact on movie attendance.

Eric Johnston died unexpectedly in 1963, leaving the MPAA temporarily without a leader of national stature. Ralph Hetzel filled in as acting president while the MPAA's board of directors sought someone who would add prestige to the organization. In the spring of 1966, the MPAA leadership selected Jack Valenti, an assistant to President Lyndon Johnson, as their new head.

Almost immediately upon taking command of his new post, Valenti was confronted with a major challenge to the rigid restrictions of the Production Code.[27] Warner Bros., one of the industry's most powerful studios, had submitted its $7-million-plus production of Edward Albee's award-winning play *Who's Afraid of Virginia Woolf?* for Code Authority approval. The film's dialogue employed language that was clearly in direct violation of the Code's provision on profanity, and contained expressions (such as "hump-the-hostess") that the faithful framers of the Production Code never imagined would be at issue. The PCA initially denied its seal but, on appeal, the film was approved when Warner Bros. made several concessions. In addition to modifying or cutting some of the objectionable dialogue ("hump-the-hostess" was not deleted), the studio agreed to advertise the film with the cautionary statement, "Suggested for Mature Audiences." Warners also inserted a clause into all contracts with exhibitors, prohibiting them from allowing anyone under 18 to see the film, unless accompanied by a parent. This innovation was a huge success. Even the National Catholic Office for Motion Pictures, reflecting its newfound liberal tendencies, rated the film "morally unobjectionable for adults, with reservations."

The MPAA's decision to approve *Who's Afraid of Virginia Woolf?* for restricted audiences foreshadowed the movie industry's general acceptance of the need for a classification system. In September 1966, the MPAA's board of directors replaced the original Production Code with a more simplified version that authorized the labeling of certain approved films as "Suggested for Mature Audiences." Although, to some extent, the new Code reflected the increasing sophistication in the tastes and sensibilities of the movie theatre audience, it still fell far short of allowing artistic expression of the full range of human experience. Michelangelo Antonioni's *Blow-Up*, which included some sex scenes that were bland by contemporary standards, was denied PCA approval soon after the new Code took effect. MGM, the film's distributor and a prominent member of the MPAA, decided to release *Blow-Up* without a seal through a wholly owned subsidiary, Premier Films. Since the subsidiary company was not a signatory of the Code agreement, MGM had not technically violated its pledge to not release films denied a seal of approval. Such hypocrisy on the part of the MPAA members soon undermined the effectiveness of the new Code in restricting films intended for mature audiences.

THE ADOPTION OF A RATING SYSTEM

The impetus for industrywide adoption of an effective classification system for motion pictures came in April 1968 when the U.S. Supreme Court, in two cases handed down on the same day, ruled that state and local authorities have the right to protect minors from exposure to subject matter deemed permissible for adults.[28] In one decision, *Ginsberg v. New York*, the high court upheld the constitutionality of a New York criminal obscenity statute prohibiting the sale of obscene material to minors under 17 years of age, even though the material in question (magazines that depicted female nudity) would not be considered obscene for adults. Justice Brennan, writing for the 6-to-3 majority, affirmed that the authority of the state over the conduct of minors is broader than its authority over adults. The court's recognition of the constitutionality of variable standards of obscenity—one standard for adults and another for children—was perceived as having far-reaching significance in the regulation of motion picture content.

The second decision, even more important to the movie industry, was *Interstate Circuit, Inc. v. Dallas*, in which the Supreme Court ruled on the constitutionality of motion picture classification. In 1965, the city of Dallas, Texas, had adopted an ordinance that established a Motion Picture Classification Board. The board classified films as "suitable for young persons" or "not suitable for young persons." A "young person" was defined as anyone who had not attained his sixteenth birthday. Interstate Circuit, a major theatre chain in the Southwest, challenged the ordinance as being unconstitutionally vague. Ignoring the board's ruling that the United Artists release *Viva Maria*, starring Brigitte Bardot and Jeanne Moreau, was "not suitable for young persons,'' Interstate deliberately exhibited the film without imposing age restrictions on the audience. A county court upheld the municipal classification board's determination and the Texas Court of Civil Appeals affirmed the lower court ruling. The U.S. Supreme Court, in reversing the decision, declared that, where expression is subjected to licensing, there must be rigorous insistence upon procedural safeguards for judicial superintendence of the censor's action. While agreeing with Interstate Circuit that the Dallas classification system was too vague, the court did not preclude the acceptance of a more carefully drafted age classification scheme for proscribing minors from viewing certain films. Echoing the ruling in the *Ginsberg* case, Justice Marshall (writing for an 8-to-1 majority) emphasized that a state ''may regulate the dissemination to juveniles of, and their access to, material objectionable as to them, but which a state clearly could not regulate as to adults.''

The potential impact of the two Supreme Court decisions was not lost on the MPAA's reigning powers. Unless the movie industry took decisive action, the proliferation of state and municipal classification boards seemed inevitable. However, the changing structure of the motion picture business now required more than the cooperation of the major producer-distributors in order to effect a meaningful change in the industry's self-regulatory scheme. Two new forces had emerged that would have to be reckoned with, the International Films Importers and Distributors of America Inc. (IFIDA) and the National Association of Theatre Owners (NATO). The latter organization represented the owners of 70 percent of all the movie theatres in the United States. In order to accommodate these disparate groups, Jack Valenti was called upon to use his talents as a negotiator. His skill stood him in good stead and, after extensive discussions, the IFIDA and NATO joined with the MPAA to establish a national system of voluntary classification.

Early in October 1968, within six months of the *Interstate* decision, the Motion Picture Rating System was publicly unveiled. Under this new system (which took effect on November 1, 1968), the members of the MPAA agreed to submit each film produced or distributed for rating prior to commercial release. The rating system, which is operated under the joint supervision of the MPAA, the IFIDA, and the NATO, is open to all producers and distributors on the same basis as members of MPAA.

With the introduction of a rating system, the Production Code Administration was replaced by the newly created Code and Rating Administration (CARA)—now referred to simply as ''the rating board.'' Originally, films submitted to CARA were classified into one of four designations: G, suggested for general audiences; M, suggested for mature audiences—adults and mature young people; R, restricted—persons under 16 not admitted, unless accompanied by parent or adult guardian; and X, persons under 16 not admitted. Early in 1970, the M rating (which was thought to be confusing) was changed to GP, general audience—parental guidance suggested. At the same time, the R and X age limits were increased to 17. Two years later, GP was changed to the current designation: PG, parental guidance suggested—some material may not be suitable for preteenagers. The ratings weren't altered again until the summer of 1984 when, primarily in response to an outcry against the PG rating assigned to Steven Spielberg's *Indiana Jones and the Temple of Doom* (in which a man's heart is ripped out of his chest), the PG-13 rating was added—''Parents are strongly cautioned to give special guidance for attendance of children under 13. Some material may be inappropriate for young children.'' While a film with a PG-13 rating goes beyond the boundaries designed for a simple PG, it does not quite fit within the restricted R category—at least, not in the view of the ratings board.

The rating board, located in Hollywood, is comprised of seven members who serve for an indeterminate period of time. The board's chairperson is selected by the MPAA's president. The chairperson, in turn, selects the other six members who serve on the rating board. The president of the MPAA (this post is still held by Jack Valenti) does not participate in, nor may he overrule, the board's decisions. The MPAA indicates that most ''entertaining, seriously intended, responsible'' (that is, nonexploitative) films made each year are submitted to the board for a rating. Makers of ''pornographic movies'' usually avoid the formal rating procedure by simply self-applying an ''X'' rating, rather than having the MPAA do so. The other symbols—G, PG, PG-13, and R—may not be self-applied, since they are registered with the U.S. Patent and Trademark Office. The MPAA's seal, which validates the rating, is withheld from any film that receives an ''X'' designation. The association is committed to defend any G, PG, PG-13, or R.

In determining a film's rating, the board evaluates thematic content, visual treatment, and use of such elements as language, violence, sex, or nudity. If a company desires a less restrictive rating, it may resubmit the film in edited form. A film company not satisfied with a rating may appeal for a less restrictive rating to an appeals board consisting of representatives of MPAA, NATO, and IFIDA. This board is the final arbiter for ratings. It is comprised of a total of 22 representatives from the three organizations. The president of the MPAA presides as chairman of the appeals board, which meets in New York. After the film in question is screened, the chairman calls on a representative of the company appealing the rating board's decision to explain why the rating received was inappropriate. The chairman of the rating board is then asked to explain the rating board's reasons for its determination. The company representative is given an opportunity for rebuttal. When the members of the appeals board have had a chance to question the two opposing parties, both contenders are asked to leave the room. Following this, the appeals board discusses the appeal and then takes a secret ballot. A two-thirds vote of those present is required to overturn a rating board decision.

It is inevitable, given the nature of motion pictures, that some rating board decisions from time to time provoke controversy. But in striking a balance between the conflicting demands for totally unrestricted expression and outright censorship, the MPAA's rating system has proven to be a reasonable compromise.[29]

SHIFTING STANDARDS

By the dawn of the 1970s, the old trinity of forces—industry self-regulators, organized religious groups, and governmental censorship boards— no longer wielded much influence in the movie industry. Only the state of Maryland and the city of Chicago still had censorship boards, and the rigorous procedural requirements established by the high court in the *Freedman* case had rendered these boards almost wholly ineffective.

The removal of many of the restrictions on moviemaking and exhibition opened the way to a new sexual explicitness on the silver screen. Before long, even hard-core sex films were receiving nationwide distribution. A sexual smorgasbord called *Deep Throat* (1972), which featured close-ups of actual copulation, fellatio, and cunnilingus, ranked among the movie industry's leading moneymakers. The film's star, a performer with the improbable name of Linda Lovelace, was propelled into the national spotlight. She appeared on the cover of *Esquire* and was the subject of a photographic essay in *Playboy*.

Although sexually explicit films had become chic, they did not go unchallenged. A number of state and municipal prosecutors brought those involved in the production and exhibition of *Deep Throat* into the courts. In New York City, soon after its premiere in June 1972 at the New Mature World Theatre, the film itself was confiscated by the police under a warrant from the New York County Criminal Court. The court calendar was crowded, however; and the trial against the theatre operator, Mature Enterprises Inc., was delayed for almost six months. Since New York requires an adversary hearing before a film can be siezed, the print was returned. While the theatre operator was awaiting trial, *Deep Throat* played to record-breaking crowds.

The *Deep Throat* case finally came before Judge Joel E. Tyler on December 19, 1972. The spectacular ten-day trial that followed became a curiosity-piquing event that received nationwide coverage. More than 1,000 pages of testimony accumulated during the trial. Among the witnesses who testified on behalf of the film was movie historian Arthur Knight, who stated that *Deep Throat* had redeeming social value because it might encourage people to expand their sexual horizons. On the other hand, sociologist Ernest van den Haag, a witness for the prosecution, testified that the film was highly antisocial because it showed "the physical use of people's bodies divorced from emotional relationships." Professor van den Haag spent four hours on the stand, describing his objections to the film. After weighing the evidence, Judge Tyler found *Deep Throat* to be "indisputably obscene by any legal measurement." He described the film as "a feast of carrion and squalor . . . a Sodom and Gomorrah gone wild before the fire . . . one throat that deserves to be cut."[30]

However, prosecutors throughout the nation found it increasingly difficult to persuade juries to curtail the exhibition of films depicting explicit sexual activity. In such diverse communities as Binghamton, New York; Cincinnati, Ohio; Houston, Texas; and Sioux Falls, South Dakota, prosecutions against the showing of *Deep Throat* resulted in acquittals or hung juries. Other sexually oriented films of the day enjoyed similar success in the courts. But the pools of Puritanism (a doctrine defined by H. L. Mencken as a terrible suspicion that somebody somewhere might be having a good time) that lie just beneath the surface of U. S. society were beginning to rise up once again.

NEW GUIDELINES FOR OBSCENITY

A major change in obscenity doctrine came in a set of decisions announced by a more conservative U.S. Supreme Court in June 1973.[31]

In the principal case, *Miller v. California*, recently appointed Chief Justice Warren Burger (writing for a five-member majority) set forth revised criteria for determining obscenity: "(1) whether the average person, applying contemporary community standards, would find that the work taken as a whole appeals to the prurient interest; (2) whether the work depicts or describes in a patently offensive way, sexual conduct specifically defined by the applicable state law; (3) whether the work taken as a whole lacks serious literary, artistic, political or scientific value."

At first glance, the court's new frame of reference for obscenity legislation and control does not seem significantly different from the three-fold definition of the *Memoirs* case. Upon closer inspection, however, the standard of "serious literary, artistic, political or scientific value" appears to hamper law enforcement officials far less in their efforts to control the content of motion pictures than the *Memoirs* criterion of "utterly without redeeming social value." The latter test had placed an almost impossible burden on the prosecution. Under the *Miller* standard, a prosecutor is only required to demonstrate that a work is patently offensive and lacks serious value. Perhaps of even more significance is the court's judgment that determination of whether material "appeals to the prurient interest" or is "patently offensive" need not be based on uniform national standards. The court specifically permitted statewide standards and implied that even local communities could make their own determinations regarding a work's alleged obscenity.

The court further limited the scope of permissible expression in four related cases, decided on the same day as the *Miller* ruling. In *Paris Adult Theatre I v. Slaton*, the five-member majority ruled that the exhibition of obscene films in an "adult theatre" is not protected by the First Amendment, even when the theatre management effectively restricts viewing to consenting adults and does not engage in "pandering or obtrusive advertising." In rendering this decision, the justices held that expert affirmative testimony on a work's obscenity is not necessary. The films themselves, said Chief Justice Burger, are the best evidence of what they represent. By so ruling, the court seemed to shift to the defense the burden of proving a work's value. In *United States v. Orito*, the court held that the constitutional protection of the possession of obscene materials in one's home does not extend to transporting them on a common carrier, even when they are intended for private use. The decision in *Kaplan v. California* held that books without pictorial content may be judged obscene under the First Amendment. In the final case, *United States v. Twelve 200-Foot Reels of Super 8mm Film*, the court ruled that the commerce clause of the Constitution empowers Congress to ban importation of obscene material, even though it may be intended for private use in the home. The same five-member majority prevailed in all five cases.

Soon after these decisions were handed down, the Georgia Supreme Court upheld a local jury's conviction of an Albany, Georgia, theatre manager named Billy Jenkins, for exhibiting Mike Nichols' critically acclaimed film *Carnal Knowledge* in violation of the state's antiobscenity laws. The Georgia court's decision was appealed by the Motion Picture Association of America to the U. S. Supreme Court, in the hope that the justices would reconsider their position allowing varying community standards of judgment. In June 1974, the Supreme Court unanimously ruled in *Jenkins v. Georgia* that *Carnal Knowledge* was not obscene.[32] Justice William Rehnquist, writing for the court, said that juries do not have "unbridled discretion in determining what is 'patently offensive.'" In discussing *Carnal Knowledge*, he noted that, although there were scenes of nudity in the film, "nudity alone is not enough to make material legally obscene under the *Miller* standards." Once again, however, the court offered no clear guidelines for determining what does constitute obscenity. Justice Brennan identified the most serious flaw in the *Miller* test when he pointed out that "one cannot say with certainty that material is obscene until at least five members of this Court, applying inevitably obscure standards, have pronounced it so." Echoing his dissenting opinion in *Paris Adult Theatre I*, Justice Brennan adhered to his view that "at least in the absence of distribution to juveniles or obtrusive exposure to unconsenting adults, the First and Fourteenth Amendments prohibit the state and Federal Governments from attempting wholly to suppress sexually oriented materials on the basis of their allegedly 'obscene' contents."

Ultimately, the high court's new guidelines proved to be no more effectively definitive than those they replaced, in permitting state and local authorities to determine what is obscene. It would seem that obscenity defies legal definition. Although all 50 states have introduced obscenity legislation since the *Miller* rulings, uncertainty, confusion, and inconsistency still prevail.

The sheer diversity of interests in the United States suggests that controversy over freedom and censorship will continue to punctuate the pursuit of profits by the movie industry. But the far-reaching revisions of U. S. mores and customs in recent decades would seem to preclude any possibility of returning to the moral strictures of the past.

4

Television's Roots in Radio

For millions of people the program fare of television provides a separate reality, one full of seemingly living images. The people who reside in this other reality are as familiar to us, in some ways, as our friends and neighbors. The very familiarity of television fare operates to make it unheeded as an influencing force. But behind the cacophony of sound and the flickering images is a complex of forces with imperatives and inclinations, which can hardly be without cultural consequences.

The policies, priorities, and products of the television industry have their roots in the earlier era of radio broadcasting. National networks, advertiser finance, government regulation, and program practices—all are a proliferation of the pattern that evolved in the first half of this century. How this pattern was formed is the object of examination in this chapter.

THE BIRTH OF BROADCASTING

Broadcasting in the United States was the progeny of a number of talented inventors and adventurous men. It was the young Italian Guglielmo Marconi who opened the way to the broadcasting era with his remarkable invention of wireless communication. In 1895, he demonstrated that through the use of a Morse key, dots and dashes could be transmitted via radio waves. The Italian Minister of Post and Telegraph expressed no interest in Marconi's invention. So, accompanied by his Irish-born mother, he sailed for England in February of the following year.

Unlike so many inventors who were technical geniuses but lacked business acumen, Marconi demonstrated an astute mind for the world of commerce and industry. In 1897, at the age of 23, he joined with a small, powerful group of British businessmen to form the Wireless Telegraph and Signal Company. The new company promoted radio transmission as an alternative to wired telegraphy wherever cable connections could not be made. Two years later, Marconi brought his service to the United States and established the Marconi Wireless Company of America. This company soon dominated the nascent U.S. radio industry.

Many competing companies were formed during radio's early years. As the industry became increasingly more complex, the number of radio patents multiplied into thousands. Among the more prominent inventors was Yale-educated Lee De Forest who, in 1906, developed what he called the "Audion"—a three-element vacuum tube that functioned as both a detector and an amplifier of radio waves. Among other things, the Audion was a key factor in the development of long-distance telephony, sound movies, and television.

As early as 1907, De Forest was broadcasting phonograph records from an experimental station in New York City. A year later, he transmitted music from atop the Eiffel Tower; it was later learned that the signal had been heard some 500 miles from Paris. In 1910, De Forest installed a 500-watt transmitter in a room at the top of the Metropolitan Opera House in Manhattan, enabling him to broadcast the magnificent voice of Enrico Caruso directly from the stage. Such feats would later lead De Forest to lay claim to the title of "Father of Radio."[1]

But De Forest's experiments were far removed from any conception of broadcasting as a fully functioning system for the simultaneous transmission of information and entertainment to millions of individual homes. Such a system would require not only the technology for transmitting high-quality speech and music simultaneously to unseen multitudes, but also millions of homes equipped with receiving units, and an organizational apparatus capable of producing a steady flow of programs. Moreover, some mechanism for financing such a system had to be found.

The system of broadcasting that emerged in the United States was the unexpected offspring of a marriage between the military and big business. During World War I, military demand coupled with a moratorium on patent disputes resulted in a dramatic improvement in the quality and sophistication of radio equipment. By the end of the war, effective long-range voice communication had been perfected.

Among the industrial giants to reap a rich financial harvest from the wartime manufacture of radio equipment was General Electric, a company formed in 1892 under the guiding hand of the Morgan banking interests through a merger between the Edison Electric Light Company and another manufacturing concern. At the war's close, General Electric, working in conjunction with Navy officials, devised a plan to force the Marconi interests out of the U.S. market. A new corporation—given the patriotic name of Radio Corporation of America—was formed with the intent of absorbing Marconi's U.S. assets and operating organization. The plan called for individual stockholders in American Marconi to receive comparable shares in the new company, and for General Electric to purchase the British parent company's stockholdings.

The Marconi interests were in an untenable position. The Navy still controlled all the American Marconi land stations; and, even if they were returned, the likelihood of receiving essential government contracts seemed remote. Under the circumstances, they decided to sell their stock in the U.S. subsidiary to General Electric.

General Electric immediately became the principal stockholder in the newly formed Radio Corporation. AT&T, which controlled the De Forest patents, established cross-licensing agreements with General Electric and RCA. Westinghouse, which managed to gain a foothold in radio through the acquisition of some important patents, was also invited to join the RCA consortium. Both AT&T and Westinghouse bought a large share of RCA stock. The complex cross-licensing agreements called for General Electric and Westinghouse to manufacture receivers and parts and to market these through RCA; AT&T was granted control over commercial telephony as well as the exclusive right to manufacture, sell, or lease radio transmitters. General Electric and Westinghouse were permitted to make transmitters for their own use, and all the companies could fill government contracts in any area.

The RCA consortium's control over the future of the electronic world seemed unchallengeable. But with peace, the demand for radio receivers and transmitters dropped sharply. As military contracts ceased, assembly lines came to an abrupt halt. However, unforeseen circumstances soon had radio manufacture booming once again.

Legend has it that the hobby of a Westinghouse engineer—one Frank Conrad—showed the way to an unpredicted profit potential.[2] As early as 1919, Conrad, who had built a powerful transmitter in his garage in East Pittsburgh, spent his Saturdays broadcasting phonograph music. A local music store provided the records in return for an occasional "plug" over the air. Conrad soon started broadcasting at regular times each week and asked anyone who heard him to send a postcard describing the reception. Not only did people respond, they even requested that particular music be played. Conrad became—in effect—broadcasting's first disc jockey.

A Pittsburgh department store decided to capitalize on Conrad's hobby by running an advertisement in a local newspaper, which described his broadcast activities and encouraged customers to purchase the ready-built receiving sets the store had in stock. The advertisement was seen by a Westinghouse executive who was quick to grasp the potential in providing entertainment as a vehicle for merchandising receiving sets. During the war, Westinghouse had manufactured an easy-to-operate, single-unit receiving set. Such sets could be sold for home use on a mass scale to buyers without any technical knowledge. The market seemed virtually limitless, but a regular program service would have to be developed and maintained to stimulate continued sales. Conrad was instructed to build a powerful transmitter on one of the taller buildings of the Westinghouse plant in East Pittsburgh. Before activating the transmitter, Westinghouse applied to the Department of Commerce for a special license to broadcast—to send out signals intended for the general public. It was assigned the call letters KDKA. On election night in 1920, KDKA broadcast the returns of the presidential race in which Warren G. Harding, the Republican senator from Ohio, defeated James M. Cox, the Democratic governor of Ohio. The spectacular debut of KDKA soon stimulated a demand for transmitting and receiving apparatuses.

It seemed as though everyone wanted to climb aboard the broadcast bandwagon. Department stores, hotels, churches, newspapers, colleges, and universities applied for licenses to operate broadcast stations. Westinghouse launched additional stations in New Jersey, Chicago, Philadelphia, and Boston. General Electric built the powerful WGY in Schenectady, New York, as well as stations in Denver and San Francisco. By May of 1922, there were 218 licensed broadcasting stations operating in the United States. Within another year, the number of stations soared to 556, with new stations springing up on a daily basis throughout the nation.

The regularly scheduled programming of many of these stations generated an enormous public demand for home radio units. Dozens of manufacturers heeded the market call and began turning out receiving sets. Some companies—Zenith and Atwater Kent, for instance—eventually negotiated licenses to use RCA patents. However, for a considerable length of time, radio manufacturers were so numerous that their very number made them immune from legal restraints. In 1922, the first year in which RCA sold radio sets for home use, its sales totaled about $11 million out of the $60 million for the entire industry. For the second year, RCA's sales amounted to some $22.5 million from an industry total of $136 million. For the third, its sales ran to $50 million, roughly one-seventh of the total sales figure for the nation.[3]

The suddenness of the broadcasting boom found RCA initially unprepared to monopolize the market in equipment and net sales. Even so, it had managed to make millions. But as sets saturated the market, some other mechanism for insuring ever greater profits would have to be found, particularly since program costs were beginning to mount.

THE WEAF EXPERIMENT

When the giants in the electronics industry had divided the radio business among themselves, the original agreements called for AT&T to manufacture transmitters, not receiving sets. Since broadcasting involves only a relatively few sending signals to great multitudes, many more receivers than transmitters were sold. How could the telephone company reap a rich harvest from broadcasting? In 1922, AT&T decided to cut loose from the RCA consortium and launch a broadcast operation on a basis quite different from that of its former allies. In August of that year, it launched WEAF in New York City as a kind of public phone booth of the air. A radio broadcast, reasoned AT&T executives, was like a telephone conversation and therefore should be paid for by the person originating it.

The first paying customer to use WEAF's facilities was the Queensboro Corporation, real estate developers of tenant-owned apartment houses in Jackson Heights, Long Island, a short distance from Manhattan. In the late afternoon of August 28, 1922, a spokesman for the real estate company made the first "commercial" broadcast. In a ten-minute presentation (some sources say fifteen minutes), he enjoined dwellers in crowded Manhattan to "get away from the solid masses of brick, where the meager opening admitting a slant of sunlight is mockingly called a light shaft, and where children grow up starved for a run over a patch of grass and the sight of a tree.''

"Hurry to the apartment complex in Jackson Heights," he urged, "near the green fields and the neighborly atmosphere, right on the subway without the expense and the trouble of a commuter, where health and community happiness beckon."[4]

The fee for this epochmaking event was $50, and the same sponsor bought several more afternoon talks and an evening presentation at $100. In September, Tidewater Oil and American Express bought evening time, bringing total revenues for the first two months of "toll broadcasting" to $550—a mere pittance compared to the millions being made from the sale of receiving sets. But from these modest beginnings would develop a moneymaking machine of unimagined magnitude.

By the end of 1922, WEAF could claim 13 sponsors, including R.H. Macy and Gimbel Brothers. Tangible evidence of a large listenership came in January 1923 when—following a talk by Marion Davies on "How I make up for the movies," which was sponsored by the beauty product of Mineralava—an autographed picture of the movie star was offered free to all who requested one. Hundreds of requests poured into the station. That same year, the Department of Commerce gave WEAF a clear wavelength, free from the interference of other stations. The gold rush was on.

At first, AT&T moved cautiously. Users of WEAF's phone booth of the air were not permitted to engage in direct advertising. Prices and even product descriptions were prohibited. A sponsored program on behalf of a toothpaste manufacturer was held up while the station management considered the propriety of mentioning on the air so intimate a matter as the care of teeth. Most sponsors merely linked their names to particular programs, much in the manner of public television today. The Browning King Company, a clothing retailer, attached its name to an orchestra. Billy Jones and Ernie Hare, two well-known vaudeville performers, became the Happiness Boys when the Happiness Candy Stores decided to sponsor their program in December 1923. The goodwill of listeners was sought for Cliquot Club Ginger Ale by broadcasting the music of the Cliquot Club Eskimos. Another orchestra featured the Ipana Troubadours to remind listeners of Ipana toothpaste. Other programs featured the A&P Gypsies and the Gold Dust Twins. Every effort was made not to offend. For instance, a vacuum cleaner manufacturer was not permitted to use the line "Sweep no more, my lady," for fear that lovers of the song "My Old Kentucky Home" might get upset.[5]

Controversial political discourse was also proscribed. In October 1923, H.V. Kaltenborn, then associate editor of the Brooklyn *Daily Eagle*, began a weekly series of "current events" over WEAF. His views on prohibition, foreign relations, and other such topics provoked angry letters of protest as well as words of praise. When the Soviet Union sought to establish diplomatic relations with the United States and the U.S. Secretary of State was curt in his response to the bid, Kaltenborn aired critical comments that proved to be too much for WEAF's management to bear. Secretary of State Charles Evans Hughes personally called a Washington representative of the telephone company to protest the broadcast. The word was relayed to New York that Kaltenborn should be taken off the air. WEAF then adopted a policy of barring all controversial material. The incident was a portent of things to come. Within a few years, Kaltenborn himself could write with some justification: "Today radio's chief purpose is to make money for those who control and use its mechanical devices. It threatens to prove as great a disappointment as the moving-picture for those who sense radio's undeveloped power as an agency of education, culture, and international good-will."[6] Critiques of businesses and banks, subjects such as socialism, and virtually any ideas likely to provoke social unrest were increasingly restricted.

NETWORKS: WEBS OF GOLD

The basic pattern for radio broadcasting—one that would later be followed by television—was firmly set during the 1920s. Soon after its entry into broadcasting, AT&T began experimenting with the use of telephone lines for station interconnection. Its first "network" was tried out on January 4, 1923, when WEAF was linked with WNAC (a Boston station owned by Shepard Stores) for a special simultaneous broadcast. The technical quality was unsatisfactory, however. This prompted AT&T to develop a high-efficiency cable specifically designed for carrying a wide range of sounds from station to station with enough fidelity so that they could be broadcast. The type of line needed was soon perfected, and by the end of 1924 AT&T could boast of a coast-to-coast hookup of 26 stations capable of simultaneous broadcasts.

Initially, AT&T maintained a monopoly on the high-efficiency lines that interconnected broadcast stations, and it refused to provide such connections to competitors. It also claimed the exclusive right to engage in toll broadcasting. Under its interpretation of the original patent agreements, AT&T argued that it had the right to manufacture broadcast receivers through its subsidiary, Western Electric.

RCA, GE, and Westinghouse attempted to counter AT&T's telephone-linked network monopoly by connecting a series of stations through the use of telegraph lines, but the quality of the broadcast signal proved inferior. In an effort to resolve their differences, all four companies agreed to arbitration. Meanwhile, early in 1924, the Federal Trade Commission (FTC) charged all the members of the original RCA consortium with conspiring to restrain competition and create a monopoly in the manufacture and sale in interstate commerce of radio equipment. With this government threat hovering in the background, AT&T (which already enjoyed a highly lucrative monopoly in the telephone industry) eventually decided that direct involvement in the broadcasting business was not worth the risk. In 1926, in a renegotiation of the cross-licensing agreements, AT&T sold its broadcast assets—including WEAF—to RCA. The price tag for WEAF was $1 million—$200,000 for the physical facilities, and the remainder apparently for the clear broadcast channel on which the station operated. This sale was the first indication that the public resource through which stations transmitted could be sold for private gain.

AT&T would continue to profit indirectly from broadcasting by leasing its high-efficiency cable lines for the interconnection of broadcast outlets. In the first year under this new arrangement, line rentals totaled $800,000. Rental fees were to rise into the many millions in subsequent years.

THE NATIONAL BROADCASTING COMPANY

In the same year the AT&T deal was consummated, RCA organized a central broadcasting subsidiary—the National Broadcasting Company. RCA, GE, and Westinghouse held 50, 30 and 20 percent of the stock, respectively, in the new company. With the acquisition of WEAF and AT&T's other broadcast assets, NBC owned two outlets in New York City and other locations. Rather than duplicate programming on two stations in the same broadcast area, NBC set up two semi-independent network operations—the "Red" network and the "Blue" network. These designations allegedly came from the colors of the crayons used by the corporate executives to outline on a map the locations of the two sets of interconnected stations within NBC's domain.

NBC was also heir to AT&T's concept of a "telephone booth" of the air, although the telephone terminology was quickly dropped. The comparison between commercial telephony and commercial broadcasting was, from the outset, a spurious one. A phone booth is available to anyone who wants to use it. The telephone industry is regulated as a "common carrier"—that is, a medium open to use by the general public on a non-discriminatory basis and at regulated rates. Broadcasters do not have common carrier status. They are enfranchised by the federal government to charge whatever the market will bear for the use of their facilities. Moreover, the broadcaster decides who shall have access to the airwaves. "Access," under these circumstances, operates somewhat like an auction, with air time going to the highest bidder.

The interconnection of stations and the centralization of programming coincided with the general consolidation and standardization of goods and services nationwide. National advertisers, who found the newly established NBC networks a most efficient sales vehicle for standardized products, soon set the scale for air time costs. Their ability to pay large amounts for access to the airwaves ensured them a privileged position in the nation's broadcast system. The phone booth of the air had become an auction block.

The appointment of Merlin H. Aylesworth as president of the new network operation did not bode well for the prospects of unfettered expression over NBC's facilities. Aylesworth came to the NBC presidency from the National Electric Light Association, the propaganda arm of the privately owned utilities. As managing director of the NELA, he had pictured public control of energy resources as tantamount to Soviet communism, had subsidized the publication of children's textbooks that reflected opposition to public power projects, and had even put compliant professors and teachers on the payroll.[7] Needless to say, NBC's programming practices did nothing to contravene the established order.

Programming costs had increased dramatically during the 1920s. Early in 1923, the American Society of Composers, Authors, and Publishers (ASCAP) demanded from WEAF a license fee in the form of royalties for the right to broadcast copyrighted music. AT&T acceded to ASCAP's demands, agreeing to pay an annual fee for the use of protected material. Other stations were not so conciliatory. That same year, the National Association of Broadcasters (NAB)—the trade association for the broadcast industry—was organized to thwart ASCAP's efforts to collect royalties. The copyright law of 1909 protected a copyright holder's right to control public performances for profit. Did the broadcasting of copyrighted music on a station owned by a commercial concern constitute such a performance? In August 1923, a federal district court ruled that copyrighted music played on WOR—the Newark, New Jersey station owned by Bamberger to promote its department store—was not eleemosynary in nature, and therefore warranted royalty payment.[8] The NAB tried to reverse this precedent, but they were unsuccessful; and, as broadcasting grew, the fees collected by ASCAP amounted to millions. Performers were also demanding greater recompense for their services.

COMPETITION FROM COLUMBIA

Around the time NBC was formed, Arthur Judson, a leading concert manager, organized the Judson Radio Program Corporation to supply talent to the broadcast medium. The roster of artists under his management included both the Philadelphia and New York Philharmonic Orchestras, most of the major conductors of the day, and a wide array of star performers—among them Jascha Heifetz, Marian Anderson, Vladimir Horowitz, and Ezio Pinza. Judson's initial aim was to provide RCA's network operation with a package of artistic talent for a fixed price per week. Rebuffed by RCA, he set out to build a rival network of stations. Early in 1927, Judson organized United Independent Broadcasters (UIB) and enlisted the aid of promoter George Coats to travel around the country and sign up stations in key cities for the fledgling network operation. The plan called for UIB to buy ten hours of broadcast time a week from each station at $50 per hour. Advertiser support was sought for the presentation of programs. Coates managed to sign up a number of stations; but AT&T at first refused to interconnect them, claiming that it might take three years to furnish lines. Coates called on his contacts at the Interstate Commerce Commission, which then had jurisdiction over the telephone industry; soon after, AT&T indicated that it would have the necessary lines ready for use by mid-September. However, advertising dollars proved to be elusive. Advertisers seemed to prefer the more prestigious NBC interconnections. To keep his operation afloat, Judson sought funding from several sources. Betty Fleischmann Holmes, heir to the Fleischmann yeast fortune, invested close to $75,000 in the new network. (Years later, she sold her stock for $3 million.) But more substantial sums had to be secured, in order for the operation to survive.

Columbia Phonograph had become alarmed by rumors of an impending merger between Victor Talking Machine and RCA. Columbia therefore decided to join the UIB venture, paying the latter $163,000 for the ten hours a week of broadcast time on its affiliated stations. Columbia planned to resell the time to other advertisers, while promoting its own products through identification with the network. The new partners set up an operating company called Columbia Phonograph Broadcasting System. The network made its debut on September 18, 1927, with a presentation of *The King's Henchman*, an American opera by composer Deems Taylor and poet Edna St. Vincent Millay. This seemed an auspicious beginning, but the sole advertiser the network had managed to secure backed out before air time.

Expenses quickly mounted. Within two months, the network was out of money and Columbia Phonograph wanted out. It sold the operating company back to UIB for $10,000 in cash and 30 hours of free broadcast time. For a while, it looked as if the whole operation was going to fold. Then, Isaac and Leon Levy of WCAU in Philadelphia (the first affiliate to join the network) decided the venture was worth saving. They persuaded their friend Jerome Louchheim, a multimillionaire subway and bridge builder, to purchase controlling interest in the network—by then called the "Columbia Broadcasting System." But Louchheim, too, decided shortly to sell his interest in the company.

One of the first major clients of the new network was the Congress Cigar Company, makers of La Palina cigars. The company was headed by Samuel Paley, Leon Levy's father-in-law; and it had used radio to promote cigar sales by sponsoring *La Palina Boy* on WCAU and *La Palina Smoker* on CBS. The network show was a startling success. In 26 weeks, cigar sales more than doubled—from 400,000 to 1 million a day. When young William Paley, the advertising manager of his father's cigar company, learned that Louchheim's shares in CBS were for sale, he leaped at the opportunity. After consultation with his father, young Paley bought the bulk of Louchheim's holdings for a price variously estimated at between $275,000 and $450,000. The Levys and other Paleys also invested in CBS. In September 1928, William Paley (at age 27) became president of the year-old network.[9]

The lessons of CBS's struggle for survival were not lost on Paley. One of his first moves was to secure strong financial underpinning for the network operation. Within a year, he managed to make an extraordinary deal with Adolph Zukor of Paramount. In an effort to buttress his expanding movie empire against potential encroachment from the newly burgeoning business of broadcasting, Zukor agreed to exchange 58,823 shares of Paramount stock—then selling at $65 a share—in return for a half-interest in CBS. The arrangement called for Paramount to buy back its shares from Paley and his associates for $5 million by March 1, 1932, provided that CBS had by then turned a net profit of $2 million or more. The deal strengthened CBS's credit line and gave the network access to movie talent.

Paramount seemed at the time to be in an impenetrable position. In 1930, its theatre chain grossed $130 million, while its film exchanges took in $69 million. However, during 1931, the economic crisis in the nation had begun to take its toll on the movie industry. Paramount's record profits of $18 million in the previous year dropped precipitously to $6 million. As the Depression deepened, the weight of empty movie theatres proved to be too much for Paramount. When the repurchase date arrived, CBS had earned nearly $3 million in profits. Faced with paying what amounted to $85 a share for stock at the time valued at $10, the movie company decided to let Paley and his associates regain their ownership by taking CBS stock in lieu of $5 million in cash.[10]

Paley proved to be an astute businessman in many ways. By 1932, the CBS network included 91 affiliated stations. Five were owned outright by CBS. Under a practice called "option time," Paley persuaded affiliated stations to relinquish large blocks of broadcast time to be programmed by the network. Unsold network air time was filled with so-called "sustaining" or unsponsored programs. NBC's practice was to charge its affiliates for sustaining shows. CBS decided to give such shows to its affiliates free of cost; however, in return, CBS could preempt any part of an affiliated station's program schedule. This gave Paley enormous leverage in dealing with prospective sponsors, since he could guarantee them broadcast outlets throughout the country. Beyond an agreement upon number of hours given over to CBS without payment, the network paid each affiliated station on an attractive sliding-scale basis for access to its airwaves. In effect, stations licensed to serve local communities had turned over their facilities to the national network. NBC was quick to follow CBS's lead when it started to lose affiliates to the rival organization. The local station had but to flick a switch, permitting programs and revenues to flow into its facilities. It could also sell time to local advertisers. Affiliation with one of the national networks turned local broadcasting into a bonanza.

OTHER STATIONS UNITE

The business success of NBC and CBS encouraged unaffiliated stations and regional networks to unite. In 1934, several advertisers urged WOR (New York City) and WGN (Chicago) to link up for simultaneous broadcasts. This arrangement allowed advertisers to reach large population centers without having to pay for coast-to-coast hookups. Soon WXYZ (Detroit) and WLW (Cincinnati) decided to join the other two metropolitan stations. That same year, all four stations officially united as the Mutual Broadcasting System. Mutual was incorporated to carry on the business of selling time to advertisers and to coordinate the exchange of programs. It did not maintain a programming division or originate its own programs. Individual stations in the network provided the programs.

The new network took on an international flavor in the fall of 1935 when WXYZ left Mutual to join NBC and was replaced by CKLW, a Windsor, Ontario, station that also served the Detroit area. The following year, the regional Don Lee Network on the West Coast and several smaller outlets joined the Mutual fold. Mutual continued to increase the number of its associated stations, adding a Texas regional network of 23 stations in 1938. By the beginning of 1939, the Mutual network included a total of 197 stations, of which 25 were also affiliated with NBC, and 5 with CBS. Mutual continued to grow, primarily by adding low wattage stations in rural areas to its hookup.

RADIO REGULATION

The rise of national networks and the growing commercialism of broadcasting coincided with the development of radio regulation. The first general legislation for radio, designed for point-to-point transmission, was the Radio Act of 1912. This same law governed broadcasting during the early years. But the broadcasting boom stimulated a demand for spectrum space, which the writers of the 1912 act had not anticipated. During the years 1922-25, the then Secretary of Commerce

Herbert Hoover convened four national radio conferences to seek advice on legislation and to formulate recommendations to Congress for more comprehensive legislation. Representatives from various segments of the radio field were invited. Proposals were made during these meetings, regarding the form that the legislation might take; but no new law resulted. Congressional committees held hearings on proposed bills, but were unable to agree on the details of new radio legislation. Lacking clear legislative authority, Hoover encouraged a voluntary system of government–industry cooperation.

Many broadcasters entered into agreements with respect to power, use of frequencies, and hours of operation; but some refused to do so. Aimee Semple McPherson, a Los Angeles evangelist, operated her station so carelessly that, after several warnings, Hoover ordered a radio inspector to seal her equipment. She swiftly informed the commerce secretary as to who had ultimate authority over the airwaves, with this telegram: "PLEASE ORDER YOUR MINIONS OF SATAN TO LEAVE MY STATION ALONE. YOU CANNOT EXPECT THE ALMIGHTY TO ABIDE BY YOUR WAVELENGTH NONSENSE. WHEN I OFFER MY PRAYERS TO HIM I MUST FIT INTO HIS WAVE RECEPTION. OPEN THIS STATION AT ONCE."[11] After agreeing to hire a competent engineer, the evangelist was permitted to reopen her station.

With the encouragement of industry leaders, Hoover set up an extralegal framework for broadcasting. His most significant action divided stations into three broad groups. The first group included high-power stations on clear channels that served large areas. The second group, less powerful, served smaller areas and were spaced so that they would not interfere with one another. The third group, low in power and often serving a small religious or educational listenership, were crammed into a crowded portion of the spectrum, which necessitated time sharing. In order to prevent interference, stations in the latter group were often permitted to operate only during daytime hours. (At night, a layer above the earth called the ionosphere contracts and acts as a reflector, bouncing some medium- and high-frequency waves back to the ground at various intervals and causing interference.)

Hoover's regulatory role did not go unchallenged in the courts. When the license of the Intercity Radio Company expired, in November 1921, the secretary of commerce refused to grant a new one on the grounds that the firm's wireless telegraphy business between New York and other cities in the United States interfered with the operation of government, commercial, and amateur stations. Intercity took the matter to court; a federal district court ruled in favor of the firm. Secretary Hoover appealed the decision; but the U.S. Court of Appeals also decided for Intercity, declaring that—while the commerce secretary might designate the channels on which the company had to operate—the issuance of a license was mandatory.[12]

Decisive legal developments in 1926 deprived the commerce secretary of any effective authority to regulate the radio spectrum. Without authorization, the Zenith Radio Corporation (which owned and operated a Chicago broadcasting station) changed its hours of operation and jumped to a channel that had been ceded to the Canadian government. Commander Eugene McDonald, Zenith's president, took this action in order to force judicial clarification of the commerce secretary's authority. (McDonald's Chicago station had been allotted only two hours a week on a channel that General Electric's station in Denver could preempt at will.) The Department of Commerce charged Zenith with criminal violation of the Radio Act of 1912. However, in April 1926, the U.S. District Court of Northern Illinois ruled that the provisions of this law were too vague and ambiguous to justify prosecution. Moreover, the court held that the commerce secretary's action to restrict channels and hours might be unconstitutional, since it had no basis in law.[13]

Since the *Zenith* ruling seemed to contradict the decision in the *Intercity* case, Hoover sought a legal opinion from the U.S. attorney general. In a memorandum released on July 8, acting Attorney General William J. Donovan replied that, under the Radio Act of 1912, the secretary of commerce did not have the discretionary power to assign hours or limit wattage; even the right to specify channels for broadcasting stations was limited. He suggested that new legislation be sought to meet both present and future needs.

No immediate action could be taken, however, since Congress was in recess at the time. A bill sponsored by Representative Wallace H. White of Maine—one that evolved from the four national radio conferences—had passed the Republican-dominated House of Representatives in March 1926. This measure authorized the secretary of commerce to serve as a "traffic cop of the air," with broad discretionary powers. A similar bill, sponsored by Senator Clarence C. Dill of Washington, passed the Democratic-controlled Senate on July 2; but the Dill bill favored the establishment of a permanent independent radio commission. A Senate-House conference committee was formed to work out a compromise. However, since the legislative session was scheduled to end the next day, no decisive action was taken. From July until December (when Congress reconvened), chaos and confusion prevailed. Stations increased their power, changed channels, and operated in accordance with schedules that suited their own needs. Soon 200 new stations crowded on the airwaves. Intolerable interference resulted.

Members of the RCA consortium had held to the position that new federal regulation should be implemented only after the business of broadcasting had established a firm economic base. The weak legal mandate of the commerce secretary had worked to their advantage. Westinghouse, GE, RCA, and AT&T were all granted favored channels. Given his tenuous position, Hoover probably could not have done otherwise. Moreover, despite public statements to the contrary, he aided and abetted the advent of broadcast advertising. At the first national radio conference, for instance, Hoover asserted: "It is inconceivable that we should allow so great a possibility for service to be drowned in advertising chatter!"[14] Yet he had given business-sponsored broadcasting a big boost by granting a clear channel to AT&T's toll station. He had also supported the interconnection of stations to develop a national service. Now, at the very time that the patent allies had resolved their differences and NBC had come into existence, the whole structure of broadcasting seemed threatened by the chaotic conditions resulting from the relegation of the Department of Commerce to a mere license bureau. Things being so, the big corporations joined with other segments of the industry in support of swift legislative action.

A NEW RADIO ACT

When Congress assembled in December, broadcasting was high on the legislative agenda. Senate and House conferees soon hammered out a compromise measure. In February of the following year, President Calvin Coolidge signed into law the resultant Radio Act of 1927. The new legislation reflected a number of Congressional concerns. Among the more significant were ownership of the airwaves, monopolistic practices, and censorship.

In the new law, the federal government's jurisdiction over the channels of interstate and foreign radio transmission was stated in unequivocal terms. The use of such channels was to be granted to licensees for only limited periods of time. It was further provided that a license did not, in any way, confer ownership. In granting a new license or permitting the transfer of an existing one, the guiding standard was to be the "public interest, convenience or necessity"—a phrase borrowed from state public-utility laws of the late nineteenth century and from the Transportation Act of 1920.

These provisions in the new radio law reflected a growing concern in the nation about private exploitation of public resources. When legislation for broadcasting was taking form, the Teapot Dome and Elk Hills scandals came to light. Secretly and without competitive bidding, Albert Fall, who was secretary of interior in the Harding administration had leased naval oil reserves in Wyoming and California to private interests in return for bribes of over $300,000. Senate investigations, governmental lawsuits, and criminal trials continued throughout much of the decade. Fall was eventually fined $100,000 and given a one-year prison term. In 1927, the U.S. Supreme Court revoked the leases, and the two big oil reserves were returned to the government.

Agitation over the RCA consortium's control of patents was one of the principal reasons that a provision in the new radio law prohibited the licensing of any person or corporation found guilty in federal court of monopolizing or attempting to restrain radio communication through the manufacture or sale of radio equipment or any other method of unfair competition. A month or so before the legislation was enacted, RCA was able to mollify many of its critics by agreeing to license a limited number of competitors to manufacture radio sets under the patents of the consortium. The royalty agreement called for RCA and its patent partners to receive 7.5 percent of licensees' gross sales or at least $100,000 a year. Some 20 set makers signed up, bringing in royalties of about $3 million in the first year. In 1928, the FTC's four-year investigation ended with the dismissal of all complaints. The big corporations seemed to be home free.

Opponents of government censorship also had an influence on the new radio law. The years immediately following World War I marked a politically turbulent time in American life. The success of the Bolshevik Revolution in Russia, in which a small political party had seized control of a backward, despotic country in the name of the proletariat, provided inspiration to the burgeoning radical movement in the United States. Factional disputes soon dissipated any possibility of effective unified action from the Left. Nevertheless, the perceived threat of communist conspiracy led to national hysteria. Mob violence, racial conflict, labor unrest, and a host of other domestic problems stemming from complex causes were increasingly attributed to Bolshevik agitation. Congress was deluged with petitions—from state legislatures, patriotic organizations, and business groups—demanding that something be done to stem the swelling tide of radicalism.

In response to the growing clamor, Attorney General A. Mitchell Palmer launched a series of raids and roundups in January 1920, in which some 6,000 suspected revolutionaries in scores of cities were arrested and held behind bars for days or weeks—often without any specific indication of the charges against them. Intolerance became the order of the day. Blacks, Jews, and aliens of all sorts were openly persecuted for not being "100 percent American." The Ku Klux Klan, whose membership had grown to well over 4 million by 1924, was able to wield great political power in several states. In many state legislatures, believers in the "letter" of the Bible—so-called "fundamentalists"—introduced bills designed to forbid the teaching of the theory of evolution. In Mississippi, Oklahoma, and Tennessee, such measures were actually signed into law.

This was not a climate conducive to free and open discussion. But by 1925, the year of the fourth national radio conference, there were some significant breakthroughs. That year, it will be recalled, the U. S. Supreme Court ruled that freedom of speech and press were among those unspecified "privileges" and "immunities" protected from impairment by the states under the due process clause of the Fourteenth Amendment. The teaching of evolution also became a national issue in 1925 when John Thomas Scopes, who taught biology at Central High School in Dayton, Tennessee, decided to challenge that state's new antievolution law. Scopes allowed himself to be caught in the act of teaching the theory of evolution to his students. This illegal deed promptly led to his arrest. No less a figure than three-time presidential candidate and ex-Secretary of State William Jennings Bryan volunteered his services to the prosecution. The Civil Liberties Union in New York secured for Scopes the legal assistance of the great Clarence Darrow. Newspapers throughout the country covered the trial. The oftentimes bizarre confrontations between Bryan and Darrow over Biblical interpretations were broadcast to large audiences by WGN (the Chicago *Tribune* station), via a "remote" pickup directly from the court. The prosecution won its case. But trial coverage gave new impetus to the advocates of greater tolerance. A proposed amendment to the new radio law, which would have banned the broadcasting of discourses on evolution, enjoyed little support in Congress.[15]

A provision in the 1927 act placed strict limits on the federal government's control over the content of radio transmissions: "Nothing in this act shall be understood or construed to give the licensing authority the power of censorship over the radio communications or signals transmitted by any radio station, and no regulation or condition shall be promulgated or fixed by the licensing authority which shall interfere with the right of free speech by means of radio communications." However, the right of free speech did not extend to "obscene, indecent or profane language." While licensees were not obliged to provide time for political candidates, they were required to treat rival candidates equally, and they were prohibited from exercising any power of censorhip over the material broadcast by candidates for office.

Ringing declarations aside, these provisions would mean little unless they were enforced. The 1927 act, reflecting an accommodation of interests between the House and Senate, established a curious division of responsibilities between the commerce secretary and a newly created Federal Radio Commission (FRC). The commerce secretary retained such powers as fixing the qualifications of operators, inspecting station equipment, and assigning call letters. The new five-member commission was given broad administrative and quasi-judicial authority over applications for station licensees, renewals, and changes in facilities, for a one-year period. At the end of that time, such authority would revert to the commerce secretary. The commission was to continue merely as an advisory and appellate body.

The new commission got off to a shaky start. The act called for the appointment of the five commissioners by the president with the advice and consent of the Senate. Each commissioner was to represent one of five designated geographic districts within the United States. But the Senate confirmed only three of the president's appointees before adjournment. Moreover, the House failed to appropriate funds for salaries or supplies. Only through an emergency allocation of funds from the Department of Commerce was the new commission able to begin its herculean task of bringing order to the airwaves.

Congress eventually confirmed a full complement of salaried members to the commission. It also extended the FRC's authority for two successive years, thereafter making it a permanent regulatory agency. But the initial temporary status of the FRC made it susceptible to all sorts of pressures. As in other areas, the interests of the already powerful prevailed.

The new law resulted in very few structural changes. Indeed, for the most part, the policies and practices of the commerce secretary were preserved. The division of the broadcasting band into low-power local, middle-power regional, and high-power clear channels was continued. Once again, the favored channels went to those organizations with ample financial resources, superior technical equipment, highly skilled personnel, and first-rate legal representation. In practical terms, this meant that commerically sponsored stations were assigned most of the regional and clear channels. Stations operated by religious, educational, municipal, and other non-profit concerns remained relegated to daytime hours on low-power local channels.

THE PUBLIC INTEREST

The 1927 act provided very few specific guidelines for utilization of the broadcasting band. Congress said curiously little about commercial sponsorship. A single reference was included in the 7,000-word document, requiring the airing of an announcement as to the person, firm, or company paying for or furnishing certain broadcast material. The FRC was authorized to make special regulations applicable to radio stations engaged in network or "chain" broadcasting; however, the rationale for such regulations was not specified.

No attempt was made anywhere in the act to explain the rather amorphous concept of the public interest, convenience, or necessity. A standard of this type can be more readily applied to public utilities where the kind of service is specific—for example, gas, water, or electricity. However, when the application of such a standard is made to broadcasting the problem becomes considerably less tractable. Is the standard applicable to programming? If so, which "public" is to be considered? In a variegated and pluralistic society like the United States, there are likely to be many different publics when it comes to programming preferences.

The FRC grappled with these issues on a case-by-case basis. In its 1928 *Great Lakes* decision, the commission made it clear that the program service rendered by broadcasters would be taken into account in granting or withholding licenses. The FRC denied the application of the Great Lakes Broadcasting Company for a license for a new station on the grounds that the proposed program service would be of value or interest to only a small proportion of the listeners living in the area to be served by the station. The commission stated that there was not sufficient room in the radio spectrum for every school of religious, political, social, and economic thought to have its separate broadcasting station. Advertising, however, was excluded from the sanctions against special interest groups because its revenues furnished the economic support for broadcasting. Moreover, the FRC seemed to imply that programs appealing to a large segment of the listening audience were by definition in the public interest, convenience, and necessity: "In the first place, the listener has a complete power of censorship by turning his dial away from a program he does not like; this results in a keen appreciation by the broadcaster of the necessity of pleasing a large portion of his listeners if he is to hold his audience, and of not displeasing, annoying, or offending the sensibilities of any substantial part of the public."[16]

Given this interpretation, the FRC's rationale for favoring profit-oriented stations selling airtime to advertisers becomes clearer: Such stations best fulfilled the public interest, convenience, and necessity standard because they presented programming designed to attract and hold the largest possible audiences. Those not served by such programming were left with the option of turning the dial. Obviously, this was not much of an option because, whether or not people listened to a profit-oriented station, they were affected by its commerical imperatives in one way or another. Those imperatives frequently worked to the detriment of minority interests.

THE BRINKLEY BAROMETER

The FRC did attempt to deal with manifestly flagrant commercial abuses. Broadcasting had attracted an amazing assortment of charlatans, fakers, and quacks. Among the more remarkable to come before the microphones, and a significant figure in the development of radio regulation, was John Romulus Brinkley—the infamous "goat-gland" surgeon.[17]

Brinkley, who had obtained a medical degree from a diploma mill in Kansas City for $100, used his broadcasting station—KFKB in Milford, Kansas—to advertise an operation involving an implant of the gonads of a young goat inside the scrotum of human patients. The operation was supposed to restore sexual vigor. Since sexual impotency is often psychological, Brinkley was able to offer his listeners testimonials of positive results. The operation became so popular that Brinkley had to arrange for a shipment of goats from Arkansas. Even several screen stars are said to have undergone the surgical procedure.

Brinkley also broadcast a program called the *Medical Question Box*, during which he diagnosed and prescribed medicines for his listeners solely on the basis of letters he received from them. "Here's one from Tillie," said the diploma mill doctor in a typical response. "She says she had an operation, had some trouble 10 years ago. I think the operation was unnecessary, and it isn't very good sense to have an ovary removed with the expectation of motherhood resulting therefrom. My advice to you is to use Women's Tonic No. 50, 67, and 61. This combination will do for you what you desire if any combination will, after three months' persistent use."[18]

To meet the growing demand for his medicines, Brinkley organized the Brinkley Pharmaceutical Association. Soon his number-coded concoctions—which contained little more than castor oil and aspirin—could be obtained from some 1,500 druggists. He also developed a thriving mail-order business. From his drug operation alone, Brinkley is estimated to have grossed in excess of $700,000 a year.

Brinkley's station had fared well in the FRC's allocations. But by 1930, powerful forces were arrayed against him. The Kansas City *Star* ran a series exposing his predatory practices, and medical authorities mounted a campaign to put him out of business. Later that year, on the basis of complaints filed by the American Medical Association, the FRC held a hearing on the renewal of the broadcasting license of KFKB. As a result of this hearing, the FRC decided not to renew the station's license. Brinkley appealed the decision in federal court, claiming that the FRC action constituted censorship.

In 1931, the U. S. Court of Appeals for the District of Columbia ruled that the FRC had acted within its powers. The commission had held that Brinkley's medical programs were inimical to public health and safety and therefore were not in the public interest. In its argument to the appeals court, the commission made it clear that there had been no attempt on its part to scrutinize broadcast matter prior to its release, and that review of past conduct did not constitute censorship. The court supported this position, holding that the commission was "necessarily called upon to consider the character and quality of the service to be rendered and that in considering an application for renewal of a license an important consideration is the past conduct of the applicant." Invoking the Biblical injunction "by their fruits ye shall know them," the court left little doubt of the licensing authority's right to consider a station's past programming when a license renewal is sought.[19] It's a precedent that prevails to this day.

Judicial affirmation of the FRC's right to review past programming practices had little immediate impact on the operations of the big commercial stations. The regulatory agency rarely refused to renew a license for anything other than the most flagrant violations. Moreover, most commissioners were not unmindful of the job opportunities open to them if they cultivated the right connections. Indeed, two of their number moved to profitable vice-presidential perches at CBS. In the years ahead, tenure with one of the regulatory agencies would often translate into a high-level position in private industry.

GROWING OPPOSITION

Not everyone in government was sanguine about the emerging system of broadcasting. Among the most outspoken critics was Representative Edwin L. Davis of Tennessee. In 1928, Davis had succeeded in adding an amendment to the radio act, which provided for a more equitable distribution of licenses, channels, power, and station time across the country. But the FRC could do little more than pay lip service to this measure. Powerful commercial stations in the major metropolitan areas were already too firmly entrenched for the agency to implement a redistribution plan without completely disrupting the existing system.

Charges of monopoly against the RCA consortium also continued to mount, despite the FTC vindication. In 1930, the Justice Department filed an antitrust suit, demanding that the alliance between RCA, Westinghouse, General Electric, and AT&T be dissolved. The patent pool was alleged to be illegal and so, the attorney general held, was GE and Westinghouse ownership of RCA stock.

Since AT&T had sold off its RCA holdings several years earlier, it was disposed to seek a separate peace with the government. Late in 1931, the giant telephone company elected to exercise its right to cancel its cross-licensing agreement, by giving the required three years' notice.

After complex negotiations, the RCA–GE–Westinghouse axis agreed to a consent decree. GE and Westinghouse divested themselves of RCA stock and withdrew their officials from its board of directors.

They further agreed to defer competing with RCA for a period of two-and-a-half years, allowing time for the radio corporation to get its new operation in order. License agreements were also modified.

The breakup of the RCA consortium did little to alter the basic structure of the broadcasting industry. The FRC's policies, following the commerce secretary's earlier example, virtually ensured commercial domination of the airwaves. Stations that sought to represent some "special interest" increasingly suffered shifts in channel assignment, restricted hours, and shared time. Educational, religious, labor, and farm groups soon found themselves edged out of the broadcasting band.

THE TWENTY-FIVE PERCENT SOLUTION

Prior to 1934, no single agency was charged with broad authority over communications. Wired and radio transmissions were partially regulated by several agencies—chiefly the Interstate Commerce Commission, the Postmaster General, and the Federal Radio Commission. The various laws governing communications were consolidated and broadened in the Communications Act of 1934 and their administration was placed under the control of one regulatory agency—the Federal Communications Commission (FCC).

When the new communications legislation was considered in the Congress, Senator Robert F. Wagner of New York and Senator Henry D. Hatfield of West Virginia proposed an amendment that called for the reservation of one-fourth of all broadcasting channels for educational, religious, agricultural, labor, cooperative, and similar nonprofit organizations.[20] These channels were to be equally as desirable as those allocated to profit-oriented operations.

The proposed amendment would have nullified existing licenses 90 days after the new act took effect. During that period, the new distribution of channels would be made by the new commission. The basis upon which the reserved channels were to be divided was not specified. Nor did nonprofit mean noncommercial; a nonprofit licensee would be permitted to sell time in order to make his station self-supporting.

Opponents of the amendment were quick to point out the unfeasibility of reallocating channels within the allotted time and the likelihood of even more advertising on the airwaves, if nonprofit licensees operating high-powered stations got into the time-selling business. CBS and NBC executives argued convincingly that, since only 30 percent or so of network programming was sponsored, there was ample time for educational and other nonprofit needs. The amendment was defeated by a vote of 42 to 23. A compromise provision was approved calling for the new commission to consider the reserved-channel idea. (No significant changes resulted.)

For commercial broadcasters, passage of the Communications Act of 1934 meant business as usual. The new legislation retained most of the provisions of the 1927 Act. As overseer of broadcasting, the new seven-member commission tended to follow the policies and practices of its predecessor agency.

THE BUSINESS OF BROADCASTING

Broadcasting became a much bigger part of advertising budgets in the 1930s. In 1928, advertisers spent some $20 million on broadcasting. Within ten years, radio advertising sales soared to $145 million. During the same period, sponsored programming came under the control of the advertising agencies representing the major advertisers. Many programs were actually produced by the ad agencies themselves.

Advertising agencies had begun to take form around the 1830s, when the penny press came into existence. At first, they mainly functioned as brokers for the sale of space in the print media. As the volume of advertising increased, they began to provide other services—writing copy, advising on strategy, and sponsoring market research.

By the early decades of the new century, a number of ad agencies were prospering. The average ad agency of the 1870s conducted its affairs from a one-room office. By the 1920s, ad agencies had become institutions of considerable resources and importance. With growing importance came a new sense of self-importance. Bruce Barton, a partner in Batten, Barton, Durstine & Osborne, was even so bold as to suggest in his best-selling book of the mid-1920s, *The Man Nobody Knows*, that if Jesus Christ were around in modern times he would be an account executive in an ad agency. The book offered an image of Jesus as a go-getter, the first modern salesman, who "picked up twelve men from the bottom ranks of business and forged them into an organization that conquered the world."[21]

The leading figures at the advertising agencies—most of which were located on Madison Avenue in New York, with branches elsewhere—tended to be highly conservative. As representatives of some of the most powerful corporations in the United States, the ad industry's political stance could scarcely have been otherwise. Albert Lasker of the Lord & Thomas agency, for instance, counted among his clients such firms as General Electric, RCA, Cities Service, Commonwealth Edison, and Goodyear. Lord & Thomas was one of the first of the big agencies to set up a radio department. J. Walter Thompson, McCann-Erickson, Young and Rubicam, Benton and Bowles, BBD&O, and scores of other agencies soon followed. For their regular services, agencies received 15 percent of the cost of broadcast time, matching the fee paid by newspapers and magazines for space sales. For putting together programs, agencies added a second fee of 15 percent of production costs to a client's bill. (Sponsors, in turn, passed these costs—hidden in the retail price of the products—on to consumers.)

So it was that agencies had the incentive to escalate the costs of broadcasting time and move into the area of programming. While the networks could decide when and what kinds of programs they would transmit, it was the agencies and their clients who held the purse strings and generally called the shots. For instance, when NBC moved into the vast Rockefeller Radio City complex in 1933, every studio had a special soundproof booth from which sponsors or their agency representatives might supervise the production of programs. In many ways, this 60-story structure, which cost $250 million and covered three square blocks, symbolized the new big business era of broadcasting.

Sponsors were highly selective in the kinds of programs they would finance. General Motors, for example, might lend its support to a symphony series, because the sponsorship of "serious" music was likely to bring the corporation prestige and public goodwill. But the giant automobile maker could scarcely be expected to promote a program on labor relations. In the early 1930s, top GM executives were paid an average of $200,000 annually. A GM worker, on the other hand, earned about $1,000 a year for fastening and tightening bolts, fenders, axles, engine blocks, and the like to car frames carried by fast-moving conveyor belts, every hour of the working day. Workers who complained about working conditions in GM plants were likely to be labeled "communist" and dismissed on some concocted charge. This kind of company picture never made it to the airwaves of the commercial networks and stations, since it would not aid product sales. To

James Rorty, a former advertising copywriter turned critic of capitalism, commercial broadcasting seemed "a conspiracy of silence regarding all those aspects of the individual and social life that do not contribute to the objectives of the advertiser."[22]

Advertising agencies produced programs designed to entertain and divert, while at the same time providing a context suitable for sales promotion. During the 1930s, advertising appeals became more frequent and more strident. Commercials preceded, interrupted, and followed programs. The old WEAF ban on the mention of product prices was lifted by NBC in the daytime hours of July 1932. In the fall of that year, both CBS and NBC decided to permit the mention of prices in nighttime, as well as daytime, presentations. Commercials for laxatives, deodorants, and other such personal products were also permitted.

ADVERTISING APPEALS

Product promotion took many forms. Dramatic situations were commonly used to support the sale of soap. The American Tobacco Company, maker of Lucky Strike cigarettes, tried a variety of sales pitches on the programs it sponsored. Women were encouraged to "reach for a Lucky instead of a sweet" as an aid to weight reduction. This firm became one of the first to buy testimonials (including one from a famous opera singer who didn't even smoke). Listeners were also reminded of the cigarette brand with a tobacco auctioneer's chant and the oft-repeated slogan: "L.S./M.F.T., L.S./M.F.T. Lucky Strike means fine tobacco. Yes. Lucky Strike means fine tobacco." Extravagant claims became common practice. The Pepsodent Company, for instance, claimed its toothpaste contained a secret ingredient of immense power called "irium"—actually a mild detergent, sodium alkyl sulphate. Products were glorified in jingles as well. Pepsi-Cola stressed economy in its singing commercial: "Pepsi-Cola hits the spot! Twelve full ounces, that's a lot. Twice as much for a nickel, too." Premium offers, usually redeemed by sending in the box top from the sponsor's product, became a prevalent sales gimmick on shows aimed at women and children. General Mills, the sponsor of *Jack Armstrong, the All-American Boy*, offered young listeners such things as whistle rings and secret decoders in return for box tops from Wheaties breakfast cereal.

Sponsors also continued to strive for a close association between product and performer. Ed Wynn was the Texaco Fire Chief. The comedy team of George Burns and Gracie Allen meant Maxwell House; ventriloquist Edgar Bergen and his wooden dummy Charlie McCarthy, Chase and Sanborn. The "personality" announcer, who could push a product and play a role in the script, became a prominent feature of many programs. Announcers like Don Wilson (*Jack Benny*) and Bill Goodwin (*Burns and Allen*) became celebrities in their own right.

THE AESTHETICS OF VAUDEVILLE

Makers of canned soups, packaged desserts, cigarettes, brand-name coffee and other such mass-produced items sought to reach the largest possible audiences. To meet advertiser demand, programmers turned to the production values of vaudeville. The repertory of this theatrical entertainment format, which was especially popular in the early twentieth century, included song-and-dance routines, acrobatics, animal acts, mimed and slapstick comedy, juggling, skits, parodies, impersonations, and monologues. A large part of the aesthetics, and a lot of the talent for commercial broadcasting (and motion pictures) came from vaudeville. Variety shows, relying heavily on the vaudeville format, became a network staple during the 1930s. These shows were usually hosted by a comedian or a singer who could be readily identified with the sponsor's product. Jack Benny, Eddie Cantor, Ed Wynn, Burns and Allen, and Jimmy Durante were among the veterans of vaudeville to gain enormous popularity on the airwaves. A juggler by the name of John F. Sullivan left vaudeville for broadcasting and, calling himself "Fred Allen," achieved lasting fame with his one-liners and clever repartee.

Budgets for popular variety and comedy shows often ran to a quarter-million or more a year. General Foods, the maker of Jell-O, paid Jack Benny $10,000 a week, 39 weeks a year, for his comedic talents.[23] Benny created the appealing on-the-air character of the self-confident skinflint who constantly makes a fool of himself. Much of his humor derived from placing this character in well-contrived situations so that laughter could be evoked not so much from what he said, but because of the circumstances in which he said it. Benny was also one of the top masters of timing. He was especially adept at the pregnant pause. In one of his most famous radio routines, Benny is accosted by a crook who snarls, "Your money or your life." Benny allowed the audience laughter to build louder and louder, before responding that he was thinking it over. This was the kind of harmless humor that sponsors could comfortably support.

Despite the apparent innocuousness of such entertainment fare, it distorted social reality in ways that were detrimental to several segments of society. To make it in big-time show business as something other than an ethnic stereotype one had to become Anglo-Saxonized. Benny, for instance, had been born Benjamin Kubelsky. This practice would be challenged, a generation later—but remnants remain, to this day. Among those who have anglicized their names are Doris Day (née Doris Kappelhoff), Tony Curtis (Bernie Schwartz), George Burns (Nathan Birnbaum), Kirk Douglas (Issur Danielovitch), Rita Hayworth (Margarita Carmen Cansino), Danny Kaye (David Daniel Kaminski), and Jane Wyman (Sarah Fulks). At a time when Jews and other ethnic minorities were being persecuted, such name changes were not without social significance.

Ethnic stereotypes—long a part of vaudeville—made the transition to broadcasting (and motion pictures) with little trouble. The very success of mass entertainment lies in the manner in which it reflects and reinforces the dominant assumptions, aspirations, and assignations of its cultural origins. During the 1930s, broadcasting's racial typologies undoubtedly served to explain, justify, and sanctify such social practices as segregation. Among the most popular shows of the period was *Amos 'n' Andy*, which featured two white ex-vaudevillians named Freeman Gosden and Charles Correll in "blackface" dialect humor.[24] Gosden and Correll played not only Amos and Andy but all the show's other characters, most of whom were supposed to be black. They also wrote their own scripts. The show made its network debut on NBC Blue in August 1929, under the sponsorship of a toothpaste manufacturer. It was on six nights a week for a time, then five—first at 11:00 p.m. and finally at an earlier hour, 7 p.m. (Eastern Time), so that it could provide a strong leadoff for the rest of the network's evening schedule. (Listeners tended to stay with the same station, because switching often involved difficulties in eliminating each station's irritating static.) If the show that followed *Amos 'n' Andy* was even mildly entertaining, there was likely to be little dial turning.

Amos 'n' Andy set the standard for a new radio form: the serialized situation comedy. Each nightly episode, sandwiched between pronouncements about Pepsodent toothpaste, lasted about ten minutes and required from 1,500 to 2,000 words. The series centered around the comic misadventures of the title characters. Amos was depicted as trusting, simple, and unsophisticated. Andy was slow, somewhat shiftless, and often domineering. The twosome owned and operated the Fresh-Air Taxicab Company, whose assets included one broken-down topless automobile, one desk, and one swivel chair for the president to "rest his brains." The action often took place in a rooming house on Chicago's South Side and frequently shifted to a lodge called the "Mystic Knights of the Sea," presided over by a scheming fellow known as "the Kingfish." All of the characters, direct descendents of the burnt-cork comics of the antebellum minstrel shows, spoke in a pseudodialect exemplified by such phrases as "Splain dat to me," "I's regusted," and "Is you mulsifying or revidin?"

During the depths of the Depression, *Amos 'n' Andy* enjoyed unparalleled popularity. A breach-of-promise suit brought against Andy by a character called Madam Queen so enmeshed audience interest that many movie theatres would stop the projector in mid-reel at 7 p.m. each weekday evening to pipe in the program to patrons who would otherwise have stayed home. Andy's fate became the topic of talk at dinner tables and on commuter trains across the nation. According to one account, on the evening of the denouement, thousands of callers who had missed the broadcast tied up the switchboards of radio stations and newspaper offices trying to find out whether "Andy got hooked."[25]

The Chicago *Daily News* syndicated a daily *Amos 'n' Andy* comic strip, and Victor promoted phonograph records featuring the popular pair. In *Check and Double Check*, a 1930 RKO release, Gosden and Correll brought their blackface characterizations to the screen. But the film failed to match their radio success. The characters they created were apparently much more appealing when one could imagine them, in the mind's eye, as actually being black.

The imaginary world created by Gosden and Correll was a far cry from the harsh reality of ghetto life. But in the segregated society of the 1930s, many people were doubtlessly unaware of the disparity. From the perspective of present-day culture, it is easy—or, at least, easier than it was at the time—to see that such a show served to legitimate the ghetto system. There were occasional calls to ban the series, but its defenders could counter with the argument that blacks seemed to enjoy the program as much as whites. One of the most perplexing aspects of socially prejudicial entertainment is that it often is not recognized as such, even by those who suffer most from its damaging distortions.

It was not until their latter radio days, and on their entry into television, that Gosden and Correll met with strong opposition from such organizations as the NAACP, who felt that the team's depiction of black life was a detriment to the realization of civil liberties and equal rights. (From 1951 to 1953, CBS ran a television version of *Amos 'n' Andy*, featuring black actors—but dropped it because of NAACP opposition.)

THE WAR AGAINST CRIME

Mass entertainment fare on commercial broadcasting also mimicked the emotionalism and sentimentality of melodramatic theatre and the plot contrivances of formulaic dime novels and magazine stories, popular art forms that had taken shape with the advent of industrialization and urbanization. Crime series, especially those featuring well-known fictional detectives, became an important staple of the networks' schedules. With rare exceptions, these series had formula plots, stereotyped characters, surface conflicts, and predictable denouements. In each episode, a noble protagonist sought to catch and/or kill some evil and villainous person or persons. The credibility of both the characters and the actions was usually sacrificed for suspenseful effect. Sophisticated use of sound served to heighten the appeal. (The same essential formula was adapted to motion pictures, and easily made the transition to television.)

Critic Charles J. Rollo saw in the detective genre the modern-day equivalent of the medieval morality play. "The hero suspects everyone, for the murderer is Everyman; the murder is the symbol of the guilt, the imperfection, that is in all of us," writes Rollo. "In his search for the hidden truth, the hero is exposed to danger, thrashes about in darkness, sometimes suffers in the flesh, for it is by his travail that the Savior looses the world of its sins."[26] Whether the detective story in general, and its dramatization on radio in particular, actually served as a substitute for sacred scripture and exegesis is highly doubtful. But it is not too farfetched to suggest that as religious faith receded before a capitalist ethos, detective fiction—with its "crime doesn't pay" dictum—served an important social function. "In a civilization established upon the principle of private ownership of property—be it in land, coin, or life—such a proclamation is a functional necessity," writes J. Fred MacDonald. The radio detective series, he suggests, served "to blend this serious lesson within a diverting context, illustrating repeatedly that anti-social villains must be reformed, incarcerated, or executed so that the society of the propertied might be secure and enduring."[27]

The 1930s saw an eruption of detective series, with nearly every fictional sleuth being presented in a radio version. There were Sherlock Holmes and Dr. Watson, Ellery Queen, Nick and Nora Charles, Philo Vance, Bulldog Drummond, Martin Kane, and even Mr. Moto. Each advertiser adapted these fictional characters to fit its own needs. In *The Adventures of Sherlock Holmes*, which early in the decade was sponsored by a coffee manufacturer, Dr. Watson would sip some of the sponsor's product before beginning his tale of adventure and intrigue. None of these shows—need one say?—made a reference to the ruinous financial crisis that prevailed throughout the nation. Sponsors shunned any suggestion that the causes of crime might have some economic roots. The basic good/bad guy formula itself served as a mechanism for such content control. The same cut-to-pattern characters and conflicts could be found in adventure series and western shows as well.

The image of law enforcement agencies was likewise bolstered by broadcasting. In 1935 Philips H. Lord, a radio actor and producer, launched the short-lived *G-Men* series with scripts based on the files of the Federal Bureau of Investigation. J. Edgar Hoover was one of the first public officials to recognize the potential of entertainment programming to promote law-and-order politics. Over the years, he came to cooperate with many producers in order to promulgate an image of the FBI as a champion of justice. But he was displeased with Lord's emphasis on gunplay at the expense of patient investigative work; so, after 26 weeks, he ended the bureau's association with the show.

Philips H. Lord lent an air of authenticity to his shows by employing actual police officials to serve as commentators. The *Gangbusters* series, which premiered in 1936, was hosted by the former superintendent of a state police force. Much of the raw material for the show's half-hour scripts came from the police reporters who covered crime cases in various parts of the country. Any of a score of free-lance writers worked on each episode, blending fact and fiction to promote "America's crusade against crime." Sirens screeching in the night, the clattering of submachine guns, and other such sound effects helped to ensure emotional participation.

Another Lord series, *Mr. District Attorney*, was loosely based on the career of Thomas Dewey in New York City. It went on the air in 1939 with Dwight Weist (soon to be replaced by Jay Jostyn) in the title role of the nameless prosecutor who served as "champion of the people, defender of truth, guardian of our fundamental rights to life, liberty, and the pursuit of happiness." At the opening of each episode, listeners were assured in ringing tones of the crusading crimefighter's unflinching dedication to law and order within a framework of justice and fair play: "And it shall be my duty as District Attorney not only to prosecute to the limit of the law all persons accused of crimes perpetrated within this county but to defend with equal vigor the rights and privileges of all its citizens."

Youngsters were also enlisted in the radio war against crime at home and abroad. In the hours after school, on Saturday mornings, and in the early evenings, the airwaves were filled with adventure programs aimed specifically at children. Comic strip characters like Terry and the Pirates, Don Winslow of the Navy, Superman, and ace detective Dick Tracy were given fuller realization on radio with the voices of actors, music, and sensational sound effects. Out of the dark recesses of some radio writer's imagination came such urban vigilantes as the Green Hornet, Captain Midnight, and that "mysterious aide to the forces of law and order," the Shadow, who was, "in reality, Lamont Cranston, wealthy young man about town who, years ago in the Orient, learned the hypnotic power to cloud men's minds so that they could not see him."

For millions of young people, the stirring sounds of the "William Tell Overture" meant another episode of the Lone Ranger—who, with his faithful Indian companion, Tonto, led the fight for law and order in the early West. At the beginning of each episode, listeners in the midthirties were told (with slight variations) that "Gun law ruled in the early West, but here and there, determined men rose up against the gunslingers and outlaws."

DAYTIME SERIAL DRAMAS

Daytime serial dramas, more popularly known as "soap operas" because of their sponsorship by soap manufacturers, also enjoyed enormous popularity during the 1930s. Such serials constituted nearly 60 percent of all network daytime programming, by the end of the decade.

Aiming primarily at women working in the home, the writers of these serials sought to develop situations with just enough suspense to draw listeners back to their radio sets each day. The basic formula was derisively described by James Thurber in gastronomical terms: "A soap opera is a kind of sandwich," wrote Thurber. "Between slices of advertising, spread twelve minutes of dialogue, add predicament, villainy, and female suffering in equal measure, throw in a dash of nobility, sprinkle with tears, season with organ music, cover with a rich announcer sauce, and serve five times a week."[28]

The most prolific and successful creators of daytime serial dramas were Frank and Ann Hummert. Among their most popular programs were *The Romance of Helen Trent; Just Plain Bill; Mary Noble, Backstage Wife; Our Gal Sunday; Lorenzo Jones; Stella Dallas*; and *Young Widder Brown*. Some of these shows had a remarkably long radio run: *Helen Trent* was on the air from 1933 to 1960. This serial told the story of a 35-year-old fashion designer who "when life mocks her, breaks her hopes, dashes her head against the rocks of despair, fights back bravely, successfully, to prove what so many women long to prove in their own lives, that because a woman is thirty-five—or more—romance in life need not be over, that the romance of life can extend into middle age, and beyond." Over the years, Helen had many amours, an unusually high number of whom met with violent death.

The Hummerts were firm adherents of an assembly-line approach to the creative process. They employed a staff of writers who worked anonymously, fleshing out with dialogue the synopsis of sequences developed by one or the other of the pair. Writers were not permitted to deviate from the basic plot line. This kind of factory-like dramaturgy enabled the Hummerts to turn out from 15 to 18 separate serials a week. The serials were produced for Blackett, Sample & Hummert, which became the leading advertising agency in total time purchases. Scores of advertisers sought serial sponsorship. Two major sponsors of such serials—Proctor and Gamble, and Lever Brothers—became the biggest time-buyers in the broadcast industry.

Serials were also beginning to arouse interest among social researchers. One study found that the average listener tuned in regularly to 6.6 different serials. What did listeners find appealing about these serial dramas? A survey conducted mainly among housewives by social psychologist Herta Herzog led her to conclude that the stories had become an integral part of many women's lives, providing temporary emotional release, escape from the dull routines of everyday life, and "a model of reality by which one is taught how to think and how to act." One woman indicated that she used a face cream advertised on *Helen Trent* "because she is using it and she is over thirty-five herself and has all these romances." Some 61 percent of those interviewed said they used merchandise advertised on the serials they followed.[29]

This kind of research was useful to the custodians of commercial broadcasting, but it necessarily ignored questions of greater cultural significance. For instance, what historical circumstances led women to turn to radio serials for emotional release, escape, or social guidance? Could there possibly be a functional link between soap operas and the romantic songs of misty-voiced minstrels, which titillated the sexual fantasies of bored aristocratic ladies in the twelfth century or thereabouts? Such broad cultural concerns are not amenable to even the most refined and sophisticated survey techniques. While useful in some areas—for determining program or product preferences, for instance—it should be clear that some knowledge simply cannot be gained by survey research. This method is limited to studying phenomena that respondents are conscious of and willing or able to disclose. Individual responses on their own—without consideration of how they might reflect broader cultural patterns, or how they might even be conditioned by the structure of society as a whole—often obscure more than they reveal.

AUDIENCE MEASUREMENT

The exigencies of advertising demanded audience data that could be quantified and generalized: Who listened to what; when; and with what commercial effect? Unlike newspapers and magazines, radio reached unseen multitudes not measurable in terms of circulation sales figures. At first, fan mail was used to determine program listenership. But by the 1930s, audience surveys based on telephone samples increasingly determined not only advertising rates but program content, as well.

One of the earliest attempts at estimating audience size was made in 1929 by Archibald Crossley, a market research specialist, using a simple recall method in which he asked respondents what programs they listened to the previous day. He called people in the early evening, finding their names in public telephone books. Those with unlisted numbers or without phones were excluded from the sample. Despite the limitations of this technique, it was met with favor by the Association of National Advertisers and American Association of Advertising Agencies. As a result, in 1930 they established a program rating service called the Cooperative Analysis of Broadcasting (CAB), under the direction of Crossley. The primary function of this service was to provide advertisers and agencies with a means of evaluating their investment in broadcasting.

A second rating service was introduced in 1934 by Clark-Hooper, Inc., a market researcher in the newspaper and magazine field. (In 1938, Clark-Hooper split into two companies, and C. E. Hooper continued the radio rating service.) Hooperatings, as the service came to be called, employed the telephone "coincidental" method (coinciding with the call), whereby a contacted individual would be asked to supply information only about the program he was listening to at the time of the call. Every day of the week, operators in 32 cities conducted coincidental interviews continuously from 8:00 a.m. to 10:30 p.m. Respondents were asked to indicate whether or not they were listening to the radio—if so, to what station they were tuned and to what program they were listening; the name of the program's sponsor; and the number of men, women, and children listening to the radio at the time the telephone rang. National ratings were established on the basis of a statistical analysis of the telephone sample. Hooper also provided ratings for programs in individual cities. Published reports were regularly provided to both the buyer and the seller of radio time. Hooperatings soon superceded CAB as the dominant rating system. (The CAB abandoned its recall method for coincidental telephone calls after 1941, but was unable to compete against Hooper and discontinued its service within five years.)

Since telephone ownership in the 1930s tended to be related to economic status, poorer households were grossly underrepresented in the Hooperatings. Nor did the sampling include rural residences. Nevertheless, advertiser-supported programs that did not do well in the Hooperatings were generally taken off the air. Not all listeners in radioland were created equal. The consequences for programming content, it can safely be said, were more conservative than revolutionary.

The A. C. Nielsen Company, a retail surveyor for food and drug firms, entered the radio ratings field in the early 1940s with a method for evaluating listening through the use of a mechanical instrument called the "Audimeter," which attached to radio sets. Designed by several MIT professors, the Audimeter made a record on tape whenever the radio set was turned on. The time of day at which the set was turned on, the length of time it was in operation, and the stations to which it was tuned could be determined from the position and length of the lines drawn on the tape. Nielsen's radio sample eventually included 1,100 households across the country. The paper tapes were collected by the company's field representatives on a biweekly basis. (The Audimeter was adapted to television and has undergone a number of refinements.)

Unlike telephone interviewing, the Audimeter did not depend on listener recall or honesty. This device also permitted audience measurement of a much greater cross section of the population. However, the Nielsen system had a number of shortcomings. The Audimeter recorded when the set was on, but it did not indicate who the actual audience was or even if anyone was listening. If someone forgot and left the house without turning off the radio, the tape would continue to register the station as having an audience. There were other more disturbing factors, concerning the composition of the sample population. From the outset, blacks and other minorities were not adequately represented, because Audimeters were not placed in ghetto households. This omission did not upset the sales strategies of the major ad agencies or their clients, because the impoverished ghetto dweller was not part of the buying public that they were trying to reach. It was a Nielsen practice that prevailed well into the television period. As a consequence, it was likely that, even if a program of special interest to those living in the nation's ghettos were to have been presented, the rating system would not have given any indication of that interest.

PROVOCATIVE PROGRAMS

The actions of the Federal Communications Commission tended to narrow program perimeters even further. In its application of the public interest standard to programming, the commission developed what came to be known as the "raised eyebrow" approach. Confronted with allegations of indecency, political bias, unfairness, and other such offenses, the commission would on occasion issue a warning statement or a letter of reprimand.

One incident involved a 1937 appearance by Mae West on NBC Red's *The Chase and Sanborn Hour* with ventriloquist Edgar Bergen and his wooden dummy Charlie McCarthy. She and the dummy traded sexual innuendoes in a sketch about Adam and Eve. West stirred up a storm of controversy with her delivery of such lines as: "Why don't you come home with me? I'll let you play in my woodpile. . . . You're all wood and a yard long." Both the network and the FCC received hundreds of complaints, many of which found their way to the *Congressional Record*. After an informal investigation, the FCC decided the sketch was, in fact, "vulgar and indecent, and against all proprieties." The commission sent a letter to NBC and its affiliates, warning that the program would be taken into account in license renewal considerations.[30]

The FCC created another brouhaha the following year, when it conducted an informal investigation of NBC Blue's radio adaption of Eugene O'Neill's Pulitzer Prize-winning play, *Beyond the Horizon*. The play told of two brothers in love with the same woman. One brother, who had wanted to seek adventure, remains home to marry the woman. The other, more prosaic brother goes to sea and later to South America. In the end, the married brother dies, embittered but happy "with the right kind of release—beyond the horizon." The broadcast script, which closely followed the original text, included such expressions as "damnation," "hell," and "Oh my God!" On the strength of its investigation, the FCC set hearings for the license renewals of 14 of the stations that had broadcast the program. These particular stations were selected because their licenses were due to expire. An outpouring of editorial protest, however, dissuaded the commission from holding its hearings. All 14 stations were granted renewal at the regular time, and there was no further official reference to the broadcast.[31] Nevertheless, such actions on the part of the commission undoubtedly had a chilling effect on attempts at innovative presentations.

CREATIVE IMPULSES

Creativity and experimentation enjoyed freer rein in unsold periods, especially at CBS. *Columbia Workshop*, launched in July 1935 under the supervision of Irving Reis, combined imaginative sound effects with innovative writing. Many of its presentations reflected the tensions of the time. In Archibald MacLeish's half-hour verse play, *The Fall of the City*, a radio announcer (portrayed by Orson Welles) gives an eyewitness account of the arrival of a conqueror. As people prostrate themselves before this armor-clad figure, his visor opens to reveal the helmet is hollow. Presented early in 1937, this play foreshadowed Hitler's march into Vienna.

The summer of 1937 saw a remarkable rivalry between CBS and NBC. Sponsored shows generally went off the air during the summer months, when listenership was thought to be low. CBS used an unsold slot on Monday evenings to present radio adaptations of the works of Shakespeare. The impressive array of actors in the principal parts included Burgess Meredith as Hamlet, Walter Huston as Henry IV, Edward G. Robinson as Petruchio, and Brian Aherne as Henry V. NBC countered with its own Monday-evening Shakespeare series, starring John Barrymore in *Hamlet*, *Richard III*, *Macbeth*, and *Twelfth Night*.

Orson Welles and John Houseman added to the cultural ferment in unsold periods, with their *Mercury Theatre on the Air*. It was presented by CBS on Sunday evenings at eight o'clock, opposite NBC Red's Charlie McCarthy show. Although CBS considered this slot unsalable, many of the *Mercury* presentations were probably heard by millions. Indications of a large listenership came on a Halloween weekend in October 1938, when the program's players presented a radio adaptation of H.G. Wells' science-fiction story *War of the Worlds*. This updated adaptation was presented in a newscast format. A news bulletin interrupted dance music "from the Meridan Room in the Hotel Park Plaza in downtown New York." Several explosions of incandescent gas had been observed on the planet Mars, occurring at regular intervals. More dance music. Another interruption. Then followed an interview with a "Princeton professor." Still another bulletin. A huge, flaming object was reported to have fallen on a farm near Grovers Mill, New Jersey. In a purported on-the-spot pickup from that location, listeners heard of the devastation being wreaked by an army of invaders from outer space brandishing death-ray weapons. The "eyewitness" account was cut suddenly—"due to circumstances beyond our control." Martians, it seemed, had landed on earth.

Thousands of listeners across the country apparently missed or did not listen to the program's introduction, which clearly stated that a dramatization of the Wells novel would follow. They also ignored three additional announcements made during the broadcast, emphasizing its fictional nature. (The first of these announcements didn't occur until a half-hour or so into the program.)

The police, newspapers, and radio stations were swamped by callers seeking advice on protective measures against the invaders.[32]

From Maine to California, terrified people were praying, crying, and fleeing frantically to escape the Martian onslaught. Some donned old gas masks. Others crowded into churches, seeking confession before the end. Sailors on shore leave were called back to their ships. Highways between New York and Philadelphia were jammed with cars. About a million people are estimated to have been frightened or disturbed by the broadcast.

Why were so many people inclined to believe such a fantastic tale? Radio was arguably more suited to the suspension of disbelief than either the print media or motion pictures. Sound effects, fine writing, and excellent acting could uniquely play on a listener's imagination, stimulating a "theatre of mind" unmatched by any other medium. In addition, unlike motion pictures or newspapers, broadcasting mingled both fact and fiction, often within seconds of one another.

A study conducted by the Office of Radio Research at Princeton University soon after the broadcast suggests a multitude of factors that may have contributed to the widespread panic.[33] High on the list of causes cited in the study was insecurity. The broadcast came at a time when Americans had endured years of economic hardship and were facing the imminent threat of another world war. Personality factors also played a part. For instance, those manifesting such characteristics as emotional instability or lack of self-confidence were more likely to believe that an invasion was taking place. The newscast format itself was a crucial factor, of course. People had come to expect that radio would be used in presenting such important announcements.

NEWS AND CURRENT AFFAIRS

In the United States, broadcasting gradually displaced newspapers in the 1930s, as the principal source of information about current events. News and opinion about national and world affairs took many forms: speeches, panel programs, regularly scheduled newscasts, commentary, news bulletins, and on-the-spot coverage of unusual occurrences.

Few politicians used broadcasting to greater advantage than Franklin D. Roosevelt. Soon after his election to the presidency in 1932, Roosevelt gave the first of his famous "fireside chats" over radio. Speaking in the midst of a banking crisis, Roosevelt assured listeners that it was safer to keep money in a reopened bank than under the mattress. Millions found his manner warm and intimate. "It was," according to one observer, "as if a wise and kindly father had sat down to talk sympathetically and patiently and affectionately with his worried and anxious children, and had given them straightforward things that they had to do to help him along as the father of a family."[34]

Roosevelt gave four radio chats during his first year in office. His patrician tone probably sounded condescending to some; but, by most accounts, the persuasive intimacy of these broadcasts did much to help propel New Deal legislation through Congress and avert a collapse of the capitalist system.

During the depths of the Depression, oracles of almost every ideological hue took to the airwaves to argue in behalf of their own social remedies. Among the most persuasive were Father Charles E. Coughlin and Senator Huey P. Long.

Father Coughlin's parish, the Shrine of the Little Flower in Royal Oak on the northern edge of Detroit, served only 28 families when he began broadcasting over WJR in Detroit in 1926.[35] His magnetic voice with its Irish brogue, and the stimulating sermons he delivered, attracted a huge following.

With the onset of the Depression, Coughlin increasingly turned his attention to political themes. For a time, CBS became the provocative priest's pulpit—at regular commercial rates. His bold attacks on international banking and his overtones of anti-Semitism prompted network officials to request advance scripts. Coughlin responded with a broadcast accusing CBS of censorship. His suggestion that listeners write to the network in protest resulted in a deluge of mail.

CBS soon worked out a plan to dispose of the increasingly demagogic priest, while at the same time seeming to open the airwaves to even greater religious freedom. A regular CBS *Church of the Air* series was scheduled. All denominations were invited to share the radio pulpit free of charge, on a rotating basis. Henceforth, no time was to be sold by the network for religious purposes. Coughlin's contract was not renewed.

When NBC likewise refused to sell him time, Coughlin organized his own hookup of stations. By the mid-1930s, he could be heard weekly throughout the nation. At the peak of his power, his income from contributions amounted to some $500,000 a year. At first, he was one of Franklin D. Roosevelt's most ardent supporters. But by 1936, he had become totally disillusioned with the New Deal. That year, he helped form the Union Party, which ran Representative William Lemke of North Dakota for president. However, Coughlin was unable to translate his own popularity into votes at the polling booth for Lemke.

Huey Long, another early Roosevelt supporter who eventually turned against the president, also built a national following through the effective use of radio. Long, first as governor of Louisiana and then as U.S. senator, often used radio to promote his controversial positions. "Hello friends, this is Huey Long speaking," he typically began. "And I have some important things to tell you. Before I begin I want you to do me a favor. I am going to talk along for four or five minutes, just to keep things going. While I'm doing it I want you to go to the telephone and call up five of your friends, and tell them Huey is on the air."[36] His *Share Our Wealth* program promised to provide every family with an income of $2,500 per year and a homestead worth $5,000, through confiscatory taxes on great fortunes. Share-Our-Wealth clubs soon spread into 8,000 cities, towns, and villages. Democrats feared that Long could poll 3 or 4 million votes on a third-party ticket, and possibly even throw the 1936 election to the Republicans. All such fears abated in September 1935, when Long was killed by an assassin's bullet. Roosevelt won reelection by a landslide.

Panel presentations provided another format in which radio listeners were able to hear about matters of current concern. Such programming found it easier to win a place on the national networks in the aftermath of the agitation over the Wagner–Hatfield amendment. Sustaining series like the weekly *America's Town Meeting of the Air*, which began on NBC Blue in May 1935, offered a wide range of opposing opinion on contemporary issues.

Early in the decade, the national networks paid scant attention to daily news coverage. But CBS's special coverage of such events as the 1932 presidential election alarmed newspaper publishers. In April of the following year, the Associated Press withdrew all service to the networks, under pressure from the publishers. The United Press and the International Press Service quickly followed suit.

The radio networks were compelled to set up their own news operations. At NBC, A.A. Schecter became virtually a one-man news department. His newsgathering for Lowell Thomas's evening newscast consisted primarily of making telephone calls. CBS set up a more extensive news organization, the Columbia News Service, under the direction of former United Press editor Paul White. White established news bureaus in major U.S. cities, and had the managers of these bureaus line up stringers (part-time correspondents). CBS also purchased the Dow Jones ticker service, which provided comprehensive financial information, and the services of the British Exchange Telegraph and the

Chinese Central News Agency for coverage of Europe, Asia, Africa, and parts of South America. General Mills agreed to pay for half the cost of the CBS-operated news service, if weekly expenses didn't exceed $3,000. The food company sponsored daily newscasts on the network.

Newspaper publishers, concerned about the success of the Columbia News Service, retaliated by dropping the program listings of local CBS affiliates. They also put pressure on the sponsors of CBS shows. These tactics got results. CBS decided to seek peace with the publishers. NBC, with its makeshift news operation, was even more amenable to negotiation. In December 1933, representatives of the broadcast and newspaper industries met at the Hotel Biltmore in New York City and arrived at a compromise. CBS agreed to disband its burgeoning news operation, and both networks promised to refrain from newsgathering in the future. At network expense, a special Press-Radio Bureau would be set up to cull material from the three wire services for broadcast use. The actual broadcasting of news was to be confined to two five-minute periods daily, one in the morning after 9:30 a.m. and the other at night after 9:00 p.m. These newscasts could not be sponsored. Radio commentators were to be restricted to generalizations and news more than 12 hours old.

The agreement seemed to signal a total victory for the publishers. But they had overlooked a simple maxim: When there is sufficient demand for something in a competitive economy, that demand—barring monopoly—will be met. And there was no monopoly on news. Non-network stations were able to attract listeners to longer newscasts; this, in turn, led to the formation of new and independent newsgathering agencies, such as the Transradio Press Service.

In 1935, the UP and INS joined the competition to sell news to radio stations. The AP, a nonprofit agency controlled by member newspapers, didn't follow suit until the end of the decade. But for all intents and purposes, the compromise agreement had come apart. Soon, even the stations that subscribed to the Press-Radio Bureau were permitted to present news summaries as early as 8 a.m. and as late as 6 p.m. After a few years, the much-maligned bureau quietly expired.[37]

RADIO IN WARTIME

In the months leading up to World War II, the networks greatly expanded their news coverage. In 1938, after the Nazis lunged into Austria, CBS began its multiple-news pickup from European capitals. William L. Shirer was in London; Pierre Huss in Berlin, Edgar Ansel Mowrer in Paris; and Edward R. Murrow in Vienna. Gradually other correspondents and stringers were added, and thus was born the CBS *World News Roundup*. This new concept in news coverage brought the war—or, rather, an audio representation of it—as near as the closest radio receiver.

Night after night, as the tension mounted, and the Nazis threatened to draw the world into war, radio reporters followed every major event. When Hitler demanded cession of a portion of Czechoslovakia called the Sudetenland, and England's Neville Chamberlain and France's Edouard Daladier sought to find a peaceful solution, the story first came to the United States by radio. During those tense days of 1938, network correspondents provided unprecedented round-the-clock coverage. NBC broadcast 147 shortwave pickups from Europe, and CBS 151. Listeners heard the live voices of Hitler, Chamberlain, and other participants. In CBS's New York studio, H.V. Kaltenborn sat before the microphone virtually every hour for 18 straight days. Between September 12 and 30, when Chamberlain returned from Munich with "peace in our time," Kaltenborn made 85 extemporaneous broadcasts about the Czech crisis.

By mid-1939, Czechoslovakia had fallen, Albania had been invaded, and both Adolph Hitler and Benito Mussolini were flaunting their aggressive intentions. On August 21, the Hitler–Stalin neutrality pact was announced; and, by the end of the month, the Nazis had invaded Poland. World War II had begun. In the spring of 1940, Hitler's armed forces invaded Denmark, overran Norway, swarmed through the Low Countries, skirted the Maginot Line, and forced the Third French Republic to surrender.

Live news and on-the-spot coverage of the fighting in Europe kept millions of people close to their radios. Special bulletins, which might interrupt at any point in a program, were presented with the sound of ticker tapes chattering in the background, or with the snap of gunfire and the rattle of tanks forming an auditory cyclorama for the disembodied voices of the radio reporters. It was the beginning of a new era in broadcasting. A 1939 *Fortune* magazine survey indicated that 70 percent of Americans relied on radio as their prime source of news. Some 58 percent of those polled thought that radio news was more accurate than that supplied by the press.[38]

Radio correspondents often scooped the newspapers with reports of major events. On June 21, 1940, when the French surrendered at Compiègne Forest in the same wagon-lit in which the German capitulation of 1918 had taken place, William L. Shirer of CBS and William Kierker of NBC were the only correspondents on hand. Later, in a joint half-hour broadcast, they provided U.S. listeners with a vivid description of the extraordinary scene.

During the London blitz, when the Nazis sent as many as a thousand planes a day to bomb the beleaguered city, Edward R. Murrow broadcast on-the-spot descriptions of the devastation. No other accounts of the air assault, writes Murrow's biographer, "so brought the reality of the conflict home to Americans, or so identified them with a cause that was becoming increasingly a common one."[39]

After the U.S. entry into the war, radio news coverage grew by leaps and bounds. For example: In 1939, NBC broadcast time gave only 3.6 percent over to news programming. By 1944, this figure had jumped to 20 percent (mainly war news, of course). The proportion was even greater on CBS, which gave more than 30 percent of its schedule to war news at the peak of the hostilities.

Radio correspondents became glamorous figures, modern-day Henry Morton Stanleys. The earnest and personal recounting of experiences by the radio men, many of whom were later to develop into deans of the news analysis business, made the war a very real and affecting experience for listeners on the home front. Especially memorable were Cecil Brown's description of the fall of Singapore to the Japanese; Larry Tighe's coverage of the invasion of Okinawa, relayed from a B-29 under heavy enemy attack; Eric Sevareid's account of parachuting out of a transport plane and trekking through the Indo-Burmese jungle; and the voice of George Hick's broadcasting from a warship on D-day.

In December 1941, an Office of Censorship was created by executive order to exercise supervision over information published or broadcast that had any relation to wartime conditions. Compliance was to be voluntary. But of course, this situation could change, if it proved unworkable. Broadcasters, in particular, were subject to stringent controls. In World War I, it will be recalled, radio had been taken over by the government. That this could happen again is spelled out in Section 606 of the Communications Act, which gives the president broad powers over radio in times of war or national emergency.

Drastic measures proved to be unnecessary. Newspapers and broadcasting stations censored themselves, withholding any information that might be of value to the enemy. Early in 1942, the censorship office issued a *Code of Wartime Practices*, in which it listed the type of materials not to be presented. For example, information concerning weather conditions was prohibited. German submarines were known to be operating off the East Coast of the United States. It was believed that weather news could be used by U-boat commanders to determine whether there would be any sailings from seaports. Also banned was information about troop, ship, or plane movements; the location of military bases or fortifications; and all but the most general reports concerning damage from enemy attacks or about casualties incurred by U.S. or Allied forces in combat with the enemy.

Broadcasters were additionally asked to eliminate any ''man-on-the-street'' or other interview-type programs in which people other than station employees or well-known local citizens could have access to a microphone. The purpose of this was to prevent the use of such programs for the transmission of coded messages. Quiz shows, telephone request programs, notices of club meetings, and amateur hours tended to disappear from the air. The networks were especially zealous in adhering to the Code restrictions.

During the war years, there was a high degree of cooperation among broadcasters and government officials. The National Association of Broadcasters promulgated a code in December 1941, forbidding the use of ''frenzied news flashes,'' vivid dramatizations of the news, and ''hysterical mannerisms'' that might unduly affect the listener's peace of mind.

In February 1942, at the suggestion of the White House, a 13-week series called *This Is War* was launched. Each of the half-hour programs in the series was written by or under the supervision of Norman Corwin, a veteran writer-director at CBS. These were carried simultaneously on 700 of the nation's 924 radio stations through the facilities of all four networks. The first program was ''How It Was with Us'' and it extolled the peace-loving, simple nature of the American people. Movie actor Robert Montgomery, as narrator, proclaimed America's essential goodness—even though ''we happen to be pretty good with a gun.'' To audiences familiar with western movies, this philosophy and attitude was easy to understand, and put the war into terms that clarified the desirable behavior and reactions. Subsequent programs saluted the armed forces and evoked the nature of the enemy. Maxwell Anderson, Stephen Vincent Benet, and Philip Wylie were among the literary luminaries who contributed scripts.

Radio was ready-made for propaganda purposes. Some 90 percent of the American people could be directly reached by radio in their homes. Moreover, the Office of War Information's domestic radio bureau enjoyed a much better relationship with the industry leaders than its counterpart did with the Hollywood impresarios.

The OWI published guideline pamphlets for the radio industry thrice monthly. These contained information about such matters of governmental concern as rumors, conservation, and absenteeism. Writers and producers could incorporate this material into scripts, but they were not required to do so. Many cooperated, nonetheless. Among the most pressing problems facing the government on the domestic front was the shortage of manpower. The United States, after years of grappling with high unemployment, found itself without sufficient workers for its war plants. The OWI, seeking to rectify this situation, suggested that serial characters be portrayed in war-related jobs. A number of producers and writers complied.[40] Peggy Farrell of *Front Page Farrell* was one of the first of the soap opera heroines to work in a war plant. Several serials soon followed suit. Stella Dallas's war plant job led to involvement with secret formulas and enemy agents. No attempt was made to determine just how many women were persuaded by these serials to enter the work force. But given the strong identificatory appeal of radio heroines, the number was probably considerable.

A number of popular radio shows adopted the practice of closing with such reminders as "Buy bonds," "Be true to your husband," "Use V-mail," "Stay on your job," and "Save kitchen fats." These appeals proved to be very effective—particularly when they related to matters in which listeners could perform an actual task, such as conservation of fats. (The accumulation of bacon drippings was recycled as glycerine, which was needed to make cannon shells.) Scripts were often adapted to include references to the war effort. On a special Jack Benny show, for instance, his wife Mary Livingston spoke of her dieting uncle, who lost 23 pounds in several days by eating nothing but soup. Playing the straight man, Benny commented, "Nothing but soup? Say, he musta had a lot of will-power." Livingston replied, "No, my aunt gave his teeth to the rubber drive."[41]

The Hummerts worked closely with the public relations division of the War Department, in an effort to reduce racial tensions. At the very same time that the United States was purportedly fighting a war against the racist doctrines of Hitler, the U.S. armed forces were fully segregated. Nazi propaganda made much of this fact; and the natural resentment of blacks was quite overt. In 1942, the cast of the popular daytime serial *Our Gal Sunday* gained the character of a black soldier. He returned intermittently during furloughs, and functioned primarily to provoke conversation between Sunday and her husband about the loyalty of black servicemen to the United States. On *The Romance of Helen Trent*, the character of a black doctor was introduced. He saved the heroine's life and eventually became a staff physician in a war factory. This plot development opened the way for several discussions of the competency, loyalty, and understanding patience of black Americans.

The war provided subject matter for a number of evening adventure shows. *The Whistler, David Harding—Counterspy, The Man Called X,* and *The FBI in Peace and War*—among others—did weekly battle with enemy agents and black-marketeers. As in the movies, the forces fighting the United States were presented in stereotyped form. The enemy seldom seemed like a threat to basic institutions. Ideological conflicts were sacrificed for sophisticated sound effects.

Many children's shows shifted to war-related themes. Dick Tracy became involved with the French underground; Captain Midnight fought the foes of freedom in Japanese-occupied China; Jack Armstrong—"the all-American boy"—was all-American in Pan-America; Little Orphan Annie was captured by the Nazis, and subsequently outwitted them; Superman did battle against the nefarious activities of domestic traitors. Youngsters were likewise urged to save fuel, collect scrap, and otherwise aid the war effort.

One of the most successful wartime radio campaigns was the marathon fund appeal made by singer Kate Smith. On September 21, 1943, CBS sponsored a War Bond Day, in which Smith spoke over the radio at repeated intervals from 8 a.m. until 2 a.m. the next day. Her pleas resulted in pledges from listeners for the purchase of about $39 million worth of government bonds. In a similar marathon a year later, the bond sales attributed to her appeals are reported to have totaled $110 million. A study conducted by social psychologist Robert Merton and his colleagues found that the content of Smith's messages was less important than her radio persona. A significant number of her listeners apparently responded as they did because, for them, she symbolized such qualities as sincerity, patriotism, and benevolence.[42]

Radio's role in furthering the war effort was facilitated by the fact that so many media personnel had entered government service. John

Harold Ryan, for instance, was in charge of the censorship office's radio division. Ryan had been general manager of a group of broadcasting stations owned by his brother-in-law, George B. Storer. Former CBS news correspondent Elmer Davis headed up the Office of War Information. OWI's radio bureau was under the command of William B. Lewis, who had been CBS's vice-president in charge of programming. William Paley himself accepted an overseas psychological-warfare assignment with the Office of War Information. Paley, who achieved the rank of colonel, aided in the preparation of recordings intended to give guidance to resistance groups in occupied lands. RCA's David Sarnoff also went on active duty as a colonel, serving the Pentagon in the capacity of communications consultant and later at the headquarters of General of the Army Dwight D. Eisenhower in Europe. Sarnoff was elevated to the rank of brigadier general in 1944.

SHIFTING STRUCTURES

Wartime relations between the broadcasting industry and government agencies were not always as congenial as they might have appeared to the casual observer. Behind the facade of unity, a bitter battle ensued. In 1941, the Federal Communications Commission concluded a three-year probe of network practices. The commission, by a vote of 5 to 2, demanded a number of reforms.[43] Since the FCC has no direct control over networks, its reform measures were aimed at affiliated stations. No station would be permitted to affiliate with an organization operating two networks; in other words, NBC Red or NBC Blue would have to go. Nor could network contracts require affiliated stations to option more than three hours in each of four day-parts, or to make option time available on less than a 56-day notice. Furthermore, affiliation contracts were to be limited to two years. Such contracts could not prevent an affiliate from accepting programs made available to it by another source. Nor could a network contract prevent an affiliate from rejecting a program it believed to be unsuitable. The networks were thus put on notice that they had better mend their ways.

CBS and NBC challenged the FCC's authority in the courts; and, in 1943, the U.S. Supreme Court found in favor of the commission.[44] NBC Blue was sold to Edward Noble, the Lifesaver candy tycoon, who changed its name to the American Broadcasting Company. Ironically, the sale of NBC Blue actually contributed to the commercialization of broadcasting; RCA had used the network primarily for unsponsored educational and cultural programs. The new management aggressively sought advertiser support.

The sponsorship of programming increased dramatically during the war years, abetted by the interaction of several factors. A wartime "excess profits tax" was enacted. The Revenue Act of 1942 raised the excess profits tax from 60 to 90 percent, the highest point in the history of the United States. Even though manufacturers had few consumer goods to sell, many of them preferred to spend excess profits, which would otherwise have been taxed, on promoting corporate trademarks and goodwill. After much political haggling and intensive lobbying by both advertisers and broadcasters, most advertising was deemed a legitimate business expense. With an eye to the time when consumerism would again be the order of the day, advertisers moved to inform the public that their products were worth remembering and waiting for. Wartime advertising expenditures invariably resulted in tax shortfalls. Since these had to be made up by individual taxpayers, advertising messages were—in effect—being subsidized by the general public. A paper shortage also moved more advertising dollars into broadcasting, since newspapers were not able to accommodate the increased demand.

Broadcasting and advertising emerged from the war more tightly intertwined than ever before. In terms of profit, war was—for radio—good business: Total advertising revenues jumped 85 percent from 1941 to 1945, resulting in before-tax profits that topped 1940 profits by 120 percent. After 25 years, asserted the president of the National Association of Broadcasters in 1945, "if the legend still persists that a radio station is some kind of an art center, a technical museum or a little piece of Hollywood transplanted strangely to your hometown, then the first official act of the second quarter century should be to list it along with the local dairies, laundries, banks, restaurants and filling stations as a member of the town's business family."[45]

The following year, the degree of commercialism in local broadcasting was documented by the FCC, in its report on the *Public Service Responsibility of Broadcasting*—generally referred to as the "Blue Book," because of the color of its cover.[46] The commission called attention to the wide disparity existing in some cases between programming promises made by the stations at the time of their original licensing or when applying for increases in power, and the actual program schedules provided by those stations. Particular stress was laid on the report of advertising abuses. One station that was cited had, in a single week, broadcast 2,215 commercial announcements—an average of almost 17 per hour of operation. Other stations that were mentioned had carried as many as five or six consecutive commercials—with no intervening program material, whatever. The report also noted the failure of affiliated stations to carry educational and cultural programs provided by the networks on a sustaining basis. In most instances, such programming was only carried by about a third of the stations to which it was offered.

The Blue Book very pointedly avoided providing any specific programming requirements. Stations were cautioned against carrying "too many" spot announcements, or against devoting "too great" a proportion of the total broadcasting schedule to advertiser-supported programs.

Release of the report brought howls of protest from the radio industry. An editorial in *Broadcasting*, the industry trade journal, characterized the report as "masterfully evasive" and "vicious." "Have we forgotten so soon," the editorial asked rhetorically, "the fanatical Pied Pipers of destruction who led the German and Italian people down a dismal road by the sweet sound of their treacherous voices on a radio which they programmed?"[47]

For months, sporadic attacks against the Blue Book appeared on *Broadcasting*'s editorial pages. The then chairman of the FCC, Charles R. Denny, Jr., asserted that the Blue Book was here to stay and would not be bleached. Despite such assertions, the standards outlined in the Blue Book were not enforced by the FCC. For most broadcasters, business as usual was the only follow-up. And what of Chairman Denny? In 1947, he resigned from the FCC to become NBC vice-president and general counsel.

Advertising revenues were used by the major broadcasting companies to develop and nurture the nascent television industry. This new form of broadcasting simply inherited the advertiser-supported network structure of its predecessor. As in the heyday of network radio, the needs and expectations of advertisers once again became the prime determiner of program policy. "If such a system had been outlined in 1927 or 1934, when our basic broadcasting laws were written it would certainly have been rejected," as media historian Eric Barnouw reminds us. "Legislative debates of those years reveal hardly a hint of the system that has developed, which has really been the product of a series of faits accomplis, gradually converting a public trust—defined in extremely idealistic terms in the early years—into a private power system firmly based on advertising."[48]

5

On Television

For most residents of the United States—child or adult, male or female—there comes a time each day when they seat themselves before the TV set, turn the knob, and—like modern-day Aladdins—say, "Entertain me." More than any other medium of expression, television fills out the idle hours, providing reassurance and relaxation. It structures not only our general perceptions of the world, but the very patterns of our social existence. The messages and images distilled through this electronic crucible reach us in our kitchens, our living rooms, our bedrooms, and sometimes even in our bathrooms.

We use television in various ways and for different purposes, and therefore presumably feel we are familiar with this medium to which many of us give almost a fourth of our waking hours. And yet, upon reflection, most people will readily recognize that they know little of how the TV industry evolved or how programming decisions are made. What social, political, economic, and technological factors have contributed to television's development? Who determines the nature of television fare? Is there some shadowy figure or, perhaps, some dastardly cabal at the summit of the system, unilaterally exercising control over content? Or can more than one center be found for different types and degrees of power and influence? These and other such questions about the character, structure, and modus operandi of U.S. television are the concern of this chapter.

A MASTER PLAN FOR TELEVISION

Television had been a technical reality since the late 1930s, but the intervention of war impeded its development. The explosive postwar growth of television found the Federal Communications Commission unprepared. In the fall of 1948, as applications for new stations began to pile up, the commission instituted a temporary freeze on the allocation of all new licenses.

At the time of the freeze, there were 108 television stations authorized to go on the air. During the freeze period, 11 cities across the country were without television service. Major cities like Houston, Kansas City, Milwaukee, Pittsburgh, and St. Louis had only one station each. However, New York and Los Angeles each enjoyed seven television stations; and, although the FCC's freeze on new allocations lasted nearly four years, it did not forestall television's ascent into the popular-culture industry's power constellation.

The freeze ended in April 1952, when the FCC unveiled its "master plan" for television. This consisted of 200 pages of fine print and was unimaginatively titled the *Sixth Report and Order on Television Allocations*.[1] Some 70 UHF (Ultra High Frequency) channels, in addition to the 12 already existing VHF (Very High Frequency) channels were authorized. Geographical assignments were included for 2,053 stations: 617 of them on VHF and 1,463 on UHF. Of that number, 242 were designated noncommerical, 80 of those on VHF. (The table of allotments has been amended several times, over the years.) The order also established three broad geographic zones, each with a separate set of requirements for mileage separation and antenna height.

Noncommercial licenses were to be issued only to bona fide, non-profit organizations and to be used primarily to serve the educational needs of the community. Licensees were to transmit cultural, instructional and entertainment programs on a purely noncommercial, non-profit basis. Typically, these licenses were awarded to local and state educational systems, colleges and universities, and community organizations. Activation of the channels went slowly, however, since there were no provisions in the plan for the funding of noncommercial television.

The financial ministrations of the Ford Foundation helped to keep noncommercial television alive in its infancy. In addition to aiding individual stations with construction grants, this foundation financed the establishment of a central agency to secure and distribute programs for the emerging system. Throughout the 1950s and early 1960s, noncommerical TV was almost entirely dependent on Ford funding for general program fare: There was no direct federal support, whatsoever; and private and other institutional financing was minimal and inadequate to sustain station operations for anything other than narrow pedagogic purposes. But despite Ford's financial transfusions, noncommercial TV remained virtually invisible to most Americans. In many large cities—such as New York, Washington, D.C., and Los Angeles—all the VHF channels were licensed to commercial broadcasters. This was a real detriment to development because most TV sets manufactured prior to 1964 required a converter in order to receive the UHF band, and reception was not clear.

In its allocation of commercial licenses, the commission assigned a maximum of three VHF channels to many major metropolitan areas. In practical terms, this meant that there would only be three national networks, since a fourth network would have to rely on UHF stations and thus operate with a severe handicap.

By 1952, NBC and CBS had already lined up their TV affiliates in many of the country's biggest and most lucrative markets. Needless to say, all were VHF stations. ABC managed to hold its own in third place. A fourth network, DuMont, died in 1955—a victim of the FCC's allocation plan.

FORMATS AND TECHNIQUES

Most of the radio's program formats and major stars made a smooth transition to network television. CBS entered the television era with a particularly large reservoir of radio stars, as a result of a competitive coup in 1948 in which William Paley "raided" NBC's comedy talent. In negotiations between CBS and MCA (the leading talent agency), a plan was worked out whereby talent would be sold as "properties" and therefore be eligible for the low capital-gains income tax rate. In the postwar years, those in high-income brackets paid taxes ranging up to about 90 percent. The financial gain from the sale of property, on the other hand, was taxed at much lower rates, ranging up to only 25 percent. In October 1948, CBS purchased *Amos 'n' Andy* outright for $2 million—$1 million to each of its creators and actors, Gosden and Correll. Within a month, CBS also acquired Jack Benny's Amusement Enterprises, which owned *The Jack Benny Show*. The reported sale price was $3.2 million. Burns and Allen, Edgar Bergen, and Red Skelton were also coaxed with capital gains deals into joining the network.

The vaudeville tradition continued on TV with such programs as the *Texaco Star Theatre* starring Milton Berle, whose zany antics made him the most watched entertainer in the nation for several years; *Your Show of Shows* featuring Sid Caesar and Imogene Coca, who offered subtle pantomimes and often hilarious character sketches; and *The Toast of the Town*, an amalgam of variety features supplemented with classical music and dance, hosted by a grim-visaged newspaper columnist named Ed Sullivan. The latter show survived on CBS for almost a quarter of a century.

Crime shows also became a television staple. Jack Webb, creator and star of *Dragnet* (which had premiered on radio in 1949), successfully transferred the low-keyed documentary style of this show to television. Loosely based on actual cases taken from the files of the Los Angeles Police Department, the series stressed the mundane nature of most police work. Its understated, matter-of-fact approach and its use of world-weary, flat-sounding voices were much imitated—and later parodied.

The *Dragnet* series, which ran on NBC-TV from 1952 to 1959, was shot on film. Most early network television shows were done live, which often caused problems in gauging time. The producers of *Man against Crime*, a popular detective series on CBS-TV from 1949 to 1953, compensated for this difficulty by including a search scene near the end of most episodes, the length of which was determined by the amount of time remaining to the close of the show.

To present a show "live"—that is, at the instant of its occurrence—generally involves the use of multiple television cameras to capture the continuous action. This procedure is quite different from traditional feature filmmaking where 50 or so master scenes are each broken down into 6 or 7 smaller scenes, making more than 300 scenes in all. Each fragment of a scene—each "take"—is set up, rehearsed, and shot separately—using a single camera. A completed feature film might consist of 700 or 800 separate shots. Cost efficiency compels a director to shoot scenes out of sequence. The action must follow the expensively constructed sets—for example— instead of the reverse, as occurs in the final editing. High-priced stars who appear only in—say—scenes 3, 8, 32, and 55 represent undue expense when kept idle, so scenes in which such stars appear are shot in close sequence.

Oscar-winning cinematographer Karl Freund pioneered a multiple-camera technique of film production for the phenomenally popular situation comedy *I Love Lucy*, which ran on CBS for six years

(1951-57).[2] This show was staged as a three-act play in front of a studio audience and photographed simultaneously with three 35-mm cameras from different angles. To accomplish this task, Freund devised an overhead lighting system that lit the entire set uniformly. This resulted in a kind of flat, low-contrast lighting effect, as opposed to the more molded, low-key lighting possible with single-camera setups. An average of 7,500 feet of film was shot for each show. In the postproduction stage, the best of the three different angles for every scene were edited together. Meticulous planning and thorough rehearsals usually eliminated the need for retakes or "pickups," as they are called in the industry. The 193 half-hour episodes of *Lucy* that were produced during its original network run can still be seen in hundreds of television markets, every day.

SMALL SCREEN CINEMA

Contrary to common belief, a great deal of what appeared on early television originated on film. Indeed, most television stations filled out their program schedules with old movies.

William Boyd made the big time in this market with his Hopalong Cassidy westerns. Boyd began working in silent pictures in 1919; and, within a few years, his leading-man facial features and prematurely white hair won him romantic roles in such epics as *The Midshipman* (1925), *The Volga Boatman* (1926), and *King of Kings* (1927).

When his career fell on hard times, Boyd donned a black hat, black shirt, black boots, and two big revolvers, and galloped onto the screen as Clarence E. Mulford's pulp-western hero Hopalong Cassidy. Starting in 1935, Boyd appeared in dozens of these inexpensively produced, quickly made westerns. He eventually bought not only the movie rights to the Cassidy character but the television rights, as well. Hopalong Cassidy became the little screen sensation of the late 1940s and a hero to hordes of youngsters across the country. The Hopalong phenomenon left little doubt about the merchandising potential of the television medium. Boyd made millions from royalties on the sale of toy guns, holsters, hats, kerchiefs, and even soap products.

Monogram Pictures released some 300 of its features to television in 1951. This tiny studio, which came into existence in the 1930s, specialized in series pictures. Among its most popular screen personalities were Leo Gorcey, Huntz Hall, Gabriel Dell, and Bobby

Jordan. These screen toughs had first achieved national fame in the film version of Sidney Kingsley's play *Dead End*, a searing indictment of the social evil of slums. After a stint at Warners, where they were featured as the Dead End Kids in such notable films as *Angels with Dirty Faces* (1938), the young actors settled in at the Monogram studio. There they made a series of cut-to-pattern pictures set in the tenements of the Lower East Side of New York City.

From the 1950s on, these films have been a staple of Saturday morning television. Leo Gorcey, who starred in such features as *Clancy Street Boys* (1943) and *Muggs Rides Again* (1945), has proved to be one of television's most enduring attractions.

The westerns of Gene Autry and Roy Rogers also provided ready-made programs for local television schedules. The two cowboy crooners had stomped the sagebrush in a long list of movies made at Republic Pictures, a production and distribution company organized in 1935 by a former tobacco executive named Herbert J. Yates. John Wayne could also claim this studio as his celluloid alma mater. Its most important female star was Vera Hruba Ralston, a former skating champion from Czechoslovakia. In its heyday, Republic ground out scores of low-budget westerns, melodramas, bucolic musicals, and chapter-plays. In 1951, it set up a subsidiary, Hollywood Television Service, to distribute its features and theatrical shorts to television. Within three years, over 350 Republic features had been telecast.

When Republic announced plans to release the feature films of Rogers and Autry to television, the two performers filed separate suits in the U. S. District Court in Los Angeles for an injunction to stop the transaction. They protested the planned release on the grounds that their contracts did not permit the presentation of the features on television for commercial purposes. The district court granted the injunction sought by Rogers, because his contract with the studio expressly forbid the use of his name, voice, or likeness for advertising without his consent. However, the same court refused a similar request by Autry, because the wording in his contract differed somewhat from that of Rogers. The district court decisions were appealed by Republic and Autry, respectively. In June 1954, the Federal Court of Appeals in San Francisco, ruling on both appeals, found in favor of the movie studio. The court permitted editing of the features to allow for commercial inserts and ruled that Republic, as producer and owner of the films, had the right to release them to television. The only stipulation was that the western stars themselves should not appear to be endorsing specific commercial products.[3] Thus judicial sanction was given to the already pervasive practice of chopping up movies into small bits to bracket commercials.

In 1955, the assets of RKO, including the studio's backlog of some 740 feature films and 1,000 short subjects, were sold to General Teleradio, a broadcasting company wholly owned by the General Tire & Rubber Company. General Teleradio wanted the RKO film library for telecasting on WOR-TV's *Million Dollar Movie* series. This non-network station had made its mark in the New York metropolitan area by taking recent movies, new to television, and showing them repeatedly for a one-week period.

The General Tire subsidiary quickly recouped some of its investment by selling the film library to a television distribution firm for $15.2 million. However, it retained rights for exclusive television showings on its owned-and-operated stations in Boston, Hartford, Los Angeles, Memphis, New York, and West Palm Beach. It also retained the first-run television rights to 150 selected features.

The exclusive rights to telecast the RKO films were sold in perpetuity to a single station in each of dozens of markets, thus enabling these stations to build their own permanent film libraries. Stations paid for the films, in part, through the exchange of advertising time. The distribution firm C&C Television had earned an estimated $25 million from the RKO library, by the middle of 1957.

The sale of RKO's backlog of films to television was the vanguard of a large-scale merchandising of film libraries: Columbia released 104 of its features (through its subsidiary Screen Gems) almost immediately after the RKO sale; Warners followed in March 1956, with the $21 million sale of 850 features and 1,500 shorts to PRM, a Canadian investment firm, and to Associated Artists, a television distributor; in June 1956, MGM announced plans to lease—rather than sell outright—750 features and 900 shorts to television; later in the year, Twentieth Century-Fox negotiated a $30 million–plus deal for the transfer of 390 feature films to National Telefilm Associates, licensee for WNTA-TV (operating on Channel 13 in the New York metropolitan area); Universal sold 600 features to Screen Gems in August 1957, with a minimum guarantee of $20 million; Paramount—the last holdout—sold 750 features to MCA outright, for a potential return of $50 million. By the end of the decade, feature films had become a mainstay of local television program schedules.[4]

The three national networks also began to dip into the rich reservoir of theatrical features, on a regular basis. In the fall of 1961, NBC inaugurated Saturday Night at the Movies with the television premiere of Fox's *How to Marry a Millionaire* (1953). Within a few years, all three networks had incorporated theatrical features into their program schedules. Television showings came to be regarded by the movie industry as an extension of the box office, part of the projected earnings for a picture.

TELEFILM PRODUCTION

Hollywood had become intimately intertwined with television in other ways, as well. As early as 1952, Columbia's wholly owned subsidiary, Screen Gems, announced a $1 million deal with Ford Motor Company to produce 39 half-hour television films—"telefilms"—for the *Ford Theatre*. Screen Gems was soon turning out such successful shows as *Rin Tin Tin*, *Captain Midnight*, and *Father Knows Best*. The latter series, which made its network debut in 1954, became the prototype for a plethora of nuclear-family fantasies.

In 1954, the Disney studio and ABC-TV announced plans for a weekly potpourri of cartoons and films, old and new, introduced by Walt himself. This series was intended to promote another Disney-ABC venture, Disneyland Park in Anaheim, California. The weekly Disney program attracted millions of new viewers to the struggling network and was followed, a year later, with an even more successful five-day-per-week series called *The Mickey Mouse Club*. This show attracted so many advertisers that the network realized its first profit.

Warners took the plunge into telefilm production in 1955 with its ABC-TV offering, *Warner Brothers Presents*. The show title was actually an umbrella for three separate series, which played on alternate weeks: *Casablanca*, *King's Row*, and *Cheyenne*. Most episodes of these shows were shot in five days or so, and studio sets were supplemented with old film footage to keep costs to a minimum. When an unknown actor named Clint Walker clicked as Cheyenne Bodie, a phlegmatic frontier scout, the other two shows were dropped. The series became *Cheyenne* and enjoyed a seven-year run on the network. Its success stimulated a spate of similar projects.

All of the big studios joined the ranks of telefilm producers. The 1955-56 season saw the entry of *M-G-M Parade* and *Twentieth Century Fox Hour*. Soon, Paramount started to turn out telefilms, too. United

Artists set up a subsidiary for the financing and distribution of independently produced telefilms. Later, UA was to absorb Ziv Television Productions, which had syndicated such successful spy series as *I Led Three Lives*. Universal's big backlot also became the home of scores of television series. In the mid-1960s, Universal made an arrangment with NBC for the cofinancing of a number of two-hour-long feature films made expressly for television. These "World Premiere" movies proved to be an expedient and resourceful way of testing the potential of possible new series. More than 30 NBC series were developed in this manner. The lines between the making of theatrical features and telefilms were becoming increasingly blurred.

ANTHOLOGY TELEVISION DRAMA

The smaller audiences of the early 1950s permitted some experimentation; and so, the variety shows, westerns, crime melodramas, and situation comedies coexisted with other formats, such as the anthology series. This format has it roots in the legitimate theatre, with each program presented as a complete drama.

Most of the anthology series were produced live, with all editing (camera switching, in this case) being done while the program was in progress. Several cameras would cover the production, from different angles and distances. Tiny studio facilities placed a premium on close-ups and intimate situations. Psychological rather than physical confrontations were stressed. Usually, scripts were selected only if they required a small cast, a minimum of set constructions, few variations in lighting, and the most elementary variety of camera shots to generate an appropriate emotional response.

There is a tendency to look back nostalgically to the anthologies presented in the 1950s as being the epitome of the medium's potential. While there were landmark offerings among these programs—many affecting audiences with impressions that endure to this day, such as *Marty*; *A Man Is Ten Feet Tall*; and *Twelve Angry Men*—anthology programs were not uniformly excellent or, for that matter, uniformly entertaining. However, the anthology series did (more than any other television form) draw upon matters of universal concern; it offered exciting glimpses of what television might aspire to in giving viewers insight into the tensions, fears, and anxieties of average people. Paddy Chayevsky's famous play *Marty*, for instance, deals with the mundane and ordinary life of a butcher from the Bronx. The main characters are typical, rather than exceptional. "I didn't want my hero handsome, and I didn't want the girl to be pretty," explained Chayevsky. "I wanted to write a love story the way it would literally have happened to the kind of people I know. I was, in fact, determined to shatter the shallow and destructive illusions . . . that love is simply a matter of physical attraction."[5]

These glimpses of reality that were permitted within the anthology format may well have contributed to the demise of this type of programming. Advertisers have always been in the business of selling magic. Commercials invariably provide, as media historian Erik Barnouw has noted, "a solution as clear-cut as the snap of a finger: the problem could be solved by a new pill, deodorant, toothpaste, shampoo, shaving lotion, hair tonic, car, girdle."[6] Barnouw suggests that the sharp contrasts between the visions shown in the commercials and the harsher realities in the content of the anthology drama caused advertisers to abandon this type of program as a sales vehicle (the contrast made the commercials seem fraudulent). Advertising and network executives alike became increasingly contemptuous of nuance and ambiguity, those shaded areas of complexity and doubt where the anthology dramas tended to dwell.

Other factors also contributed to the demise of the format. The possibility of expansion into foreign markets created a demand for programs that were easily transplantable to other cultures. England, for example, had adopted a commercial television system in 1955 to supplement the noncommercial British Broadcasting Corporation. Japan and several Latin American countries had also launched commercial systems. Television was about to begin in scores of other countries, as well. The most successful authors of anthology dramas and adaptations—such as Paddy Chayevsky, Rod Serling, Reginald Rose, and Gore Vidal—were naturally sensitive to verbiage and masterfully caught the shadings and subtleties of everyday American speech—but these nuances were often incomprehensible to an overseas audience. On the other hand, series de-emphasizing dialogue in favor of action could be dubbed with little difficulty.

There was also a spreading dearth of quality scripts. Writers for the anthology programs were poorly paid, on the whole. Initially, they welcomed the opportunity to showcase their works; but once they became established, they moved on to movies for more lucrative endeavors. Producers, directors, and actors, too, sought employment in Hollywood, having made their mark in the venturesome moments that appeared more often in the anthology than in other types of programs. When advertisers did invest more money in the anthology (most noticeably as they moved from live to filmed production and, later, to videotaped production), they demanded big-name performers in return for the larger bankroll—which shut out newer talent from the scene.

There was an even more compelling reason for the jettisoning of the anthology. As television audiences began to increase with the sale of more and more sets, the percentage of the viewing audience watching anthology programs began to drop. The growth of a mass audience also meant that a median level of sensibilities had to be presumed by the advertiser; and this sensibility had to be protected from insult, to avoid retaliation in the marketplace. There was less likelihood of offense—philosophical, political, or otherwise—being aroused by a quiz show or an action-adventure series. This was not an insignificant consideration, given the cultural climate of the period.

SEEING RED

The House Un-American Activities Committee—the Congressional agency designated to ferret out communist infiltration into high, potentially influential places—descended on the movie industry early in 1947, in a series of closed hearings.[7] The following October saw the beginning of public hearings, in which a number of "friendly" witnesses outlined what they believed to be examples of communist influence on motion picture content. These witnesses offered very little of substance, and an almost circuslike atmosphere prevailed. Some 19 "unfriendly" witnesses were also subpoenaed to appear. Of these, only 11 were actually called; and the eleventh, denying any communist affiliation, made a precipitous retreat to East Germany. The remaining, mostly screenwriters, refused to cooperate with the committee in any way. Labeled the "Hollywood Ten," they were all eventually tried and convicted of contempt of Congress.

The fledgling medium of television was easily traumatized. Three ex-FBI agents, sensing an opportunity, were quick to capitalize on the trepidations rife in this developing branch of the popular arts.[8] They published a widely circulated newsletter called *Counterattack*, which listed the alleged communist activities and sympathies of those prominent in commerce and industry. Executives in the advertising and television industries responded with particular alacrity to the accusations being made, prompting the *Counterattack* forces to focus most of their energies on the entertainment field. A special edition of *Counterattack* was issued, called *Red Channels*, which read like a virtual *Who's Who* of show business. It listed 151 performers, with "citations" of their alleged communist activities and sympathies. Fear permeated the television industry. Performers were dropped from shows without explanation. Actors, writers, directors, and producers found themselves unemployable, as media organizations began to compile blacklists. Industry personnel were made accountable for their actions and affiliations. Those called upon to explain their citations were only employable if their responses to the inquisitors proved acceptable. Many were given neither the opportunity to contest the charges nor the opportunity to gain further employment. Writers could—and did—find work under pseudonyms; the plight of actors and actresses was particularly onerous, since the only salable thing they had was their identity. Many turned to alcohol. Some, in total desperation, committed suicide. It was a sorrowful period for the entertainment industry.

Television's marketplace perspective had made it particularly susceptible to the frenzy of fear gripping the nation. Not only were the best practitioners hobbled by the witch-hunting atmosphere, but creativity in any form was suspect. The fear of reducing audience numbers or associating the advertisers' products with causes or individuals that might be deemed offensive crippled creativity and impelled a further retreat to formula programming.

SEE IT NOW

Some advertisers—perhaps seeking to gloss their corporate images—were willing to support prestigious programming, even if it attracted a small viewership or provoked public controversy. Alcoa, for instance, backed the *See It Now* broadcasts through several years of intermittent controversy.[9]

This news documentary, which featured Edward R. Murrow, made its debut over the CBS Television Network in November 1951. In the first show, Murrow noted in his introductory remarks that he and coproducer Fred Friendly were "an old team trying to learn a new trade.'' Murrow and Friendly had collaborated on a record album called *I Can Hear It Now*, a forty-minute ''scrapbook in sound,'' which began with Will Rogers discussing the Depression and concluded with General Douglas MacArthur accepting the surrender of the Japanese aboard the battleship *Missouri* in 1945. They had also put together a weekly radio show for CBS called *Hear It Now*, a potpourri of topics of current concern. The premiere telecast of *See It Now*, which was presented as part of the ''cultural ghetto'' of Sunday afternoon programming, featured a live, simultaneous showing of the Golden Gate Bridge and the Brooklyn Bridge. It also included substantive subjects, such as Murrow conversing with CBS correspondents about alleged atrocities taking place during the military conflict in Korea. Gradually the program series, which moved to an early evening time slot during the 1952-53 season, tackled ever more sensitive topics.

During the fall of 1953, the Murrow–Friendly partnership put on *The Case of Milo Radulovich AO589839*. This program dealt with a 26-year-old University of Michigan student who had been asked to resign his Air Force Reserve commission because of unidentified accusations that his sister and father had radical leanings. When he refused to resign, Radulovich was separated from the service, because he was considered a security risk. Although the charges against the young Air Force reservist may now seem absurd, it took courage for Murrow and Friendly to present this case in the chilling cultural climate of the 1950s. Through the exposé of an individual situation, the news team was casting a critical light on the outrages of that whole political phenomenon called ''McCarthyism.''

McCarthyism is the catchall term for the paranoia that prevailed in the United States during the 1950s. The junior senator from Wisconsin, Joseph R. McCarthy—whose name came to symbolize the era—was particularly zealous in his pursuit of alleged communists and subversives in U.S. public and private life. But the practices that McCarthy's name stand for arguably had more to do with postwar expansionism than with the abusive activities of any one individual.

Buttressed by the wartime boom, U.S. businesses began to move aggressively into new markets around the globe. The concept of a ''free world'' became the corporate creed. Freedom—of the seas, markets, trade, and the media—was the pennon of the postwar period. Through such measures as the Truman Doctrine, U.S. foreign policy aimed to curtail and contain the spread of communism, while simultaneously expanding U.S. business interests abroad. Not infrequently, this necessitated the instituting of unpopular measures, such as the shoring up of the regimes of odious dictators. This policy of expansionism abroad required justification at home. A war-ravaged Soviet Union was therefore presented to the U.S. people as posing a direct threat to their national security. The military was especially active in whipping up a tempest of fear.

Murrow and Friendly were never so bold as to expose the roots of postwar paranoia, but they did take on the junior senator from Wisconsin. On the evening of March 9, 1954, *See It Now* presented a special report on Senator Joseph R. McCarthy. The program consisted primarily of juxtaposed McCarthy film footage that highlighted his inconsistencies and his often wild, unsubstantiated accusations. McCarthy was shown browbeating witnesses at Congressional committee hearings, contradicting himself, and resorting to innuendo and malicious remarks.

A key sequence involved the testimony of Reed Harris, an employee of the U.S. Information Agency, who appeared before McCarthy's Senate Permanent Subcommittee on Investigations to answer questions about, among other things, a book he had written in 1932 while an undergraduate at Columbia University. The footage from this hearing, which was referred to as "a sample investigation," showed the junior senator at his browbeating worst. McCarthy singled out a passage from the book, which referred to the institution of marriage as an antiquated and stupid religious phenomenon. Harris had been suspended from his Columbia classes as a result of the book, and McCarthy established that the American Civil Liberties Union had supplied him with an attorney. He asked if Harris was aware that the ACLU was listed as a subversive front. Murrow pointed out that neither the attorney general, the FBI, nor any other federal government agency had ever listed the ACLU as subversive. Throughout the telecast, Murrow did not pay even lip service to journalistic objectivity. There could be little doubt left, at the close, that strongly held convictions motivated him when he said: "This is not the time for men who oppose Senator McCarthy's methods to keep silent. We can deny our heritage and our history, but we cannot escape responsibility for the result."

The following week, a second McCarthy exposé was presented, which showed the senator and his minion Roy Cohn badgering and bullying a seemingly bewildered witness named Annie Lee Moss, who was suspected of being a communist. When Mrs. Moss was asked if she had ever heard of Karl Marx, she responded: "Who's that?" The Senate hearing room regaled with laughter—not at her but, as Fred Friendly explained it, "at the ludicrous situation of this pathetic, frightened woman, suspended from her job, being interrogated as though she were Mata Hari."[10] The program clearly reinforced McCarthy's image as a dangerous demagogue. However, it should be noted that, four years later, the Subversive Activities Control Board reported that Annie Lee Moss had indeed been a member of the Communist Party.[11]

Early in April, McCarthy, accepting an offer of free time, presented a filmed half-hour rebuttal that strongly attacked Murrow. He characterized the journalist as "the cleverest of the jackal pack which is always found at the throat of anyone who dares to expose individual communists and traitors." There's a certain irony in this attack, because Murrow clearly had cold-warrior credentials. He was an ardent supporter of the Truman Doctrine, favored more spending on armaments, argued for a stronger military presence in Europe, and even advocated the right of a president to send military forces abroad without congressional approval.[12] It's testimony to the tenor of the times that a man like Murrow would be labeled a communist sympathizer.

Viewer response to the McCarthy programs was immediate and polarized. CBS was deluged with thousands of telegrams and telephone calls. The general reaction was one of praise for the position taken against McCarthy, but there were also bitter denunciations of Murrow and the network. Threats were even made against Murrow's eight-year-old son Casey; and, for years afterward, the boy always had to be met at school and escorted home.

The McCarthy–Murrow encounter became a national spectacle. Murrow was regarded in some circles as "that traitor." Some months after the McCarthy telecasts, Murrow was the principal speaker at the annual Junior Chamber of Commerce ceremony to honor the year's "ten outstanding young men." As he rose to speak, one of the young men walked out in protest. He was Robert F. Kennedy—who, for several months, had served as counsel to the senatorial committee of Joseph McCarthy.[13]

Throughout the continuing controversy, Alcoa remained steadfast in its sponsorship of *See It Now*. It even held firm when the tobacco industry, a major purchaser of aluminum foil, objected to a two-part report on cigarettes and lung cancer. But its priorities were changing.

Competition in the aluminum industry was increasing, and the company had decided to enter the consumer market. Since it would no longer be just a wholesaler, public controversy assumed much greater importance. At the end of the 1954-55 season, Alcoa bowed out and *See It Now* was dropped from the weekly network schedule.

THE NETWORKS TAKE CONTROL

The loss of *See It Now* from the weekly schedule was all the more pronounced because it had been the only show of its kind on network television. The prime viewing hours were fast being drawn down an ever-widening whirlpool into mediocrity and sameness.

As the number of stations increased, and there was a general rise in viewership, prime-time slots in the program schedule became ever more valuable—that is, they could be sold for higher fees. When the tab for a whole series began to exceed the advertising budgets of all but the biggest sponsors, control over programming gradually shifted from the ad agencies to the networks.

Pat Weaver of NBC led the network forces with his "magazine concept," whereby advertisers bought insertions in programs produced and controlled by the network. The *Today* show, which premiered on NBC-TV in 1952, was set up on this basis. This early morning series, hosted by Dave Garroway, featured a charismatic chimpanzee named J. Fred Muggs. Weaver also established a late-hour beachhead for the new approach with the *Tonight* show, which began as a local program in New York and went on the network in 1954, hosted by Steve Allen. The show became a smash hit in 1957 when an outspoken and emotional conversationalist named Jack Paar took over the hosting chores.

With the shift to network control came a discernible decline in quality and diversity of prime-time programming. "Audience flow" became the order of the day. Evening schedules were carefully constructed to carry over as large an audience as possible from one time period to the next. Such well-regarded shows as *Voice of Firestone* (classical and standard popular music) and *Armstrong-Kaiser Circle Theater* (sophisticated drama) were canceled by their networks for low ratings, despite sponsor willingness to continue support.

The struggle between the networks and the agencies for control over programming came to a climax in the late 1950s with the infamous "quiz show scandals," a series of disclosures that highly popular quiz shows were rigged.[14] Relatively inexpensive to produce and requiring only simple facilities, quizzes shows began to crowd network schedules in the mid-1950s.

In radio, the top prize on quiz shows was usually $64; television upped the ante a thousandfold. On *The $64,000 Question*, which debuted on CBS-TV in 1955, a losing contestant would get a new Cadillac as a consolation prize. Developed by the newly formed Norman, Craig & Kummel agency and then sold to Revlon, this show transfixed viewers with the spectacle of a contestant in an ''isolation booth'' spouting miscellaneous esoterica for big money prizes. Its success soon spawned several imitators, including an NBC-TV offering called *Twenty-One*, which pitted contestants against each other.

It was around the latter show that the first whiffs of fraud and hoax began to surface. Articles in *Time* in April 1957 and in *Look* the following August raised allegations of collusion and question slanting. Herbert Stempel, an early winner on *Twenty-One*, charged that his opponent had been primed with answers. The producers of the show apparently thought that Stempel lacked the kind of personality that would hold viewers, but they were unable to find anyone knowledgeable enough to beat him. Network and advertising agency executives, as well as former contestants, all vehemently denied any rigging. But in 1959, after probing by a New York grand jury and a House of Representatives special subcommittee on legislative oversight, the charges were confirmed. The climax came when Charles Van Doren, a Columbia University professor who had won $129,000 on *Twenty-One*, confessed to the House subcommittee that the show's producer had given him the questions—and sometimes the answers—before his appearance. He admitted that he had even been coached to feign nervousness during the questioning. Other big money quiz shows were also found to be rigged, and several people were indicted for perjury. Those in television's top echelon continued to insist that they had known nothing about the rigging. High-sounding pronouncements were issued, and all such shows were scrapped.

The quiz shows had been the last stronghold of independent production and single sponsorship. In the aftermath of the scandals, the networks assumed a viselike grip over the programming process. With few exceptions, a producer with a prime-time series to sell would now deal only with a network. Final approval of scripts, cast, and virtually all other creative and administrative matters rested with one of three buyers—CBS, NBC, or ABC.

Network executives, most of whom had come up through the ranks via sales, became increasingly committed to programming of the most vacuous sort. The few social-minded weekly series developed and offered by the networks—*The Defenders* (the nature of the justice system); *East Side, West Side* (the cases of a social worker); *Slattery's People* (a state legislator's problems); and *That Was The Week That Was* (lighthearted but sharp topical satire)—were gone by the middle of the decade. In their stead, viewers were offered weekly series with cardboard characters whose exploits rarely raised questions about race or poverty or social justice.

The new breed of executive cadre that assumed power at the networks was exemplified in the extreme by James T. Aubrey, Jr. Named president of CBS-TV late in 1959, the Princeton-educated Aubrey acquired network programming that stressed rural settings, sexy women, and simplistic plots. Typical of his efforts were *The Beverly Hillbillies* (down-home folk who outsmart the city slickers); *Mister Ed* (a talking horse prone to hypochondria); and *Petticoat Junction* (a hotel proprietress with three voluptuous daughters)—all creations of Filmways, a telefilm firm that had started as a producer of commercials. During his years at CBS, Aubrey's cold decisiveness and unsentimental detachment, coupled with his almost inaudible voice, earned him the sobriquet of "the Smiling Cobra." He often lived up to this reputation. When Jack Benny's ratings began to slip, for instance, Aubrey dismissed the comedian with a curt and unceremonious: "You're through." In 1965, Aubrey himself was summarily fired, when several of his shows failed to score.[15]

THE PROGRAMMING PROCESS

Since the early 1960s, there has been unremitting pressure on those who make the programming decisions at the three networks. Jobs are constantly on the line; and television programmers—representing a transitory elite, as they do—know that, if entertainment fare fails to resonate with a mass audience, the axe will surely fall.

Harried executives, seeking ways to predict program success or failure, came to rely on the kinds of data supplied by ASI (Audience Studies Inc.). This Hollywood-based firm tests the "pilots" (sample programs) of proposed series in its Sunset Strip auditorium—a 400-seat theatre with a full-size theatrical screen. Each seat is equipped with a hand-held, black plastic oval case. The dial on the face of the case permits a viewer to turn to any of five positions: Very Dull, Dull, Fair, Good, and Very Good. As the viewer moves the dial to the setting of his choice while watching a presentation, corresponding impulses feed into a computer that instantly registers his reactions on a scale of 1 to 1,000. When viewers fail to turn the dials for any length of time, they are reported to the control booth by ASI personnel patrolling the aisles; and these derelict dial-turners are electronically expunged from the sample. Test audiences are invited to attend in a somewhat random fashion—that is, tickets are distributed at shopping malls, the Universal studio tour, and other places frequented by tourists. ASI also seeks a more stratified sample through telephone invitations.

Although ASI calls its theatre Preview House, the more popular appelation in the industry is "*Magoo* House." This name was given in recognition of the cartoon *Mr. Magoo Goes Skiing*, which has been shown to test audiences prior to the pilot program. If a given audience's responses to the vintage cartoon are atypical, the findings can be adjusted accordingly. At the end of the pilot presentation, questionnaires are passed out: Did you like the show? Do you want to see it as a series? Would you watch it against this or that competition? Over the years, both ABC and NBC have relied on ASI's program tests. CBS has its own similar setup for pilot testing.

ASI-type testing is open to easy criticism. For instance, the assembled group is watching in the knowledge that their dial twisting is being monitored. Also, large screen viewing in a theatre among strangers cannot give the same perceptions as home viewing. Additionally, the limited response options are more suitable for visually oriented, simplistic action than for complex character development. Even more stultifying to creativity and diversity is the inherent bias toward the already familiar. How much we comprehend and what we enjoy depends, in large measure, on what we bring to the viewing situation— our reservoir of everyday experiences and our previous encounters with expressive forms having similar content and conventions. The new and unusual takes time—and often guidance—to appreciate. The initial response of any sample audience representing a cross section of the population to something out of the ordinary is likely to be unfavorable. Yet most pilots are tested—and most series make it on the air—as a result of favorable test data.

Once a network has decided which pilot presentations are likely to draw large audiences, it usually orders 13 episodes for each program series. These new series are then integrated with the survivors from the previous season along with "mini-series" (that is, short-term offerings), "specials," and movies to form the new season's program schedule.

In what has become an annual rite of spring, the networks offer up the new program schedule to the affiliates for their examination. This is most often done in a kind of Saturnalia—presenting the shows and their stars in an ambiance of festive bibulation and revelry. The chant of the networks to their affiliates is: "This year will bring us all the largest number of enthralled audiences ever, if you affiliates will but clear these shows. Your—our—audiences will love the schedule and us, and our advertisers will too. We will harvest the largest profit in our history."

In most instances, the affiliate is more than happy to accept network programming, because the slick, professionally produced offerings of the network attract the large audiences that enable each affiliate to demand high rates from its local advertisers. The network makes time available in each program for the affiliates to sell to advertisers. For carrying (the industry term is "clearing") its programs and commercials, the network generally gives the affiliated stations approximately 30 percent of the rate that they would receive by selling to advertisers directly. An affiliated station, it should be noted, does not make most of its profits from this network compensation. The bulk of a station's revenue derives from two sources: the sale of local time in and around the network programs; and the sale of local time on its own presentations, in those hours when the network programs are not carried. Although the affiliate is dependent on the network for program material, the arrangement is symbiotic: Without the audiences provided by the local stations, the networks could not reach the mass audiences that "validate" the high advertising rates that constitute the profit income. Collectively, the affiliates wield a certain power over the networks, since by law they are able to reject any network offering. If a substantial number of affiliates reject a network program, it can mean a drastic reduction in advertising revenue, because what the network is selling to the advertiser is people. Network expenses are fixed, regardless of the size of the audience. It costs no more to reach 40 million people than it does to reach 10 million people. Affiliate clearance, then, means bigger and bigger profits: Full clearance means maximum profits. To assure affiliate clearance, the networks tend to avoid programs that might cause problems. A proposal for a program on "The Life and Times of Tom Hayden," for instance would most likely not move beyond the concept stage.

Each of the three television networks has its own standards and practices department, which is responsible for clearing all material to be aired. Entertainment programs, as well as commericals, are generally reviewed from script through final production and editing. Whenever a particular show or series or made-for-television movie is expected to include sensitive or controversial subject matter, discussions are held with the producer to ensure that the final product will conform with network standards. Advertisers, in turn, must provide the network with substantiation or documentation for all affirmative claims made for a particular product. All three networks, along with many stations, exercise a right to reject issue-oriented commercials.

INNOVATIVE PROGRAMMING

Of course, commercial imperatives can conspire with, as well as against, those seeking to place innovative programming on the networks. By the late 1960s, for instance, demographic data had become more important to network advertisers than gross head counts. Most advertisers sought programs that appealed to economically active viewers—people with money, people with flexible tastes, people open to advertising's blandishments. As a result, the networks started to stress prime-time shows aimed at urban and suburban residents in the 18- to 49-year-old range, because they—presumably—spend the most money.

NBC hit the new demographic target with such shows as *Rowan and Martin's Laugh-In*, which assaulted viewers with a rapid-fire kaleidoscope of one-liners, song fragments, silly skits, and graffiti painted on the undulating body of a go-go dancer. Much of the humor was of a sexual nature. Scatologically suggestive catch phrases like "Look that up in your Funk and Wagnalls" and "Sock it to me!" were oft repeated. Comedians Dan Rowan and Dick Martin lent a continuity of sorts to the visually complex collage. The show was the smash hit of the 1968-69 season.

All three networks scrapped shows that appealed primarily to older, poorer, and rural people. CBS made the most sweeping changes: *The Beverly Hillbillies, Petticoat Junction, Gomer Pyle, Mayberry RFD*. All these popular pastorals disappeared from the network's evening lineup in the early 1970s. The shows of Red Skelton and Jackie Gleason were also canceled, because advertisers considered the two comedians over-priced for the kind of demographics they delivered. Instead, CBS sought programming with the potential to tap the young adult and urban market. A notable result of this new approach was the series *All in the Family*.

This show was modeled after a hit BBC-TV series, *Till Death Do Us Part*, in which the central character is a cockney hatemonger. Bud Yorkin and Norman Lear, a producing-writing-directing team with a long list of credits, bought the adaptation rights and took the concept to ABC. This network financed two versions of a pilot episode at a total cost of $250,000. Both tested poorly, and the project was dropped as too risky and unorthodox.[16]

The second version of the pilot featured the now familiar cast, whose fine acting has since made so many viewers care about the well-drawn characters and situations. Carroll O'Connor was especially ef-fective as Archie Bunker. Camera close-ups captured every nuance of emotion in his marvelously expressive face—incredulity, exasperation, astonishment, and even vulnerability. It was the latter trait that seemed to belie the character's blunt language and blasphemies. For all his surface simplicity, the bigoted Bunker was a complex comic crea-tion.

The subject matter dealt with many topics that were taboo on television. In the opening scene, for instance, son-in-law Mike Stivic tries to persuade his wife Gloria to have Sunday morning sex while her parents Archie and Edith Bunker are in church. When the Bunkers come home early—Archie didn't like the sermon—they are greeted by Mike zipping up his trousers as he descends the stairs from the second-floor bedrooms. Interspersed throughout the episode were Archie's at-tacks on welfare chiselers, Jews, blacks, and atheists—among others. His epithets included: "If your spics and your spades want their rightful share of the American dream, let them get out there and hustle for it, just like I done. . . . I didn't have no million people marchin' and protestin' to get me my job." Such bigoted outbursts were softened somewhat by Edith's humorous responses: "No, his uncle got it for him." Later, Archie asserts: "I wouldn't call your black beauties lazy. It just happens their system is geared slower than ours, that's all." When Mike objects to the racial reference, Edith offers: "It's nicer than when he called them coons." The expletive "goddam" was also used several times.

This kind of stuff was not likely to score well in television's testing system. But Norman Lear, the guiding spirit behind the show, was not deterred. His agent took the pilot to Robert D. Wood, the recently installed president of CBS-TV, who was groping toward an approach to programming that would capture the desired demographic composition. The pilot tested below average at CBS's small screening room in New York City, but Wood sensed a potential smash and decided to buy the series, anyway. It was scheduled early in 1971 as a mid-season replacement; the pilot was used as the premiere episode, although the zipping of the pants and the profanity were deleted.

Anticipating clearance problems, CBS arranged a special showing for its affiliates. Extra switchboard operators were hired, to handle any possible public protest that the premiere telecast might provoke. Moreover, a voice-over commentary was run with the opening credits: "The program you are about to see . . . seeks to throw a humorous spotlight on our frailties, prejudices and concerns. By making them a source of laughter we hope to show—in mature fashion—just how absurd they are." CBS received relatively few complaints and even some compliments. The initial reviews were mixed, however. *TV Guide*'s Cleveland Amory waxed enthusiastic: "Not just the best-written, best-directed and best-acted show on television, it is the best show on television." The strongest condemnation came from John Leonard, writing under the by-line "Cyclops" in *Life* magazine. He called it "a wretched program" in which "bigotry becomes a form of dirty joke."[17]

Network brass had little vested interest in such reviews. Commercial television is in the business not of creating critically acclaimed programs, but of supplying audiences to advertisers. "To the critic," as industry analyst Les Brown has noted, "television is about programs. To the broadcast practitioner, it is mainly about sales. This explains why most critics have nothing important to say to the industry and why, among all the critics in show business and the arts, the television reviewer is probably the least effective."[18]

All in the Family was a slow starter; but, by summer reruns, it took the lead in the ratings race. In its first full season, it was the most watched series in the nation, a position it held for five years. While maintaining its situation comedy format, the show tackled such serious topics as bigotry, molestation, impotence, menopause, draft evasion, cancer, and death.

Like all weekly series, *All in the Family* eventually became routine and predictable. But individual episodes provide clear proof that popular culture can be both pointed and entertaining. Weekly series such as *The Mary Tyler Moore Show* (the trials and tribulations of a 30-ish career woman working in a Midwestern TV newsroom), *M*A*S*H* (the high jinks of some cynical civilian surgeons who have been drafted for service in the Korean War), and *Hill Street Blues* (the grim reality of police work in an urban ghetto) also broke new ground. The latter show, in particular, deftly handled disturbing issues while maintaining a sense of humor. Its emphasis on characters rather than cases, and its convincingly realistic dialogue and insightful but restrained pathos, served to underscore the stubborn sameness of a large part of the television schedule.

The risks and the potential rewards of producing for network television are great. The producer of a prime-time series rarely recovers expenses on the initial network sale, because the license fee paid by the network covers only about 75 or 80 percent of the production cost. However, after two showings on the network, the rights generally revert back to the producing company. Assuming the series is a success, the producer can later make syndication deals—selling the show on a station-by-station basis. A 100-program package of a popular series can bring as much as $100 million or more in domestic and foreign sales. A smash hit such as *The Cosby Show* may eventually earn $400 million, when it is sold in syndication. However, the period from initial network presentation to eventual profits from syndication is a long one. Generally, a show must run on the network for at least four seasons before there are enough episodes to make it salable in the syndication market.

The high-stakes marketplace of network television operates systematically to consolidate the position of those producers who are already well established. Those without a substantial capital base simply cannot hope to participate effectively. In consequence, most network shows are produced by the big studios and a score (or so) of smaller companies that have managed to make a mark in the industry. There is a definite aversion to outsiders—despite the fact that, in some seasons, as many as two-thirds or more of all new series vanish because of inadequate audience numbers.

PLAYING BY THE NUMBERS

Once a program is on the air, the two sets of numbers that provide the quantitative yardstick of success or failure are known in the industry as the "rating" and the "share."

The rating represents the percentage of households tuned to a particular program in a given time period, from the universe of households equipped to receive television signals. For a national or network program, the universe is the total number of television-equipped households within the contiguous 48 states; for local ratings, it is the number of TV households in the station's coverage area. If *Murder She Wrote* has a national average audience rating of 26.1, for example, this figure means that an estimated 26.1 percent of the nation's 86 million or so TV households were tuned to that program during an average minute of its telecast.

The share (short for "share of audience") is a comparative and, hence, competitive figure—representing how programs performed, relative to the other programs in the same time period. Whereas the rating is a percentage of all TV households, the share is based only on those households using television at a specific time. Let's say, for purposes of illustration, that there are 100 TV households in the United States and that 30 of them are tuned to *Miami Vice*. This means that *Miami Vice* has a 30.0 rating. But of those 100 TV-equipped households, only 60—say—are actually using television during *Miami Vice's* time slot, which means that *Miami Vice* has 30 out of the 60 households with sets in use, or a 50.0 share of audience.

The A.C. Nielsen Company, which was acquired by Dun & Bradstreet in 1984, emerged as the most influential audience measurement service in the television industry. Nielsen Audimeters are attached to television sets in 1,700 sample households nationwide and are able to record when each set is turned on and to which channel it is tuned. Sets are monitored continuously at one-minute intervals, in order to keep accurate track of channel switchings. Each meter is linked by means of telephone lines to Nielsen's main computer center in Dunedin, Florida. At least twice a day, a central office computer dials each meter in the sample and retrieves the stored data. A processing computer organizes the data and generates the many reports that the research company issues. Nielsen is able to provide rating and share information within a time period that ranges from overnight to one to two weeks.

Since the Audimeter is unable to specify who (if anyone) is watching, Nielsen uses a second sample of 3,200 households that keep diaries one week a month, on a rotating basis. When the television set is on, each diary household is expected to record in a printed ledger such information as the age and sex of each family member who is watching. The demographic data culled from the diaries are used to compile a profile of the viewing audience for each program.

Network executives use the Nielsen data to determine national advertising costs. Individual television stations establish their local advertising rates and their network programming compensation based on the results of what the industry calls "sweeps"—ratings that are compiled simultaneously for virtually every station in the nation, four times a year. The local viewing data from each sweep are used by the stations to establish their advertising rates for the next quarter. Each sweep covers a four-week period, and the samples are drawn from telephone directories—in contrast to Nielsen's national samples, which are drawn from U. S. Census Reports plus interim census updates. A number of large markets are also metered, to provide daily and weekly reports on estimated audiences. (Arbitron, a rating service in business since 1948, also surveys over 200 television markets each fall, winter, and spring and summer.)

An industry organization known as the Electronic Media Rating Council—made up of representatives from the networks, stations, cable companies, and ad agencies—keeps watch on the operations and methodology of Nielsen and the other rating services. Its main objective is to maintain and improve the quality and credibility of audience measurement techniques.

The Nielsen numbers are a key factor in virtually every decision made in the television industry. Not only do programs rise and fall by these figures, but so also do the careers of administrators, producers, directors, writers, and actors. Who advances, how far, and when rides on the ratings, because the loss of a single rating point in a network's seasonal rating average can mean a difference of many millions and millions of dollars. Even the stock market prices of the networks' parent companies rise and fall according to the ratings.

The seemingly small samples used by Nielsen to estimate the viewing habits of more than 86 million households are statistically sound within a small margin of error, provided that the sample is random—that is, each and every member of the population being measured has an equal chance of being included in the sample. An estimated 30 percent or so of the households asked by Nielsen refuse to allow the Audimeter to be installed. On top of this, many diaries are not usable, because they are filled out incorrectly or not returned, at all.

The unresolved question is whether or not people who refuse to have a meter on their sets or neglect to return the diaries have viewing habits different from those who effectively participate in the sample.

The accuracy of diary data is further diluted by the dozens of choices now offered by cable television: Respondents are simply less able to remember and record accurately the decisions they make about viewing. Moreover, the growing use of video cassette recorders, allowing viewers to rearrange personal television schedules for their own convenience, has spawned increased doubt about both meter and diary data. This new technology is particularly perturbing to advertisers, because viewers who tape programs off the air to watch later can use their fast-forward button to whiz past commercials.

The tax that new technology has put on old audience research techniques has thrown the television industry into turmoil. Pressure from advertisers has prompted the introduction of new ways of determining the size and composition of television audiences. In December 1984, Audits of Great Britain Research (AGB), the dominant television research company in Europe, began tests in the United States of a sophisticated electronic device colloquially called the "people meter"—a small hand-held keypad, on which viewers punch a code to indicate their presence in front of a television set. When a viewer stops watching or steps away from the set, he is expected to punch the keyboard to record his activities. Arbitron and A. C. Nielsen have since introduced their own versions of the people meter. How many and what kinds of households will choose to participate in people-meter polling remains to be seen. In any case, even if the people meter does provide a more accurate indication of the atomized viewing habits of the 1980s than the data from diaries, it will doubtlessly do little to diminish the avarice behind the use of audience research.

As long as profit is the prime motivation for programming, rating and share figures will continue to be studied with fervid intensity, in a numbers game that has little to do with audience enfranchisement. If a network comes in third in the competition for share of audience (even if its program offering has attracted millions of viewers), this will be regarded as nonmaximization, since network nabobs will surmise that advertising revenues could have been greater. According to an industry rule of thumb, a show must have a share of at least 25.0 to survive. (The networks' combined share of the national prime-time audience has dropped in recent years, from 90 to 75 percent.) Series that consistently fall below that figure are usually removed from the schedule, sometimes after only four or five episodes have played.

In today's competitive environment, series such as *The Mary Tyler Moore Show* (1970-77), *All in the Family* (1971-79), *M*A*S*H* (1972-83), and *Hill Street Blues* (1981-)—all of which started out slowly—would probably not have the opportunity to build their audiences. "As on Broadway and in the bookstores, a combination of profit pressure, fierce competition, and rising costs gives new goods less and less time to prove themselves," notes Todd Gitlin in *Inside Prime Time*. "All the more pressure on the medium to cater quickly, unambiguously, to whatever composition of audience taste seems to rise to the surface at a given moment and holds out the possibility of being measured simply."[19]

THE NIGHTLY NEWS SHOWS

Commercial television's overarching concern with delivering people to advertisers affects the style, form, length of treatment, sequencing, and overall duration of news presentations, as well.

Network newscasts did not enjoy a high priority in the fledgling television industry. CBS and NBC offered modest news presentations at the early edge of prime viewing hours. CBS's 15-minute news program was called *Television News with Douglas Edwards*. On NBC, suave, boutonniered John Cameron Swayze went "hop-scotching the world for headlines" on the 15-minute *Camel News Caravan*. Both shows relied heavily on newsreel organizations for pictorial content. The government also supplied film footage about world events.

In 1954, when ABC set up light entertainment to compete with the CBS and NBC newscasts, those two networks showed a drop in viewership. To win back viewers, they shifted their news programming to an earlier hour and quickly substituted entertainment shows in the slots formerly held by the news.

NBC and CBS did not lose all viewers, but—again—the goal for any network or station is to attract and hold the maximum number of viewers. That is the bait for advertising dollars. The public virtue in offering news programs at hours of prime viewing yielded (with no struggle) to the private acquisition of more money. Nor, in the commercial system, could any other action have been considered feasible. Not only the networks, but their affiliated stations, demanded (and still demand) programming that will draw the largest possible percentage of the viewing audience.

However, the financial considerations were not so simple as they may at first seem. Networks had generally provided their affiliates with 3½ hours of evening programming, beginning at 7:30 Eastern Time. (The amount of programming that an affiliate might accept from the network in prime time was not reduced by the FCC to three hours until 1970.) When the networks moved their news programs to an earlier hour, the network news usurped profitable local programming. As a rule, the affiliates utilized the time before the network offerings for locally originated news programming. Local news not only meets the Federal Communications Commission criterion of ''serving the public interest,'' but it is also profitable in itself. These programs can boast of a fairly high viewership, and the advertising revenue from local programming goes directly to the station. The preemption of local time for network news programming, then, often means a loss in local advertising income. The further the local news offering is moved from the prime viewing hours, the less profitable it becomes, since fewer people are in the viewing audience.

Each network, for its own part, would like to expand its nightly news show. The cost of gathering the news is prodigious. To justify this expense, in 1963 the networks increased their evening news from 15 minutes to a half hour. (ABC did not go to the half-hour format until 1967.) While this move meant that the networks could sell more advertising time to meet the costs of their news operations, it resulted in a further shrinking of the time available for local news scheduling. The networks would actually like to expand their national news programs to 45 minutes or even a full hour. This expansion would give the networks greater utilization of their highly paid on-camera personnel (some of whom make upwards of two million dollars a year), and would bring in still more money from advertisers. This prospect is especially appealing to network organizations because the added cost of expanding the news would not be significant at all. And even an extra quarter-hour of news time would bring in many millions in expanded advertising fees.

However, while (on the whole) accepting the expansion of the national news coverage to a half-hour, the local stations served notice that no further violations of their financial territory would be tolerated. And managements of the affiliated stations continued to express their opposition to any further extension of network news time. As a CBS-TV affiliate executive dramatically declared in 1976 when the network was making one of its periodic pushes for expanded coverage, ''If CBS announced it was going to 45 minutes this fall, and wouldn't make 15 minutes optional, I'd cut my wrists and jump out the window."[20] Most affiliates still oppose the idea, some vehemently.

Wounds in the treasuries of affiliated stations have been soothed somewhat by the growing popularity of network newscasts. Television does not require the concentration of reading; and, through the use of arresting images, the viewer can receive the impression of being closer to national and international events than any newspaper can hope to accomplish. Nor can newspapers ever expect to compete with the timeliness of network news presentations. The launching of Telestar I in 1962, followed by other more sophisticated satellites, has made it possible to transmit news instantaneously from almost anywhere in the world directly to a network broadcast center.

It is little wonder that, since 1963, the network newscasts have become the primary source of information on national and world affairs for the majority of people in the country. To support this growing stature, the network news organizations try to give the impression that they are girdling the globe with their cameras and crews. The blunt truth is that many places are just too expensive to reach or to transmit from, or too distant from the newsgathering teams that are based (for reasons of economy) only in the major centers of the world.

Within the limits of their budgetary leash, journalists and camera crews look for the eye-catching moments that will capture the viewer: This footage is then refined by film (or video) editors, who remove all less-active moments—trimming and pruning the existing material to underscore its action appeal. The emphasis is on the visual. Events that do not lend themselves to visual representation tend to be short-changed. The eye of the viewer must be amused, amazed, and mesmerized.

This emphasis on the visual results in a particular style of news, a particular type of news—that which is visually full of drama or emotional appeal. This visual presentation operates to put the strongest emphasis on shocking the senses, not on challenging the intellect; favoring crude action and reaction over perceptive thought; focusing on happenings rather than concepts. Subtlety and nuance are sacrificed for the broad visual sweep in network television's presentation of news.

The appeal of network newscasts is further enhanced by the authoritative presence of "anchor persons." The title far exceeds their actual contribution to intelligibility or coherence in the news; but their mellifluous tones and pontifical manner, creating an aura of reasoned intellect, make them extremely valuable show-business assets. Dan Rather, Tom Brokaw, and Peter Jennings are stars—and are paid and treated as such. Their personal followings help to draw large numbers of viewers to the television tube. Earnestly or masterfully, they disguise the patchwork composition of the news, giving it a semblance of continuity, cohesion, and congruence.

Even the venerable Walter Cronkite has bemoaned the inflated role of the anchor in television news. "I think," he said, "that it would be absolutely splendid if you got rid of the anchor person entirely and found some other way—subtitles or voice-over—to do the broadcast."[21] His remark is a telling one. Television network anchors often do little more than read headlines. National Public Radio's *Morning Edition*, with Bob Edwards, has demonstrated that an anchor can contribute significantly to making the news something more than merely an array of isolated tidbits. But network television's predilection for slick packaging precludes the possibility of a more substantive role for on-camera news personnel.

Local news shows are even more show-business oriented than their network counterparts. A random sampling of local news shows could easily lead one to conclude that the only criterion necessary for on-camera personnel is a fortuitous arrangement of facial components. The theatrical element in local news is becoming increasingly apparent. Male as well as female newscasters are carefully coiffured and garbed in what are perceived to be the audience's conception of the latest fashions. What the local station managements strive for is the creation of an image: the up-to-date newscaster who is seen by the audience as sophisticated, scintillating, suave, and—above all—the epitome of show biz. The rising numbers who habitually rely on the television medium for news and information are of increasing importance to the local stations, as well as to the networks. As a consequence, the scramble for local news audiences has become fiercely competitive. Local news can no longer be left in the hands of "newspersons" who have little or no training in how to build an audience. Audience popularity is now as important a criterion for employment of the local on-camera news reporter as it is for performers in entertainment programs.

As local news programming has become a more profitable vehicle for advertising, these programs have expanded from 15-minute to half-hour or one-hour shows and even (in New York City, for instance) to two hours. This increase in program time should not be interpreted merely as an increase of news coverage. Primarily, the expansion makes available more opportunities for commercial "messages," thereby steadily increasing revenue to the station. Obviously, the responsibility for maintaining programming that will attract and hold large audiences could no longer be safely entrusted to professional news directors and producers, alone. As media critic Ron Powers has noted, "The biggest heist of the 1970s never made it on the five o'clock news. The biggest heist of the 1970s *was* the five o'clock news." What he meant was, he continues, "The salesmen took it. They took it away from the journalists slowly—and with such finesse that nobody noticed until it was too late."[22]

Unscheduled news events such as a presidential assassination or a space shuttle disaster are resented by sales divisions at both the network and station level, and are regarded as intruding into the entertainment schedule—because preemptions result in interrupted and diminished flow of profit. Only in exceptional instances of unquestionably essential newsworthiness does the news event itself dictate the amount of its own exposure. When this does happen, a great deal of time may be expended on coverage of the event, but it remains just that—an event.

At the network level, those who are officially in charge of news are not permitted to make decisions unilaterally. Permission to run beyond the regular half-hour news stint requires approval by executives higher up in the corporate structure. Anyone who might wish to ascend the heights inside the news division must have sensitivity to profit-and-loss ledgers; so, in fact, conflicts over preemption rarely arise. When a dispute may chance to occur, it seldom reaches the ears of the outside world. Network policies are generally implemented quietly and effectively, attracting little or no publicity that might disturb the public picture of reassuringly authoritative unanimity.

Although many journalists of integrity and quality still toil in television land, they do so tightly hobbled by the strictures of the medium's mercantile orientation. The illusion is created of a freewheeling system with great tolerance for freedom of the press; in practice, the styles of news presentation, taken together with the stringent limitations of time and the frequent commercial intrusions, too often act—in themselves—as powerful censors.

THE RELUCTANT REGULATORS

This preoccupation with profitability raises perplexing problems of freedom, control, and responsibility. Under the Communications Act of 1934, as amended, the Federal Communications Commission would appear to have broad and extensive powers: It may issue cease-and-desist orders, impose monetary forfeitures, deny license renewals, and even revoke licenses in mid-term. However, its actions must be reconciled with constitutional and statutory limitations. Moreover, most of its members have shown little interest in change or reform. Indeed, the commission (whose members are appointed by the president with the advice and consent of the Senate) has gained a reputation for being—by turns—timid, vacillating, and overly protective of industry interests in carrying out its regulatory responsibility. For the most part it has treated licenses as private property—although they are not, in law—and, short of deliberate deception or flagrant infractions of its rules and technical requirements, renewal has been almost automatic.[23]

Some commissioners have even been corrupt. In January 1958, the House Committee on Interstate and Foreign Commerce's Special Subcommittee on Legislative Oversight began an investigation of the regulatory commissions and agencies, including the FCC. New York University professor Bernard Schwartz was brought to Washington to conduct the probe.[24] Professor Schwartz found that the chairman of the FCC, John C. Doerfer, was himself guilty of improprieties: Files and expense vouchers indicated that Doerfer had billed the government for travel expenses that had already been reimbursed by industry groups, on his speaking engagements. Schwartz also found evidence that FCC commissioner Richard Mack had accepted a bribe for his vote on a disputed Florida television channel assignment. When the subcommittee seemed unlikely to act on his findings, Schwartz "leaked" his evidence to the New York *Times*; he was summarily fired. Nevertheless, his action caused continuation of the investigation, and both Doerfer and Mack were eventually forced to resign.

THE MINOW MOMENT

Not all commissioners have been totally ineffectual, however. Take, for example, the case of Kennedy appointee to the chairmanship of the FCC, Newton Minow. Named to the post in 1961, Minow immediately began to build a reputation as anything but a rubber-stamp bureaucrat for broadcasting interests. His first speech to the National

Association of Broadcasters, one of the capitol's most powerful lobbies, reminded the assembled broadcasters that: "You earn your bread by using public property. When you work in broadcasting, you volunteer for public service, public pressure, and public regulation." After warning NAB members that his purpose was not to "make life easier" for the owners and operators of broadcasting stations, Minow chided the assemblage that their TV offerings were formulaic; full of unbelievable characterizations, unnecessary mayhem, and violence; and over-burdened with commercials—in short, a "vast wasteland." Reminding his audience that they knew how to present better material, Minow bluntly stated: "Gentlemen, your trust accounting with your beneficiaries is overdue. Never have so few owed so much to so many." The new FCC head made clear to his listeners that license renewal would no longer be a matter of routine.[25]

In the first year of his term, Minow (adroitly maneuvering) managed to force the sale of a commercial channel in the New York metropolitan area to a committee of prominent citizens organized under the name Educational Television for the Metropolitan Area (ETMA). When National Telefilm Associates (the licensee of WNTA-TV on Channel 13 in Newark, New Jersey), announced in February 1961 that the station was up for sale, ETMA made an offer of $4 million. The rejection of this offer set in motion a series of bids, counterbids, and various intentions to bid. Producer-performer David Susskind, with the support of Paramount Pictures, offered $6 million. A group headed by Ely Landau, who had recently resigned his post as NTA's board chairman, submitted a bid of $7 million. Former film star Frances Langford and her husband Ralph Evinrude, the head of Outboard Marine Inc., also expressed an interest in the station. Meanwhile, ETMA had increased its bid to $5.5 million.

Determined to see the educational group win out, Minow came up with an effective way to circumvent legislative limitations on the FCC's role in license transfers.[26] Exercising its prerogative under Section 403 of the Communications Act, the commission issued a "notice of inquiry" and it scheduled hearings to assess the possibilities of securing noncommercial VHF television outlets in New York and Los Angeles. Applications for license transfers in those cities would be held in abeyance until the inquiry was completed. The prospect of lengthy hearings persuaded Susskind and Landau to withdraw their bids. NTA, which was in dire financial straits, decided to accept ETMA's offer. The agreed-upon price for the license and facilities was $6.2 million. Most of New York's commercial stations—in an obvious effort to eliminate a potential competitor for advertising revenue—made contributions to the educational group. These stations received assurances from the Department of Justice that the contributions would not be construed as restraint of trade. The only other obstacle to Minow's maneuver was Governor Robert Meyner of New Jersey, who attempted to block the transfer because ETMA planned to center production in New York City. (Channel 13's transmitter was already atop the Empire State Building.) Meyner's efforts were unsuccessful but he did manage to win some concessions, including pledges of service to New Jersey viewers and the addition of representatives from that state to the station's board of directors. In December 1961, Minow had the satisfaction of seeing Channel 13 transferred to ETMA. Effective entry into the New York City area was a major breakthrough for noncommercial television.

In the following year, Minow advocated and saw the passage of the Educational Television Facilities Act of 1962. This legislation authorized $32 million in matching grants over five years to aid the construction of university, school, state-agency, and community-controlled stations. With this financial foundation in place, the number of noncommercial outlets on the air jumped from 75 in 1962 to 124 at the close of 1966. In another move to encourage a more open television system, Minow and the FCC convinced Congress in 1963 that all sets manufactured after April 1964 should have reception facilities for UHF channels. This reopened competition, since all desirable VHF channels had been granted.

While Minow's accomplishments cannot be denied, they did little to change the basic character of commercial broadcasting. In truth, even the most diligent FCC member could do little to alter prevailing practices. Minow himself later joined a law firm that represents the broadcast industry; he is currently a member of CBS's board of directors.

CONFLICT OF INTEREST

Many commissioners, well before their tenures expire, look to high-paying positions in the communications field for future employment. From 1945 to 1970, there were 33 commissioners of the FCC; of these 21 became affiliated in one way or another, subsequent to their terms of office, with industries for which they had had regulatory responsibility.[27]

Of course, the number of commissioners who have consciously used their appointments as stepping-stones to more lucrative private sector jobs cannot be confirmed with any certainty. However, relatively few commissioners serve out their full seven-year terms; the average length of service of an FCC chairman has been a little over two years. A 1952 amendment to the Communications Act prohibits commissioners who resign early from practicing before the agency for one year. But, by many accounts, this restriction is not strong enough to insulate commissioners from career considerations when they are promulgating rules or making decisions. And no such restriction is placed on FCC staff members, who—more often than not—actually make the decisions that the commissioners later approve. As might be expected, large staff turnover is a common occurrence at the agency.

THE WLBT CASE

How regulatory policy can be shaped to suit the requirements of the regulated has been illustrated by the way the FCC handled the granting or renewal of licenses. Prior to 1966, the commission refused to allow citizen groups to intervene in these proceedings. Its policy was to permit only those parties who alleged economic injury or electrical interference to bring forth evidence or testimony in the decision-making process affecting the use of publicly owned airwaves.

However, under Section 402 (b) of the Communications Act, appeals from FCC decisions in broadcast licensing matters may be filed with the U.S. Court of Appeals for the District of Columbia Circuit. In March 1966, this appeals court overruled the FCC in a historic case, and opened the way for active public particpation in broadcast regulation.[28] In 1964, the FCC had granted a license renewal to the Lamar Life Broadcasting Company, licensee of WLBT-TV in Jackson, Mississippi. In taking this action, it had rejected a petition from the Office of Communications of the United Church of Christ on behalf of local citizens, asking that the license renewal be denied on grounds of racial discrimination. The church group, together with two local black leaders, claimed that WLBT-TV's management had consistently discriminated against black viewers, who constituted about 45 percent of the station's potential audience. The station had no black employees, carried no programming of particular interest to blacks, did not deal with local problems as they concerned blacks, and—it was reported—occasionally interrupted the network newscast when it was covering civil rights. Moreover, the station promoted the segregationist views of the White Citizen's Council, which maintained that the civil rights movement was communist inspired.

Although the FCC denied the petitioners official "standing" (a legal term that defines the parties who have a right to participate), it did take their claims into consideration. It extended the station's license for a probationary period of one year, instead of granting the customary three-year renewal (now, five years for television and seven years for radio). Two of the seven (now, five) commissioners dissented.

The petitioners promptly challenged the decision in the appeals court. In 1966, a three-judge panel headed by Judge Warren Burger (later to become chief justice of the U.S. Supreme Court) unanimously ruled that civic associations, professional societies, unions, churches, educational institutions, and other such responsible community organizations did indeed have legal standing in license renewals. The FCC was ordered to hold a renewal hearing in which the petitioners could participate. A hearing examiner (now called an "administrative law judge") was duly appointed; and, after hearing the charges of the United Church of Christ and examining the evidence, the examiner recommended granting a full three-year license renewal—which the FCC did, in 1968, with a 5-to-2 vote.

Once more, the church group was compelled to turn to the appeals court; and, in 1969, this court again overruled the FCC and ordered it to "vacate" Lamar's license. The FCC was required to consider a plan for an interim operation of the station, and to accept new applications for the license. The court did not disqualify Lamar from filing a new application; but for the commission to grant the license to the same organization would have been sheer effrontery. This was especially so, because this decision (also written by Judge Burger) constituted as stern a rebuke of the FCC's conduct as any court had ever administered. Judge Burger expressed "profound concern" over the commission's entire handling of the case and, in no uncertain terms, criticized its "impatience" with the petitioners and its "hostility" toward their efforts.

WLBT-TV was permitted to remain on the air, on an interim basis, under the supervision of a newly formed nonprofit organization with a biracial board of prominent members of the community. A black general manager was hired, and the station became quite financially successful. However, the caretaker organization was required to pay $30,000 a month to the former licensee, Lamar Life, for the use of its facilities, equipment, and broadcast tower. It was not until late 1979 that the commission finally awarded a new license to a largely local Jackson group controlled by a black majority.

THE FAIRNESS DOCTRINE

One of the principal issues in the *WLBT* case involved the FCC's failure to fully enforce its own "fairness doctrine." This doctrine has its roots in a 1949 policy statement on editorializing. At that time, the FCC stated that stations were permitted to editorialize, but only if they offered opportunities for opposing points of view. The doctrine has since been expanded to cover controversial matters in news and public affairs programming. Broadcast licensees are required: (1) to devote adequate time to controversial issues of public importance; and (2) to do so fairly by affording reasonable opportunity for contrasting points of view.

In most circumstances, the licensee has considerable discretion as to the format to be used in presenting an issue, the different shades of opinion to be presented, and the amount and nature of the time to be afforded—although two aspects of the fairness doctrine, relating to personal attacks and political editorials, were codified more precisely in the form of FCC regulations in 1967. In essence, these special fairness rules hold that, if—during the presentation of views on a controversial issue of public importance—an attack is made on the honesty, character, or integrity of an identifiable person or group (except on bona fide newscasts, news interviews, and on-the-spot coverage of news events), the station broadcasting the attack must notify the target within one week, provide a script or tape (or an accurate summary, if these are not available) of the attack, and offer time for reply. Similar steps must be taken within 24 hours, should a broadcaster oppose or endorse a legally qualified candidate for public office.

The fairness doctrine should not be confused with Section 315 of the Communications Act, which requires that equal opportunities be afforded all legally qualified candidates for all public office. The fairness doctrine itself was never specifically voted into law, although—when Congress amended Section 315 in 1959 to exempt candidates who appear in bona fide newscasts, news interviews, news documentaries, and on-the-spot coverage of news events—it did accord legislative recognition to the concept of fairness.

FAIRNESS AND THE FIRST AMENDMENT

The constitutionality of the fairness doctrine and its component personal-attack and political-editorial regulations were upheld by the U. S. Supreme Court in 1969.[29] The high court ruled on two separate appeals simultaneously, issuing a single opinion. The first case involved the application of the fairness doctrine to a particular broadcast. In November 1964, WGCB in Red Lion, Pennsylvania, carried a syndicated program called *The Christian Crusade*, which featured an attack by the Reverend Billy James Hargis on a book by journalist Fred J. Cook, entitled *Goldwater: Extremist of the Right*. During the 15-minute broadcast, Hargis alleged that Cook had been fired by a New York newspaper for making false charges against city officials; that he had then worked for a Left-wing publication; and that he had written articles absolving Alger Hiss and attacking J. Edgar Hoover, the FBI, and the CIA.

Aided and abetted by the Democratic National Committee, which was seeking to counter conservative criticism, Cook requested free rebuttal time from WGCB and the more than 200 other stations that had broadcast the Hargis attack.[30] When the Red Lion station refused his request, Cook turned to the FCC for redress. Following a lengthy study by its examiners, the commission ruled that the station was required to give Cook reply time, whether or not he was willing or able to pay for it. WGCB went to court to appeal the order, and the National Association of Broadcasters supported the station. In 1967, the appeals court in the nation's capital upheld the FCC's application of the fairness doctrine.

Soon after its victory in the appellate arena, the FCC adopted regulations making the personal-attack aspect of the fairness doctrine more precise, and detailing the rules relating to political editorials. The promulgation of these regulations prompted CBS, NBC, and the Radio-Television News Directors Association to file challenges in the appeals courts. CBS and NBC filed in New York, the news group in Chicago. (Appeals for review of FCC rule-making may be filed in any of the 11 circuit appeals courts.) Since the news group filed first, the

Chicago court was awarded jurisdiction. In a unanimous opinion, this appeals court found the regulations at issue to be a violation of the free speech and free press guarantees contained in the First Amendment.

The decisions of the court of appeals are subject only to review by the U. S. Supreme Court upon issuance of a discretionary writ of certiorari—a formal order issuing from a superior court, calling up the record of a proceeding in an inferior court for review. The high court had granted certiorari to WGCB but then postponed it, pending the decision of the Chicago appeals court. In early 1969, the Supreme Court consolidated the two cases.

In a landmark decision, a unanimous Supreme Court (seven justices voting) affirmed the District of Columbia appeals in its ruling that the FCC had the right to order WGCB to grant Fred Cook reply time, and reversed the Chicago circuit court opinion that the personal-attack and political-editorial regulations were a violation of the First Amendment. Justice Byron White, writing on behalf of his brethren, stated without equivocation that a broadcaster has no constitutional right to monopolize a scarce resource, use of which has been denied to other citizens by the government: "There is nothing in the First Amendment which prevents the Government from requiring a licensee to share his frequency with others and to conduct himself as a proxy or fiduciary with obligations to present those views and voices which are representative of his community and which would otherwise, by necessity, be barred from the airwaves."

Justice White did acknowledge that the First Amendment is relevant to radio and television. But he also stated that "it is the right of the viewers and listeners, not the right of the broadcasters, which is paramount. . . . It is the right of the public to receive suitable access to social, political, esthetic, and other ideas and experiences which is crucial here."

This romantic vision of the public's First Amendment rights has had little effect on actual programming practices. The three television networks and most major stations already had a policy of presenting contrasting viewpoints on any issue that could conceivably be construed as controversial, although—all too often—this was done within a framework designed to entertain, rather than enlighten. And entertainment shows per se do not fall within the purview of the fairness doctrine. Even though situation comedies, melodramas, teleplays, and action-adventure shows undoubtedly play a major role in shaping attitudes and ideas—including controversial ideas—the FCC has not interpreted the fairness doctrine to include such entertainment fare.

The commission did apply the fairness doctrine to cigarette commercials; but, in a 1974 policy statement, it took great pains to limit the reach of this ruling. (Congress banned all cigarette commercials from the airwaves, effective January 2, 1971.) Now, only those commercials that openly argue about some significant issue can trigger a fairness obligation.

PROMOTING PROGRAM DIVERSITY

Of late, the FCC has decided to dismantle decades of regulatory structure, in favor of the old orthodoxy of marketplace rule. Requirements for a minimum amount of news and public affairs programming, guidelines for commercials and children's programming, obligations to ascertain community needs and maintain program logs for public inspection—all were eliminated in the early 1980s.

The few rules that remain have done little to promote programming outside the cultural mainstream. In 1970, for instance, the commission promulgated a rule (put into force the following year) that restricted the amount of network programming carried by TV affiliates in the top 50 markets to a maximum of three of the four evening hours between 7 and 11 p.m. (6 and 10 p.m. in the Central and Mountain Time Zones). Since network-affiliated stations generally used a half hour of prime time for their own local news, the net effect of the rules was to open up a half hour for non-network programming, each night of the week. All three networks opted to give up the 7:30–8 p.m. time slot. The rule was later revised to exempt network-originated children's, public affairs, and documentary programs. However, the networks have tended to take advantage of this exemption only on Sunday evenings. CBS, for instance, moved its newsmagazine series *60 Minutes* to the Sunday 7-8 p.m. time slot in 1975.

In addition to effectively making the half hour at 7:30 p.m. off limits to CBS, NBC, and ABC, the FCC prohibited the networks from engaging in domestic syndication and restricted their foreign distribution to the sale of their own productions. Another provision prevented the networks from acquiring a percentage of profit or ownership in an independently produced program, a pervasive practice in the 1960s.

The stated aim of the prime-time access rule was to stimulate competition among existing and potential program producers, but the implicit objective was to promote program diversity. Yet, a survey of current programs aired during the evening time slot now known as "access time" indicates that the principal dividend of the rule has been the return to prime time of the game/giveaway show. Many stations have adjusted to the rule by "stripping" such shows—that is, carrying them five days a week. One of the biggest access-time hits of the 1980s has been *Wheel of Fortune*, a nationally syndicated game show on which three contestants take turns spinning a large wheel for the chance to guess the letters of a mystery word or puzzle.

The rule did spawn a thriving syndication industry, turning the sale of programs directly to stations into a big business. Those companies associated with *Wheel of Fortune* have done especially well. King World, which bought the show's syndication rights in 1982, saw its revenues shoot up from $8 million to $80 million in two years. Merv Griffin Enterprises, *Wheel*'s producer, was purchased by the Coca-Cola Company in 1986 for a reported $250 million.

As was to be expected, very few stations took advantage of the access-time period to produce original programming of their own. Most stations simply found it far more profitable to procure nationally syndicated program fare. Affiliates came to love the rule, when their coffers began to fill up with added profits. Nor were the networks hurt by the loss of a half hour at the early edge of prime time. The reduction of commercial time available on the networks created a sellers' market, driving up the national advertising rates year after year.

PROTECTING THE PUBLIC MORALITY

The reluctance of the FCC to take a more active role in programming matters stems, in part, from its conflicting mandate. The same Communications Act that empowers the commission to regulate in the public interest also prohibits the agency from engaging in censorship. Section 326 states emphatically that "no regulation or condition shall be promulgated or fixed by the Commission which shall interfere with the right of free speech by means of radio communication."

The commission does have some latitude in controlling programming that threatens to undermine the public morality. Specifically, it may enforce Section 1464 of the criminal code, which prohibits the broadcasting of "any obscene, indecent, or profane language."

In exercising its authority to impose sanctions under this statute, the commission has consistently contended that broadcasting is subject to tighter strictures than other media, since it is available at the flick of a switch to young and old alike. In 1973, for instance, the FCC imposed a $2,000 fine on the Sonderling Broadcasting Corporation, licensee of WGLD-FM in Oak Park, Illinois. The station featured a midday talk show with a male moderator who invited women to call in and discuss the intimate details of their sex lives on the air. The commission concluded that a broadcast dealing with a detailed discussion of oral sex met the prevailing definition of obscenity in that it appealed to a prurient interest in sex and was patently offensive to contemporary community standards. The FCC stressed that this definition was being applied to the special case of radio broadcasting: "This is peculiarly a medium designed to be received and sampled by millions in their homes, cars, on outings, or even as they walk the streets with transistor radio to the ear, without regard to age, background or degree of sophistication."[31]

The licensee elected to pay the forfeiture, and did not appeal. But the Illinois Citizens Committee and the Illinois Division of the American Civil Liberties Union petitioned the Federal Court of Appeals in Washington, D. C., for review. This court found in favor of the FCC, noting that the probable presence of children in the audience is relevant to a determination of obscenity.

Does the pervasive presence of radio and television justify a more limited First Amendment protection for broadcasters than for print practitioners? The first full U. S. Supreme Court review of the issue came in 1978.[32] The case on which the high court ruled involved a broadcast by WBAI-FM, a listener-supported station in New York City. Early one afternoon in 1973, the station had featured a 12-minute selection from a comedy album by George Carlin, in which the comedian discussed the "seven dirty words" that could not be said on radio or television. The words describe female organs, excrement, sexual intercourse, sodomy, and incest. Carlin gave examples of their current usage and varying meanings, and provided a bit of etymological background on some of them. For instance, in commenting on the ancient Anglo-Saxonism for the sex act, Carlin noted: "It's a great word, fuck, nice word, easy word, cute word, kind of. Easy to say. One syllable, short u, fuh ends with a kuh. Right? A little something for everyone. Fuck. Good word. Kind of a proud word, too. Who are you? I am FUCK. FUCK OF THE MOUNTAIN. Tune in again next week to FUCK OF THE MOUNTAIN."

The comedy monologue, preceded by a warning about the potentially offensive words, had been played during a program about contemporary society's attitudes toward language. The FCC received a complaint from a man who happened to hear the broadcast on his car radio. The man noted that his young son was with him when he heard the broadcast and that "any child could have been turning the dial and tuned in that garbage." (It later turned out that the man was a member of the media watchdog group Morality in Media and that the "young son" whom he said was with him in his car when they heard the monologue was 15 years old at the time.)

Acting on that single complaint, the FCC ruled that the language used in the Carlin monologue was "indecent," because it depicted sexual and excretory activities and organs in a manner patently offensive by contemporary community standards for the broadcast media at a time of day when children were likely to be in the audience. The commission reprimanded the station and issued a "declaratory order" forbidding the broadcast of indecent language.

The Pacifica Foundation, licensee of WBAI-FM, appealed the FCC order; and, in March 1977, the Court of Appeals for the District of Columbia ruled that the agency's ban was an unconstitutionally vague and overbroad exercise in censorship. The FCC then appealed the decision to the U. S. Supreme Court.

In July 1978, in a decision that aroused considerable controversy, a five-member majority of the high court held that the FCC may regulate the broadcasting of words that are patently offensive, even though they are not obscene. Associate Justice John Paul Stevens, writing for the narrow majority, cited the broadcast media's "uniquely pervasive presence in the lives of all Americans" and the fact that broadcasting is "uniquely accessible to children, even those too young to read" as the reasons for restricting the First Amendment rights of broadcasters. In so supporting the FCC action, the majority seemed to affirm a more restrictive rationale for broadcast regulation, based on the intrusiveness of radio and television rather than on the scarcity of spectrum space. "Patently offensive, indecent material presented over the airwaves confronts the citizen, not only in public," wrote Justice Stevens, "but also in the privacy of the home, where the individual's right to be let alone plainly outweighs the First Amendment rights of an intruder."

Civil libertarians could find some consolation in the court's emphasis on context, as well as content. Justice Stevens suggested, for instance, that an occasional expletive in the telecast of an Elizabethan comedy would not justify the imposition of sanctions. Time of day was also an important consideration. The court implied that the case for regulation would be far weaker if allegedly patently offensive material was broadcast late at night. Recalling an earlier case in which it was noted that a "nuisance may be the right thing in the wrong place—like a pig in the parlor instead of the barnyard," Justice Stevens stated: "We simply hold that when the Commission finds that a pig has entered the parlor, the exercise of its regulatory power does not depend on proof that the pig is obscene."

In a sharply worded dissent, Associate Justice William J. Brennan pinpointed the cultural conflicts inherent in any FCC foray into the regulation of program content. "As surprising as it may be to individual Members of this Court," he asserted, "some parents may actually find Mr. Carlin's unabashed attitude towards the seven 'dirty words' healthy, and deem it desirable to expose their children to the manner in which Mr. Carlin defuses the taboo surrounding the words." He accused the majority of "a depressing inability to appreciate that in our land of cultural pluralism, there are many who think, act and talk differently from the Members of this Court, and who do not share their fragile sensibilities."

Prior to its ruling in the "dirty words" case, the high court had been besieged with briefs from CBS, NBC, ABC, the National Association of Broadcasters, and other powerful media organizations; they challenged the constitutional authority of the FCC to restrict the broadcast of words—regardless of redeeming literary, social, or artistic value. No one concerned with fostering a free marketplace of ideas can fail to be alarmed by the FCC's enforcement of statutory prohibitions that are so broad, vague, and potentially all-encompassing. But it is difficult to take seriously the constitutional claims that are based on profitable speech, not free speech. The real threat of television censorship comes not from the government, but from the industry itself. The ideas of the marketplace, as former FCC commissioner Nicholas Johnson has noted, do not make a marketplace of ideas.

THE PROMISE OF PUBLIC TELEVISION

The ideology of the marketplace has penetrated the nonprofit television system, as well. Lacking both an adequate funding strategy and a basic programming philosophy, this system has been principally shaped by the demands or preferences of those in society who possess a preponderance of power or opinion or numbers.

A Carnegie Commission manifesto—issued early in 1967—provided the basic blueprint for the present-day service.[33] It called for the support and development of a system devoted in the broadest sense to public service and cultural enrichment—one that would be national in scope while, at the same time, maintaining a local orientation. This system would be managed by a federally chartered, nonprofit, nongovernmental corporation that would receive and disburse funds for station inter-connection and programming. It suggested adoption of the term "public television" to encompass "all that is of human interest and importance which is not at the moment appropriate or available for support by advertising, and which is not arranged for formal instruction."

Central to its recommendations was the need for some automatic source of revenues, such as a manufacturer's excise tax on the sale of television sets. The report estimated that $270 million a year would be needed to maintain a strong national system.

The Carnegie document arrived in the midst of the Great Society initiatives of President Lyndon B. Johnson and, within less than a year, many of its recommendations were translated into legislation—as the Public Broadcasting Act of 1967.

The new law established a nonprofit, nongovernmental organization—the Corporation for Public Broadcasting (CPB)—chiefly charged with administering funds for the system and keeping it free from political influence. Its functions include: facilitating the development and production of programs from diverse sources, arranging for the interconnection of stations (both radio and TV), encouraging the development of new stations, and conducting research and training programs.

The CPB's 10-member board is supposed to be selected by the president, with the advice and consent of the Senate, from among citizens who have achieved eminence in such fields as education, cultural and civic affairs, or the arts. However, the first appointees were not exactly men and women whose stature was attributable to their cultural accomplishments or artistic sensibilities.[34] CPB's first board chairman, for instance, was Frank Pace, Jr., a former secretary of the Army and chief executive officer of General Dynamics, one of the country's largest military equipment manufacturers. John Macy, Jr., an old Washington hand who had served in a variety of governmental and military positions, was the first president of the CPB. Other appointees added little in the way of ideological diversity to the board. The token woman was Oveta Culp Hobby, onetime director of the Women's Army Air Corps and vice-president of the Hobby Foundation (reportedly, a conduit for Central Intelligence Agency funds). The lone artist on the board—one presumes that the appointment was made to meet the legislative specifications of the board's composition—was Erich Leinsdorf, then conductor of the Boston Symphony Orchestra.

Any expectation that the CPB could operate in an environment free from ideological bias or political influence has proven unfounded. In fact, the process of board selection has lent itself to increased politicization, to the point where appointments are sometimes made purely on the basis of political considerations. For instance, President Richard Nixon packed the CPB with his political pals, expressly to influence it for his own purposes. Several board members and Henry Loomis, a former deputy director of the United States Information Agency who was then CPB president, cooperated with the White House inner circle in its efforts to eliminate what it saw as excessive centralization of the public television system. To many observers, this emphasis on decentralization seemed motivated by Nixon Administration objections to the supposedly liberal tenor of the news and public affairs programs put on by the Public Broadcasting Service (PBS)—the agency set up by CPB in 1969 to manage the national distribution apparatus and to select much of the programming for it.

The Public Broadcasting Service itself had been created partially in response to the perceived progressivism of National Educational Television (NET), the New York-based program supplier that had grown out of the Ford Foundation's early efforts. Prior to the creation of PBS, NET had been the principal source of general programming material for noncommercial stations. Throughout most of the 1960s, banks of videotape machines at NET's Ann Arbor, Michigan, reproduction facilities ran around the clock seven days a week, duplicating drama, performing arts, public affairs, and children's programs—which were then mailed to the organization's affiliated stations.

NET's public affairs programs, in particular, ran into well-developed pockets of parochialism and pusillanimity. Its scheduling in early 1968 of a 49-minute segment from *Inside North Vietnam*—a British documentary film that depicted the devastation of North Vietnamese towns and villages by U.S. bombers—was greeted with a barrage of protest. One letter of opposition that was addressed to the president of

NET and described the documentary as "nothing more or less than Communist propaganda," was signed by 33 congressmen—none of whom had seen the film.[35] Although NET presented the program anyway, it took some pains to point out the documentary's political coloration. A discussion following the film featured both a critic and a defender of U.S. policy in Vietnam. Most NET affiliates carried the program, but local opposition to the nascent network was growing. (In 1970, NET merged with the community group operating Channel 13 in New York City, to form WNET.)

The fate of another Ford-founded project, called *PBL* (*Public Broadcasting Laboratory*), provides an illustrative example of how non-commercial operations—often working under boards of directors who are pillars of the local power structure—can be as conservative as commercial stations, when it comes to scheduling programs that might provoke an adverse reaction. The producers of *PBL* planned to provide a weekly 2½-hour program, designed to demonstrate the cultural and public affairs possibilities of an adequately financed system freed from commercial constraints. Starting in the fall of 1967, it was to be made available on Sunday evenings (when many stations went dark, because of budget limitations) to nearly all the nation's noncommercial stations, through AT&T interconnections.

The first installment in the series, which debuted in November 1967 opposite such offerings on the commercial channels as Ed Sullivan, *The FBI*, and *Bonanza*, concerned racial problems in the United States. Its centerpiece was a bizarre off-Broadway hit by Douglas Turner Ward, called *Day of Absence*, about a Southern town from which all the black residents have departed. The whites in the town, finding themselves unable to function, plead with the blacks to return. The play's ironic edge was sharpened by the fact that the white townspeople were portrayed by blacks in "whiteface" makeup. Some 33 southern stations refused to carry the program.[36]

The series' other sojourns into the angry subculture of the late 1960s also met with local resistance, from big city operations as well as rural ones. The *PBL* project expired after two years, having failed dismally in its efforts to consolidate local outlets.

Differences in basic outlook, in funding strategies, and even in operational details made it difficult for public television stations to achieve consensus on what constituted proper programming objectives. There was a sharp division in noncommercial circles between proponents for a network-oriented operation and advocates of a strong local service, and between station managements who would emphasize education and instruction and those who wanted to provide a broad range of programming. The seeds for these divisions were sown in the way that noncommercial TV evolved. Stations that were owned and operated by universities or state educational authorities and those that were under the control of nonprofit corporations dependent on community contributions often had little sense of common purpose, aside from that of seeking greater financial security.

The Carnegie Commission's proposal for an insulated, long-term source of federal funding for public television failed to account for the political practicalities involved at the time. No support for a dedicated tax was forthcoming in Congress, which appropriated only $5 million to CPB in fiscal 1969. By 1972, the appropriation had risen to only $35 million. That year Congress passed a two-year, $155 million authorization for CPB; but President Nixon vetoed it. In his message accompanying the veto, he cited evidence that public broadcasting had become too centralized, and made it plain that approval of long-term funding was contingent upon a return to the concept of localism.

The Nixon administration's stress on the primacy of the local outlet over any national or network service coincided with the views of many station managers and their boards of directors. Primed to protect programming prerogatives and desperate for federal dollars, the leadership of the stations took steps to decentralize the system. PBS's power as a central programming entity was dissolved and replaced by a station-by-station voting mechanism, called the Station Program Cooperative. Under this plan of operations, station representatives select the programs that they will help finance from a catalog of proposals prepared by PBS. Each station's share of the cost of a program is calculated according to the size of its CPB grant. If enough money is pledged to cover the production costs of a show or series, then the project is incorporated into the PBS schedule. Only stations that contribute to the cost of a program are permitted to carry it.

The new plan fit well with the expectations of the White House, since the entire programming responsibility now rested squarely with the local station. Not long after this plan was put into effect, President Gerald Ford—who had succeeded Richard Nixon following the Watergate revelations—signed legislation authorizing a potential $634 million in federal funds over a five-year period. The Public Financing Act of 1975, as this legislation was called, retained the matching principle—government monies were to be released at a ratio of $1.00 for each $2.50 raised by public broadcasters from other sources. A follow-up bill, passed in 1978, authorized federal funding into the early 1980s with a somewhat less stringent matching formula.

With greater certainty about their budgets, local, regional, and national programmers were better able to make long-term plans. But the public broadcasting system was still beset by bureaucratic inefficiency and, more distressingly, by local broadcasters seemingly incapable of daring vision. There was wholesale duplication of effort between CPB and PBS; and far too much of the television budget was spent on administration rather than programming. Station managements, for their part, tended to support only mainstream programs with proven track records.

By January 1979, an assessment of the system was long overdue when the Carnegie Commission on the Future of Public Broadcasting (dubbed "Carnegie II" by the industry) concluded an 18-month-long investigation of every major aspect of public broadcasting: structure, funding, the application of new communications technologies, and programming.[37] "We find public broadcasting's financial, organizational and creative structure fundamentally flawed," the commission's report flatly declared. "There is little likelihood that public television and radio might consistently achieve programming excellence under the present circumstances."

This new Carnegie manifesto called for sweeping structural changes—beginning with the elimination of the CPB and its replacement by an ostensibly better-insulated body, to be called the Public Telecommunications Trust. This mouthful of an organization would set goals for the system, evaluate performance, and function as a fiduciary agent—but would have no voice in programming decisions. On a national level, these decisions would be the province of another new organization, the Program Services Endowment, which would operate as a semi-autonomous division of the trust. Its principal mission would be to promote the unconventional and the untested, although it would lack the authority to impose its programming projects on local stations. Appointments to the governing boards of these new organizations would be made in ways intended to ensure insulation from political pressures.

To support this reorganized system, the report recommended annual funding of $1.2 billion a year, with about half to come from the federal government and the remainder from viewers and listeners, business corporations, foundations, and state and local educational agencies. Washington's share was to be offset by the imposition of fees on commercial broadcasters and other users of the airwaves. Once again, the federal government's contribution would be in the form of matching grants.

The Carnegie recommendatons failed to win Congressional support. But even if they were to be turned into legislation in the latter half of the 1980s, many of the old problems would still persist. For instance, continued reliance on matching funds would leave the local station dependent on well-to-do viewers and business corporations and would discourage programs that might offend them. Moreover, this formula for funding fosters periodic preemption of programming for protracted on-the-air appeals—known derisively in the industry as "begging with an electronic tin cup." The prospect of increased federal revenues would probably be a stimulus to expand this practice even more.

Although financial infusions from large corporations have been very helpful to public television—and programming has noticeably improved as a result—these corporations are highly selective of the kinds of programs they are willing to underwrite. For instance, the corporation that has funded *Masterpiece Theatre* has been very partial to the past—preferably pageantry with a British accent.

Perhaps the most basic flaw in the Carnegie-proposed infrastructure is that it would keep the cornerstone of localism intact. It would still be the local broadcaster who determines whether or not a national program was appropriate for his viewing area, even though audience interests often defy any such geographical circumscription. This primacy of the local station in programming matters—as in the case of commercial television—translates into the power of censorship.

Given the state of affairs in public television, it is little short of remarkable that the system can claim some definite triumphs: outstanding presentations of music, dance and opera; distinguished dramas; informative documentaries; excellent children's programs such as *Sesame Street*; films of historical and aesthetic value; and comprehensive coverage of news and current events. But what's still missing from the schedule—on a regular basis, at least—is what Carnegie II referred to as "innovative and untried programming ideas in a wide range of genres devised by producers working inside and outside the present system." All too often the offerings are cautious and bland, catering to what might be called traditional cultural tastes. Producers of probing, committed, or provocative programs frequently find the system closed to them.

The leadership's reluctance to take risks heightened in the 1980s when the Reagan administration—in its slashing of social programs—vetoed funding authorizations for public broadcasting. The prospects of continued federal funding looked dim. When deep cuts are being made in health, education, welfare, and environmental programs, it becomes increasingly difficult to make a case for funding public broadcasting. Commercial stations should, arguably, pay for their very profitable use of the public airwaves—especially when noncommercial outlets are starving for funds and must beg for survival. But as long as the National Association of Broadcasters maintains one of the most effective lobbies in Washington, this measure is likely to find little congressional support.

President Reagan did sign a bill (after two vetoes) that included federal funding for public broadcasting—authorizations for CPB to rise from $200 million in 1987 to $254 million in 1990; and for facilities, from $24 million in 1986 to $32 million in 1988. Since authorization and appropriation are separate considerations, however, public broadcasting's leadership remains relegated to the role of self-serving lobbyist.

Some stations have become convinced that they can only survive through the sale of advertising time. This flat-out embrace of marketplace precepts was sanctioned by Congress, which—in 1982—authorized ten public television stations to take part in a 15-month experiment with on-the-air advertising. The legislation authorizing the experiment stipulated that ads could not interrupt programs; could not exceed two minutes in length; and could not promote political, religious, or other ideological points of view. A concerted effort on the part of several stations to extend the experiment did not receive congressional blessing. But given the difficulty of securing subscriber, underwriter, and government support, the idea of advertising on public television as an alternative means of funding is likely to remain with us.

THE EMERGING ELECTRONIC ENVIRONMENT

For many prognosticators, the new panoply of electronic marvels—satellites, cable systems, video cassettes, and the like—presages an end to the problems that have persisted in conventional television.

Dazzling new delivery systems are already in place. Satellites, set in geosynchronous orbits (that is, the speed of the satellite matches that of the earth's rotation) some 22,300 miles above the equator, blink scores of television programs to several thousand parabolic dish antennas sprinkled across our country. The antennas of these "earth stations" relay the signals to more than 5,000 cable TV systems—which, in turn, carry them into nearly half of the nation's 86 million or so television households.

The American landscape is additionally dotted with more than 1½ million "backyard" satellite dishes. The owners of these unsightly antennas can select from the hundreds of hours of programming—country and western music, rock video marathons, foreign language shows, general and financial news services, and ever more movies—that are being beamed by satellites each week (although some pay services now scramble their satellite transmissions, permitting only those dish owners who purchase a decoder and pay a monthly fee to capture clear pictures from the sky).

The availability of geosynchronous orbiting satellites has also spawned media hybrids—such as WTBS-TV (Atlanta), a broadcast station whose signal is available to cable systems across the country via satellite transmission. Other such "superstations" currently "on the bird" include WPIX-TV (New York) and WGN-TV (Chicago). National newspapers—such as *USA Today*—are another media hybrid made possible by satellite technology. Newspaper copy is converted into electronic signals, transmitted to a satellite, and beamed to printing plants across the country.

Through the purchase or rental of tapes, owners of video cassette recorders (VCRs) can supplement standard TV fare with programs ranging from big-budget theatrical releases to hastily produced erotic enticements to an assortment of self-help offerings. This electronic gadgetry, which is fast becoming a standard household item, has an added advantage in that it permits viewers to select their own show date and curtain time.

The television set itself is undergoing a transformation. Experiments with high-definition television (HDTV), which uses 1,125 lines to create the video image, are underway in both Japan and the United States. Doubling the number of scanning lines produces a startlingly clear picture. But the transmission potential of this system is limited, because it requires a great deal of spectrum space and its general implementation would render obsolete the millions and millions of 525-line (625 in Europe) television sets currently in use. However, sets with new digital circuitry, which improves the sharpness and color of television pictures without increasing the number of lines, are now available. Stereophonic TV sets, too, are now a mass market item; and an ever-growing number of stations are modifying their equipment to transmit stereo sound.

Contributing to the tempest is the appearance on the horizon of the hair-thin optical fiber. For almost two decades, the promise of fiber optic technology has hung like an enticing mirage—always just out of reach. But steady improvements in this technology may soon permit the creation of a greatly expanded nationwide communications web. Optical fibers carry television and myriad other signals in the form of light pulses. The source of the light, which is actually invisible infrared, is the light-emitting diode or the semiconductor laser (*l*ight *a*mplification of *s*timulated *e*mission of *r*adiation). Hair-thin, light-carrying fibers have many advantages over the copper wire used in coaxial cable: The principal one is that of channel capacity. A single strand of optical fiber, for instance, can potentially carry 100 or more television signals. A bundle of such strands may make possible more than 1,000 channels. In addition, fiber optic material is immune to electrical interference, and can carry light pulses for several miles—even around curves and corners. Optical fibers are already being put into telephone trunk lines, and the near future promises the possibility of local links with homes and offices.

At the epicenter of these explosive developments is the integrated circuitry of the so-called "miracle chip." Computer functions are now being etched onto tiny silicon chips, half the size of a fingernail. Each chip has a calculating capability equal to that of a room-size computer of 35 years ago. And unlike the cumbersome vacuum tubes and tangles of wires from which it evolved, the chip is cheap, easy to mass-produce, fast, infinitely versatile, and convenient. With the present generation of chip-based computer technology, vast amounts of information can be stored, manipulated, and transmitted at blinding speed.

The advent of these new and glittering technologies both reflects and intensifies the convergence and integration of the formerly disparate fields of information and entertainment. The whole character and definition of the mass media are changing—as network nabobs, movie magnates, and publishing pooh-bahs jockey for position and form new alliances.

All three of the major television networks were pursued by corporate suitors in the mid-1980s. Early in 1986, American Broadcasting Companies (ABC-TV's corporate parent) merged with Capital Cities Communications (one of the nation's most profitable owners of newspaper, television, and cable properties) in a deal valued at more than $3.5 billion. That same year, RCA (longtime owner of NBC-TV) was absorbed by General Electric (a huge, diversified company with worldwide interests) in a $6.28 billion takeover—the largest such transaction ever, outside the oil industry.

CBS caught the eye of upstart media mogul Ted Turner, who offered to buy two-thirds of the company's stock in a complex cashless deal that involved the exchange of so-called "junk bonds" (high-yield and higher-than-normal-risk debt securities). In a series of defensive maneuvers designed to defeat Turner's takeover attempt, CBS purchased 21 percent of its own stock for close to $1 billion and encouraged Loews' chairman Laurence A. Tisch to increase his firm's share of CBS stock from 12 to 25 percent. (Tisch became the CBS president and chief executive officer, titularly under the once-and-current chairman, octogenarian William Paley.) CBS got rid of the unwanted suitor, but it was out a lot of money. To help finance its antitakeover tactics (Tisch, in effect, did take over the company), CBS decided to sell its book and music publishing units and its television outlet in St. Louis. It also sliced more than 1,000 personnel off the payroll.

Twentieth Century-Fox owner Rupert Murdock launched a new commercial television network in 1986—the Fox Broadcasting Company (FBC)—which competes with ABC, CBS, and NBC in some time periods. His seven owned-and-operated television outlets form the core of a 90-plus station satellite hookup. (Many new television stations have come into being, in recent years.) Murdock's News Corporation also owns one of the world's largest newspaper chains, as well as the European Sky Channel (a cable-to-satellite network) and an Australian television network. Among his publishing interests in the United States are the Boston *Herald*, the Chicago *Sun-Times*, the New York *Post*, *New York* magazine, and the *Village Voice*.

Most of the major newspaper publishers have acquired substantial holdings in other media. The giant Gannett Company not only owns dozens of dailies, but several television and radio stations, as well. It also publishes the hybrid newspaper *USA Today*, which has a national circulation of about 2 million or so. The Times-Mirror Company owns book publishers, magazines, television stations, and cable TV systems—as well as the Los Angeles *Times*, *Newsday* (on Long Island,

New York), the Dallas *Times-Herald*, and other newspapers. The Hearst newspaper empire, too, encompasses broadcasting and other media interests. In 1985, the Hearst Corporation paid a reported $450 million for Boston's WCVB-TV, a former Metromedia station briefly owned by Rupert Murdock's News Corporation. The Tribune Company, whose publications include the Chicago *Tribune* and the New York *Daily News*, also owns superstations WGN-TV and WPIX-TV. This Chicago-based firm anted up a record-setting $510 million in 1985 for KTLA-TV, an independent station in Los Angeles. The New York Times Company is likewise a media conglomerate involved in magazines, books, and broadcasting—in addition to newspapers. The Washington Post Company, publisher of the leading newspaper in the nation's capital, owns *Newsweek* magazine and is in the radio and television business, as well. In 1985, the already powerful Post Company expanded its influence by purchasing the 53 cable systems of Capital Cities for $350 million.

Cable television, too, is fast becoming the private preserve of a few media giants. This technology had its inception in the late 1940s in rural areas, where the terrain interfered with broadcast signals. By running coaxial cable from a high, central antenna to each individual home, it was possible to bring signals clearly where none were received before. Increased channel capacity (state-of-the-art systems now offer upwards of 100 channels) made possible not only the importation of distant broadcast signals, but the origination of programs, as well. The expense of construction, coupled with restrictive FCC regulations (imposed largely at the behest of broadcasters), stalled the development of cable in big cities. However, the climate for urban cable improved considerably in 1975, when Home Box Office (HBO)—a wholly-owned subsidiary of Time Inc.—began to transmit programming to cable systems via satellite. HBO's ability to deliver movies into the home, uncut and without commercial interruption, created a clear demand for cable interconnection in densely populated urban and suburban areas. (HBO's subscribership jumped from under 60,000 in 1975 to more than 13 million a decade later.) The profusion of cable-satellite programming services produced by HBO's success further promoted the proliferation of urban cable systems. By the mid-1980s, virtually every big city in the nation was wired or about to be wired for cable.

Competition to cable up the cities became fierce. To win urban franchises, companies often promised to install large-capacity systems with two-way capability. A subsidiary of Warner Communications (a conglomerate involved in various aspects of the entertainment business) pioneered two-way interactive cable with its much ballyhooed "Qube" system, which began operations in Columbus, Ohio (a popular test market, because its demographics roughly parallel those of the country at large), in December 1977.

Subscribers could select from 30 channels, by means of a touch-pad control. Ten of the channels operated on a "pay-per-view" basis and provided current and old movies, football games, opera performances, and an assortment of self-help courses. A second row of ten buttons gave access to on-the-air commercial and public television stations, a public access channel, and a program guide channel. A third row of ten buttons provided so-called "community" channels, where viewers were encouraged to interact with their sets. Each channel was dedicated to a particular type of program fare: consumer information; stock and business news; religious offerings; and programs for specific audiences—doctors, lawyers, teachers, union members, and so forth. In addition to the 30 channel-selector buttons, there were five more buttons, which accommodated viewer instant reaction to questions posed from Qube's studio building. (This building—the "head end"—housed three TV studios and the heart of the interactive system—the "polling" computer—which gathered billing and response information from subscribers.) By merely pressing one or the other of the first two buttons, viewers were able to respond "yes" or "no" to questions. All five could be used in answering multiple choice questions, or in punching up number codes to indicate—for example—a selection of products displayed on the screen by local retailers.

This merchandising potential helps to explain why American Express, the giant credit card company, decided to buy 50 percent interest in the Warner cable operation in 1980. The newly named Warner Amex Cable Communications became one of the most aggressive companies in the competition for urban franchises. Its pie-in-the-sky promises won Warner contracts to wire Dallas, Houston, and Pittsburgh—and parts of St. Louis, Chicago, and New York's outer boroughs.

However, big city construction proved to be far more expensive and problematical than the cable company had expected. On top of this, subscribers showed scant interest in the pay-per-view channels—the principal source of profit. The programming glamour and novelty that these channels once held fell victim to the video cassette boom. Prerecorded cassettes, which can often be purchased for as little as a dollar or two, have cut deeply into Qube's profit potential. (The wide proliferation of VCRs and video rental outlets has also slowed the growth of HBO and other national pay services.) In consequence, the cable company has had to renegotiate franchising agreements—abandoning many of the extravagant claims made in the heat of the contest. Once the most compelling coming attraction in the cable industry, Qube has fallen far short of its revolutionary potential.

In 1984, Warner-Amex sold the franchise for its Pittsburgh system to Tele-Communications Inc. (TCI), a cost-cutting Denver-based firm, which continues to swallow up cable systems all over the country. The new owner quickly removed the interactive apparatus and closed down four of the five community stations.

TCI is the current colossus of the cable industry. It owns more than 500 cable systems in more than 40 states, and serves upwards of 4 million subscribers.[38] This market clout gives the company considerable say over what programs make it on cable. TCI itself has extensive investments in such cable program services as Black Entertainment Television (religious and family fare, music videos, and talk shows aimed at minority audiences), The Discovery Channel (shows about nature, science, technology, and exploration), and American Movie Classics (far-from-classic feature films). It also owns stock in Ted Turner's Turner Broadcasting Systems, whose holdings include superstation WTBS-TV (Atlanta), the Cable News Network (24-hour news), and CNN Headline News (24-hour news updates).

Time Inc. owns American Television & Communications, the second-largest cable operator in the country. This publishing-based firm also owns Home Box Office and its sister-service Cinemax, and is part owner (with Paramount and MCA) of the advertising-supported USA Network. Viacom International Inc., another big multiple-system cable operator, owns Showtime and The Movie Channel (the major competitors of the HBO/Cinemax combine) and MTV Networks (operator of such cable-satellite services as Music Television and Nickelodeon).

These vertically integrated structures would seem to hold the real or potential threat of restraint of trade and curtailment of competition. But the winds of antitrust have shifted considerably since the late 1940s, when Justice Department trustbusters forced the dismantling of the major studios. (The studios are again acquiring theatres.) In the laissez-faire era of the 1980s, the federal government is not likely to thwart the centralizing tendencies of the cable industry. In fact, the Cable Communications Policy Act of 1984 frees cable operators from most federal requirements and severely limits state and local interference with the play of market forces.[39]

The pyramiding of control into fewer and larger entities is evident in virtually every aspect of the industry of mass communication. "The industry has become so concentrated, and the companies have so assiduously purchased other firms among their competitors, customers and suppliers," notes *Channels* magazine in its 1987 survey of the electronic media, "that the 25 biggest now include owners of: all three TV networks, as well as the Fox Broadcasting Company network; nine of the ten TV station groups with the greatest potential audience; seven of the ten most extensive cable system holdings, serving more than a third of U.S. cable subscribers; 11 of the 15 top syndicators of TV programming; and seven of the ten top publishers of pre-recorded video-cassettes, with some two-thirds of sales."[40]

Concentration of control over the central channels of mass communication is compounded by the fact that most of the parent corporations of the major movie studios, cable TV systems, group station operators, newspaper chains, and television networks have directors who also serve on the boards of the big banks, insurance companies, investment firms, and major industries that organize and manage much of the world's resources. "Almost every major industry whose activities dominate the news of the 1980s—the leading defense contractors and oil companies—sit on the controlling boards of the leading media of the country," writes Ben H. Bagdikian in *The Media Monopoly*. "There is hardly a major international bank or insurance or investment company that is not represented on the boards of directors of the major media that control most of what we learn about the economy."[41]

Just how far the potential for corporate control of mass communication content is actually realized in practice—or how it may operate, and in whose interests—remains uncertain. Whatever the case, the logic of the market and profit maximization have thus far operated to keep most programming well within the cultural mainstream. Video cassette outlets tend to mainly stock proven Hollywood product and what is euphemistically called soft-core pornography. Pay cable networks already resemble conventional television—albeit with more movies, more sports, and more risqué entertainment specials. The schedules of superstations and advertising-supported cable channels consist largely of old movies and vintage network fare. "Too many cablecasters," notes New York *Times* television critic John J. O'Connor, "have apparently decided the future lies nostalgically in old network series or in new sitcoms badly imitating old network sitcoms."[42]

But familiar formulas notwithstanding, the contours of the emerging electronic environment are not yet wholly predetermined or settled. Applications of the new media will undoubtedly alter the existing cultural landscape. To predict just how pervasive or how profound the changes will be would require us to set out on a path beset with pitfalls and difficulties. Who could have foretold, for instance, the far-reaching cultural transformation that ensued from the invention and widespread use of the printing press? To be sure, the mere technical existence of a satellite or a cable system will not—in itself—alter sensibilities or social arrangements. Who uses it, and what it is used for—these will be the decisive factors.

In a world facing the threat of nuclear annihilation, irrational violence, and ecological disaster, the who and the what of mass communication are not inconsequential concerns. The study of developments in the art and industry of communicating with large, heterogeneous, geographically dispersed, anonymous audiences is becoming increasingly urgent, not just for its own sake, but for an essential understanding of the social relationships and social processes in which these developments are taking place.

Notes

CHAPTER 1

1. Lucien Fèbvre and Henri-Jean Martin, *The Coming of the Book: The Impact of Printing 1450-1800*, trans. David Gerard (London: New Left Books, 1976), p. 17.

2. Harold Innis, *Empire and Communications* (Toronto: University of Toronto Press, 1972), p. 138.

3. Fernand Braudel, *The Structures of Everyday Life*, trans. Sîan Reynolds, vol. 1 (New York: Harper and Row, 1981), p. 401.

4. See Barbara Tuchman, *A Distant Mirror: The Calamitous 14th Century* (New York: Alfred A. Knopf, 1978).

5. Ibid., p. 27.

6. See S. H. Steinberg, *Five Hundred Years of Printing* (Harmondsworth, Eng.: Penguin Books, 1961).

7. Ibid., p. 27.

8. Ibid., pp. 21-22

9. See Braudel, *Structures of Everyday Life*, pp. 497-99.

10. Elizabeth L. Eisenstein, *The Printing Press as an Agent of Change: Communications and Cultural Transformations in Early-modern Europe*, vol. 1 (Cambridge, Eng.: Cambridge University Press, 1979), p. 391.

11. Innis, *Empire and Communications*, p. 10.

12. See Fèbvre and Martin, *Coming of the Book*, p. 262.

13. Elizabeth L. Eisenstein, "Some Conjectures about the Impact of Printing on Western Society and Thought: A Preliminary Report," *Journal of Modern History* 40 (1968): 8.

14. Marshall McLuhan, *The Gutenberg Galaxy: The Making of Typographic Man* (Toronto: University of Toronto Press, 1962) p. 161.

15. Quoted in ibid., p. 183.

16. Steinberg, *Five Hundred Years*, p. 68.

17. Ibid., p. 102.

18. McLuhan, *Gutenberg Galaxy*, p. 198.

19. Ibid., p. 233.

20. Ibid., p. 234.

21. Eisenstein, *Printing Press*, p. 132.

22. Quoted in ibid., p. 306.

23. Steinberg, *Five Hundred Years*, pp. 103-04.

24. Fèbvre and Martin, *Coming of the Book*, p. 294.

25. See Steinberg, *Five Hundred Years*, p. 77.

26. Lawrence Stone, "Literacy and Education in England, 1640-1900," *Past and Present* 42 (February 1969): 78-79.

27. Lawrence Stone, *The Crisis of the Aristocracy, 1558-1640* (New York: Oxford University Press, 1965), p. 36.

28. Elizabeth L. Eisenstein, "The Emergence of Print Culture in the West," *Journal of Communication* 30 (Winter 1980): 103.

29. Lawrence Stone, "The Educational Revolution in England, 1500-1640," *Past and Present* 28 (July 1964): 42.

30. Stone, "Literacy and Education," p. 86.

31. John Milton, *Areopagitica and Other Prose Works of John Milton* (New York: E. P. Dutton, 1927).

32. See James Curran, "Capitalism and Control of the Press, 1800-1975," in *Mass Communication and Society*, eds. James Curran, Michael Gurevitch, and Janet Woollacott (Beverly Hills, Calif.: Sage Publications, 1979).

33. See Raymond Williams, *The Long Revolution* (New York: Harper and Row, 1961), ch. 3.

34. Ivon Asquith, "The Structure, Ownership and Control of the Press, 1780-1855," in *Newspaper History: From the 17th Century to the Present Day*, eds. George Boyce, James Curran, and Pauline Wingate (Beverly Hills, Calif.: Sage Publications, 1978), p. 116.

35. An intricate interlacing of terrestrial and submarine telegraph cables was constructed along already established transportation routes. Subsequent developments in communications technology tended to follow the basic pattern set down by the expanding colonial system, a notion developed very well by Phil Harris, "News Dependence: The Case for a New World Information Order" (Unpublished Final Report: UNESCO, 1977), ch. 2.

36. Anthony Smith, *The Geopolitics of Information: How Western Culture Dominates the World* (New York: Oxord University Press, 1980, p. 75.

37. Quoted in ibid., p. 25.

38. Ibid.

39. Ibid., p. 79.

40. See Oliver Boyd-Barrett, *The International News Agencies* (Beverly Hills, Calif: Sage Publications, 1980).

41. Quoted in Frank Luther Mott, *American Journalism: A History*, 3rd ed. (New York: Macmillan, 1962), p. 6.

42. See Vincent Buranelli, ed., *The Trial of Peter Zenger* (New York: New York University Press, 1957). See also Leonard W. Levy, ed., *Freedom of the Press from Zenger to Jefferson* (Indianapolis: Bobbs-Merrill, 1966).

43. Leonard W. Levy, *Legacy of Suppression* (Cambridge, Mass: Harvard University Press, 1960). For a more recent version of Levy's views, see his *Emergence of a Free Press* (New York: Oxford University Press, 1985).

44. Michael Schudson, *Discovering the News: A Social History of American Newspapers* (New York: Basic Books, 1978), p. 44.

45. See Frank M. O'Brien, *The Story of the Sun* (New York: Appleton-Century-Crofts, 1928).

46. Quoted in Mott, *American Journalism*, pp. 232-33.

47. Quoted in Willard G. Bleyer, *Main Currents in the History of American Journalism* (Boston: Houghton Mifflin, 1927), pp. 194-95.

48. O'Brien, *Story of the Sun*, p. 53.

49. Quoted in Dan Schiller, *Objectivity and the News: The Public and the Rise of Commercial Journalism* (Philadelphia: University of Pennsylvania Press, 1981), p. 78.

50. See Robert Luther Thompson, *Wiring a Continent: The History of the Telegraph Industry in the United States 1832–1866* (Princeton: Princeton University Press, 1947).

51. Matthew Josephson, *The Robber Barons* (New York: Harcourt, Brace, and World, 1962), p. 208.

52. See Victor Rosewater, *History of Cooperative News-Gathering in the United States* (New York: Appleton-Century-Crofts, 1930).

53. See W. A. Swanberg, *Pulitzer* (New York: Charles Scribner's Sons, 1967).

54. Daniel Boorstin, *The Image* (New York: Harper and Row, 1961), p. 12.

55. See John Tebbel, *The Life and Good Times of William Randolph Hearst* (New York: E. P. Dutton, 1952). See also W. A. Swanberg, *Citizen Hearst* (New York: Charles Scribner's, 1961).

56. See Sidney Kobre, *The Development of American Journalism* (Dubuque, Iowa: William C. Brown, 1969) for a detailed study of many leading twentieth-century newspapers.

57. Boorstin, *Image*, p. 13.

CHAPTER 2

1. See Gordon Hendricks, *The Edison Motion Picture Myth* (Berkeley: University of California Press, 1961) for the argument that Dickson deserves full credit for the creation of the first motion picture camera.

2. See Russell Merritt, "Nickelodeon Theatres 1905-14: Building an Audience for the Movies," in *The American Film Industry*, ed. Tino Balio (Madison: University of Wisconsin Press, 1985), ch. 4.

3. See Robert Anderson, "The Motion Picture Patents Company" (Ph.D. dissertation, University of Wisconsin, 1983) for an emphasis on the positive contributions of the MPPC.

4. See Benjamin B. Hampton, *A History of the Movies* (New York: Covici-Friede Publishers, 1931), p. 210.

5. Leo Rosten, *Hollywood: The Movie Colony and the Movie Makers* (New York: Harcourt, Brace, 1941), p. 19.

6. See Robert M. Henderson, *D. W. Griffith: His Life and His Work* (New York: Oxford University Press, 1972).

7. Lewis Jacobs, *The Emergence of Film Art* (New York: Hopkinson and Blake, 1969), p. 50.

8. Vachel Lindsay, *The Art of the Moving Picture* (New York: Macmillan, 1915).

9. Hugo Münsterberg, *The Photoplay: A Psychological Study* (New York: D. Appleton, 1916).

10. Siegfried Kracauer, *From Caligari to Hitler: A Psychological History of German Film* (Princeton: Princeton University Press, 1947).

11. See Richard Abel, *French Cinema: The First Wave, 1915–1929* (Princeton: Princeton University Press, 1984).

12. See Sergei Eisenstein, *The Film Form*, trans. and ed. Jay Leyda (New York: Harcourt, Brace, 1949) for the great director's ideas about filmmaking.

13. See Maurice Bardiche and Robert Brasillock, *The History of Motion Pictures* (New York: W. W. Norton, 1933), p. 199.

14. See J. Douglas Gomery, "The Coming of Sound to the American Cinema: A History of the Transformation of an Industry" (Ph.D. dissertation, University of Wisconsin, 1975).

15. See Michael Conant, *Antitrust in the Motion Picture Industry* (Berkeley: University of California Press, 1960).

16. See Upton Sinclair, *Upton Sinclair Presents William Fox* (Los Angeles: Upton Sinclair Publishing, 1933).

17. F. D. Klingender and Stuart Legg, *Money behind the Screen* (London: Lawrence and Wishart, 1937), p. 79.

18. See "Paramount Pictures, Inc.," *Fortune* (March 1937): 87–96 +.

19. See Douglas Gomery, *The Hollywood Studio System* (New York: St. Martin's Press, 1986) for an analysis of the business aspects of the studio system.

20. See Bosley Crowther's *The Lion's Share: The Story of an Entertainment Empire* (New York: E. P. Dutton, 1957) and *Hollywood Rajah: The Life and Times of Louis B. Mayer* (New York: Holt, Rinehart, and Winston, 1960) for an anecdotal account of the studio in its heyday.

21. Aljean Harmetz, *The Making of the Wizard of Oz* (New York: Alfred A. Knopf, 1977), pp. 28–29.

22. See François Truffaut, "A Certain Tendency of the French Cinema," *Cahiers du Cinéma* 31 (January 1954): 15–29, trans. in *Movies and Methods*, ed. Bill Nichols (Berkeley: University of California Press, 1976), pp. 224–36. See also James Hillier, ed., *Cahiers du Cinéma The 1950s: Neo-Realism, New Wave* (Cambridge, Mass.: Harvard University Press, 1985).

23. See Andrew Sarris, "Notes on *Auteur* Theory in 1962," in *Film Theory and Criticism*, 3rd ed., eds. Gerald Mast and Marshall Cohen (New York: Oxford University Press, 1985), pp. 527–40.

24. See Nick Roddick, *A New Deal in Entertainment: Warner Brothers in the 1930s* (London: British Film Institute, 1983) for an overview of the working conditions at this studio.

25. See David Bordwell, Janet Staiger, and Kristin Thompson, *The Classical Hollywood Cinema: Film Style and Mode of Production to 1960* (New York: Columbia University Press, 1985).

26. Lewis Jacobs, *The Rise of the American Cinema*, rev. ed. (New York: Teachers College Press, 1968), p. 468.

27. See "Twentieth Century-Fox," *Fortune* (December 1935): 85–93 +.

28. Richard H. Pells, *Radical Visions and American Dreams* (New York: Harper and Row, 1973), p. 280.

29. Arlene Croce, *The Fred Astaire and Ginger Rogers Book* (New York: Galahad Books, 1972), p. 135.

30. See Robert L. Carringer, *The Making of Citizen Kane* (Berkeley: University of California Press, 1985).

31. Robert Sklar, *Movie-Made America: A Social History of American Movies* (New York: Random House, 1975), p. 210.

32. Pells, *Radical Visions*, p. 270.

33. See Tino Balio, *United Artists: The Company Built By the Stars* (Madison: University of Wisconsin Press, 1976).

34. See Rudy Behlmer, ed., *Memo from David O. Selznick* (New York: Viking Press, 1972).

35. See "The Big Bad Wolf," *Fortune* (November 1934): 88–95 + for an excellent description of how Disney's cartoon shorts were made. See also Richard Schickel, *The Disney Version* (New York: Simon and Schuster, 1968) for a caustic critique of the Disney studio operation.

36. See Raymond Fielding, *The American Newsreel, 1911–1967* (Norman: University of Oklahoma Press, 1972).

37. See David Robinson, *Chaplin: His Life and Art* (New York: McGraw-Hill, 1985) for a comprehensive biography of the great comedic actor.

38. Quoted in Lewis Jacobs, "World War II and the American Film," *Cinema Journal* 7, (Winter 1967–68): 6.

39. See Balio, *United Artists* p. 164.

40. Gerald P. Nye, "Our Madness Increases as Our Emergency Shrinks," *Vital Speeches* 7 (September 15, 1941): 720-21.

41. U.S. Congress, Senate Subcommittee of the Committee on Interstate Commerce, *Propaganda in Motion Pictures* (Washington, D.C.: Government Printing Office, 1942), p. 423.

42. See Allan M. Winkler, *The Politics of Propaganda: The Office of War Information 1942-1945* (New Haven: Yale University Press, 1978).

43. Walter Wanger, "OWI and Motion Pictures," *Public Opinion Quarterly* 7 (Spring 1943): 100.

44. Clayton R. Koppes and Gregory D. Black, "What to Show the World: The Office of War Information and Hollywood 1942-1945," *The Journal of American History* 64 (1977): 103.

45. See Richard Dyer MacCann, *The People's Films* (New York: Hastings House, 1973), ch. 6.

46. Cited in "Walt Disney: Great Teacher," *Fortune* (August 1942): 94.

47. See Richard Allen Shale, "Donald Duck Joins Up: The Walt Disney Studio during World War II" (Ph.D. dissertation, University of Michigan, 1976) for a detailed study of the Disney studio's propaganda output during World War II.

48. The U.S. military employed a team of social scientists to measure the persuasive effectiveness of these films on soldiers. The findings indicated that the films produced large increases in "factual" knowledge and modest amounts of opinion change on certain specific points. But more general attitudes toward the war, its aims, and why the United States was involved in the conflict remained largely unaffected. See Shearon Lowery and Melvin L. De Fleur, *Milestones in Mass Communication Research* (New York: Longman, 1983), ch. 5, for a summary and analysis of these studies.

49. See Dorothy B. Jones, "The Hollywood War Film," *Hollywood Quarterly* 1 (October 1945): 1-19.

50. Statistics taken from Lawrence W. Lichty and Malachi C. Topping, eds., *American Broadcasting: A Source Book on the History of Radio and Television* (New York: Hastings House, 1975), p. 522.

51. See *United States v. Paramount Pictures, Inc. et al.*, 344 U.S. 131 (1948).

52. See Steven Bach, *Final Cut: Dreams and Disaster in the Making of Heaven's Gate* (New York: William Morrow, 1985) for a fascinating account of the *Heaven's Gate* fiasco.

53. See David McClintock, *Indecent Exposure: A True Story of Hollywood and Wall Street* (New York: Dell Publishing, 1982) for an insightful analysis of the inner workings of Columbia Pictures Industries and the movie industry in general.

54. Ibid., p. 49.

CHAPTER 3

1. See Susan Sontag, *On Photography* (New York: Farrar, Strauss, and Giroux, 1977).

2. David Robinson, *Hollywood in the Twenties* (Cranbury, N. J.: A. S. Barnes, 1968), p. 33.

3. Quoted in Terry Ramsaye, *A Million and One Nights* (New York: Simon and Schuster, 1926), p. 259.

4. *Mutual Film Corporation v. Industrial Commission of Ohio*, 236 U.S. 230, 244 (1915).

5. U.S. Congress, House of Representatives, *Federal Motion Picture Commission*, 1916, H. Rept. 697, p. 2.

6. See Raymond Moley, *The Hays Office* (New York: Bobbs-Merrill, 1945) for a detailed description of industry attempts at self-regulation.

7. Robert Warshow, "The Gangster as Tragic Hero," in *The Immediate Experience* (New York: Atheneum, 1972), pp. 127–33.

8. Alexander Walker, *The Celluloid Sacrifice* (New York: Hawthorn Books, 1967), p. 72.

9. See Hortense Powermaker, *Hollywood: The Dream Factory* (Boston: Little, Brown, 1950), ch. 3.

10. Frank Capra, *The Name of the Title: An Autobiography* (New York: Macmillan, 1971), pp. 320–21.

11. See Pauline Kael, *The Citizen Kane Book* (Boston: Little, Brown, 1971), pp. 5–9.

12. Murray Schumach, *The Face on the Cutting Room Floor* (New York: William Morrow, 1964), p. 53.

13. Ibid., p. 59.

14. Ibid.

15. *Motion Pictures Classified by National Legion of Decency, 1936–1959* (New York: National Legion of Decency, 1959), p. 13.

16. Quoted in the New York *Times*, December 24, 1956, p. 14.

17. Ibid.

18. Quoted in the New York *Times*, December 30, 1956, p. 24.

19. *Joseph Burstyn, Inc. v. Wilson*, 343 U.S. 495 (1952). See also Alan F. Westin, *The Miracle Case: The Supreme Court and the Movies*, Inter-University Case Program No. 64 (Alabama: University of Alabama Press, 1961).

20. *Times Film Corp. v. Chicago*, 365 U.S. 43 (1961).

21. *Freedom v. Maryland*, 380 U.S. 51 (1965).

22. *Roth v. U.S.*, 354 U.S. 476 (1957).

23. *Jacobellis v. Ohio*, 378 U.S. 184 (1964).

24. *Memoirs v. Massachusetts*, 383 U.S. 413 (1966).

25. *Variety*, April 12, 1961, p. 4.

26. See Richard S. Randall, *Censorship of the Movies* (Madison: University of Wisconsin Press, 1968), pp. 181–84.

27. See Jack Vizzard, *See No Evil* (New York: Simon and Schuster, 1970), pp. 320–24.

28. *Ginsberg v. New York*, 390 U.S. 629 (1968); *Interstate Circuit v. Dallas*, 390 U.S. 676 (1968).

29. See Stephen Farber, *The Movie Rating Game* (Washington, D.C.: Public Affairs Press, 1972) for a critical assessment of early rating-board applications.

30. See Richard Smith, *Getting into Deep Throat* (Chicago: Playboy Press, 1973) for a detailed discussion of this decision.

31. *Miller v. California*, 413 U.S. 15 (1973); *Paris Adult Theatre I v. Slaton*, 413 U.S. 49 (1973); *Kaplan v. California*, 413 U.S. 115 (1973); *U.S. v. Twelve 200-Foot Reels of Super 8mm Film*, 413 U.S. 123 (1973), *U.S. v. Orito*, 413 U.S. 139 (1973).

32. *Jenkins v. Georgia*, 418 U.S. 153 (1974).

CHAPTER 4

1. Lee De Forest, *Father of Radio* (Chicago: Wilcox and Follett, 1950).

2. See Erik Barnouw, *A Town in Babel: A History of Broadcasting in the United States, Volume I: To 1933* (New York: Oxford University Press, 1966), pp. 66–72.

3. Figures cited in Gleason Archer, *Big Business and Radio* (New York: American Historical Company, 1939), p. 19.

4. See Gleason Archer, *History of Radio to 1926* (New York: American Historical Society, 1938), pp. 397–98, for the full text of the first sponsored message.

5. See William Peck Banning, *Commercial Broadcasting Pioneer: The WEAF Experiment 1922-1926* (Cambridge, Mass.: Harvard University Press, 1946), pp. 149–50.

6. Hans V. Kaltenborn, "Radio: Dollars and Nonsense," in *Problems and Controversies in Television and Radio*, eds. Harry J. Skornia and Jack William Kitson (Palo Alto, Calif.: Pacific Books, 1968), p. 303.

7. See Ernest Gruening, *The Public Pays: A Study of Power Propaganda* (New York: Vanguard Press, 1931).

8. *Witmark v. Bamberger*, 291 Fed. 776 (1923).

9. See Robert Metz, *CBS: Reflections in a Bloodshot Eye* (Chicago: Playboy Press, 1975) for a fascinating history of this organization under Paley's stewardship.

10. Ibid., p. 26.

11. Quoted in Barnouw, *Town of Babel*, p. 180.

12. *Hoover v. Intercity Radio Company*, 286 Fed. 1003 (1923).

13. See Marvin R. Bensman, "The Zenith Case and the Chaos of 1926–27," *Journal of Broadcasting* 14 (Fall 1970): 423–40.

14. Herbert Hoover, *The Memoirs of Herbert Hoover: The Cabinet and the Presidency, 1920-1933* (New York: Macmillan, 1952), p. 140.

15. See Barnouw, *Town in Babel*, p. 197.

16. Federal Radio Commission, "In the Matter of the Application of Great Lakes Broadcasting Co.," in the *Third Annual Report* (Washington, D.C.: Government Printing Office, 1929).

17. See Maurice E. Shelby, Jr., "John R. Brinkley: His Contribution to Broadcasting," in *American Broadcasting: A Source Book on the History of Radio and Television*, eds. Lawrence W. Lichty and Malachi C. Topping (New York: Hastings House, 1975), pp. 560–68. See also Gerald Carson, *The Roguish World of Doctor Brinkley* (New York: Rinehart, 1960).

18. *KFKB Broadcasting Association, Inc. v. Federal Radio Commission*, 47 F. (2d) 670 (1931).

19. Ibid., p. 672. See also Andrew G. Haley, "The Law on Radio Programs," *George Washington Law Review* 5 (January 1937): 1–46.

20. See Eric Barnouw, *The Golden Web: A History of Broadcasting in the United States, Volume II: 1933 to 1953* (New York: Oxford University Press, 1968), pp. 22–26.

21. Bruce Barton, *The Man Nobody Knows* (Indianapolis: Bobbs-Merrill, 1924), pp. i–v.

22. James Rorty, *Our Master's Voice: Advertising* (New York: John Day, 1934), pp. 73–74.

23. Cited in Lichty and Topping, *American Broadcasting*, p. 334.

24. See Charles J. Correll and Freeman F. Gosden, *All about Amos 'n' Andy* (New York: Rand McNally, 1929). See also Arthur Frank Wertheim, *Radio Comedy* (New York: Oxford University Press, 1979), ch. 3.

25. Ben Gross, *I Looked and I Listened* (New York: Random House, 1954), p. 156.

26. Charles J. Rolo, "Simenon and Spillane: The Metaphysics of Murder for the Millions," in *Mass Culture: The Popular Arts in America*, eds. Bernard Rosenberg and David M. White (New York: Free Press, 1957), p. 174.

27. J. Fred MacDonald, *Don't Touch That Dial: Radio Programming in American Life from 1920 to 1960* (Chicago: Nelson-Hall, 1979), p. 158.

28. James Thurber, "Onward and Upward with the Arts," *New Yorker*, May 15, 1948, p. 34.

29. Herta Herzog, "On Borrowed Experience: An Analysis of Listening to Daytime Sketches," *Studies in Philosophy and Social Science* 9 (1941): 65–95.

30. *Broadcasting*, December 20, 1937 and January 25, 1938. See also "Dummy and Dame Arouse the Nation," *Broadcasting-Telecasting*, October 15, 1956, p. 258.

31. *Broadcasting*, October 15, 1938, p. 22.

32. See Howard Koch, *The Panic Broadcast: Portrait of an Event* (Boston: Little, Brown, 1970).

33. Hadley Cantril, *The Invasion from Mars: A Study in the Psychology of Panic* (Princeton: Princeton University Press, 1940).

34. Quoted in MacDonald, *Don't Touch That Dial*, pp. 299–300.

35. See Sheldon Marcus, *Father Coughlin: The Tumultuous Life of the Priest of the Little Flower* (Boston: Little, Brown, 1973). See also Alan Brinkley, *Voices of Protest: Huey Long, Father Coughlin, and the Great Depression* (New York: Alfred A. Knopf, 1982).

36. Quoted in Ernest G. Bormann, "This is Huey P. Long Talking," *Journal of Broadcasting* 2 (Spring 1968): 116.

37. See George E. Lott, Jr., "The Press-Radio War of the 1930s," *Journal of Broadcasting* 14 (Summer 1970): 275–86.

38. Cited in Llewellyn White, *The American Radio* (Chicago: University of Chicago Press, 1947), p. 47.

39. Alexander Kendrick, *Prime Time: The Life of Edward R. Murrow* (Boston: Little, Brown, 1969) p. 174.

40. See George A. Willey, "The Soap Operas and the War," *Journal of Broadcasting* 7 (Fall 1963): 339–52.

41. Quoted in Allan M. Winkler, *The Politics of Propaganda: The Office of War Information 1942–1945* (New Haven: Yale University Press, 1978) p. 61.

42. Robert K. Merton, *Mass Persuasion: The Social Psychology of a War Bond Drive* (New York: Harper and Bros., 1946).

43. Federal Communications Commission, *Report on Chain Broadcasting* (Washington, D.C.: Government Printing Office, 1941).

44. *National Broadcasting Co. v. United States*, 319 U.S. 190 (1943).

45. Quoted in Charles A. Siepmann, *Radio's Second Chance* (Boston: Little, Brown, 1946), pp. 186–87.

46. Federal Communications Commission, *Public Service Responsibility of Broadcast Licensees* (Washington, D.C.: Government Printing Office, 1946). See Richard J. Meyer, "The Blue Book," *Journal of Broadcasting* 6 (Summer 1962): 197–207 for a general overview of this document.

47. Quoted in Richard J. Meyer, "Reaction to the 'Blue Book'," *Journal of Broadcasting* 6 (Fall 1962): 296.

48. Eric Barnouw, *The Image Empire: A History of Broadcasting in the United States, Volume III: From 1953* (New York: Oxford University Press, 1970), p. 336.

CHAPTER 5

1. Federal Communications Commission, *Sixth Report and Order on Television Allocations*, 41 FCC 148 (1952).

2. See Bart Andrews, *The "I Love Lucy" Book* (New York: Doubleday, 1985) for a detailed description of virtually every aspect of this series.

3. *Republic Pictures Inc. v. Rogers*, 213 F. (2d) 662 (1954); *Autry v. Republic Pictures Inc.*, 213 F. (2d) 667 (1954).

4. See Amy Schnapper, "The Distribution of Theatrical Feature Films to Television" (Ph.D. dissertation, University of Wisconsin, 1975) for detailed documentation of the pervasiveness of movies on television.

5. Paddy Chayefsky, *Television Plays* (New York: Simon and Schuster, 1955), p. 173.

6. Eric Barnouw, *The Image Empire: A History of Broadcasting in the United States, Volume III: From 1953* (New York: Oxford University Press, 1970), p. 33. See also William Kenneth Hawes, Jr., "A History of Anthology Television Drama through 1958" (Ph.D. dissertation, University of Michigan, 1960) for a detailed study of the rise and fall of this television format.

7. See John Cogley, *Report on Blacklisting I: Movies* (New York: Fund for the Republic, 1956). See also Larry Ceplair and Steven Englund, *The Inquisition in Hollywood: Politics in the Film Community, 1930–1960* (New York: Anchor Press/Doubleday, 1980).

8. See John Cogley, *Report on Blacklisting II: Radio-Television* (New York: Fund for the Republic, 1956). See also J. Fred MacDonald, *Television and the Red Menace: The Video Road to Vietnam* (New York: Praeger Publishers, 1985).

9. See Daniel J. Leab, "*See It Now*: A Legend Reassessed," in *American History/American Television*, ed. John O'Connor (New York: Frederick Ungar Publishing, 1983) for a recent reassessment of this much-analyzed series.

10. Fred W. Friendly, *Due to Circumstances beyond Our Control* (New York: Random House, 1967), p. 48.

11. Cited in Alexander Kendrick, *Prime Time: The Life of Edward R. Murrow* (Boston: Little, Brown, 1969), p. 60.

12. See A. M. Sperber, *Murrow: His Life and Times* (New York: Freundlich Books, 1986).

13. Incident related in Kendrick, *Prime Time*, p. 378.

14. See Meyer Weinberg, *TV and America: The Morality of Hard Cash* (New York: Ballantine Books, 1962). See also Kent Anderson, *Television Fraud: The History and Implications of the Quiz Show Scandals* (Westport, Conn.: Greenwood Press, 1978).

15. See Merle Miller and Evan Rhodes, *Only You, Dick Daring!* (New York: William Sloane Associates, 1964) for a witty and caustic account of Aubrey's reign at CBS.

16. See Richard P. Adler, ed., *All in the Family: A Critical Appraisal* (New York: Praeger Publishers, 1979). This work contains several scripts.

17. Quoted in ibid., pp. 89–91.

18. Les Brown, *Television: The Business behind the Box* (New York: Harcourt Brace Jovanovich, 1971), p. 58.

19. Todd Gitlin, *Inside Prime Time* (New York: Pantheon, 1983), p. 55.

20. Quoted in "Longer News: A Bitter Pill Stations Brace to Swallow," *Broadcasting*, June 28, 1976, p. 19.

21. Quoted in Tony Schwartz, "Are TV Anchormen Merely Performers?," *New York Times*, August 1, 1980, p. C3.

22. Ron Powers, *The Newscasters* (New York: St. Martin's Press, 1977), p. 1.

23. See John H. Pennybacker, "The Character Standard: Will It Survive RKO?" *Journal of Broadcasting & Electronic Media* 29 (Spring 1985): 161–74 for a discussion of the complicated 1980 case in which the FCC voted to strip RKO General of its television licenses in Boston, New York, and Los Angeles. Congress came to RKO's rescue in 1982, when it passed a tax bill with a rider requiring the FCC to automatically renew the license of any VHF television station that agreed to move to a state without such a station. RKO relocated its New York City outlet, WOR-TV, to nearby Secaucus in New Jersey—one of the few states in the nation that did not have a VHF television station. (RKO sold the station in 1986 to MCA for a reported $387 million.)

24. See Bernard Schwartz, *The Professor and the Commissions* (New York: Alfred A. Knopf, 1959) for a detailed description of the findings of this investigation.

25. See Newton M. Minow, *Equal Time: The Private Broadcaster and the Public Interest*, ed. Lawrence Laurent (New York: Atheneum, 1964), pp. 46–64.

26. Congress amended Section 310(b) of the Communications Act in 1952, requiring the FCC to approve a license transfer request unless it can be established that the proposed beneficiary of this public trust is unqualified—in some serious way—to operate a radio or television station. Such policies have turned the sale of television stations into a continuing auction, in which only the economically powerful can participate. (The sale of TV stations accelerated in the 1980s, when the FCC rescinded

its rule requiring a broadcaster to operate an outlet for three years before putting it on the block. The commission also increased the number of TV stations that any single entity may own from 7 to 12, providing the total reach is no more than 25 percent of the potential national audience.)

27. Cited in Roger Noll, Merton J. Peck, and John J. McGowan, *Economic Aspects of Television Regulation* (Washington, D.C.: Brookings Institution, 1973), p. 123.

28. See Fred W. Friendly, *The Good Guys, The Bad Guys and the First Amendment: Free Speech vs. Fairness in Broadcasting* (New York: Random House, 1975) for a different slant on this case. Although the judicial outcome of this case triggered many more petitions to deny license renewals, there have been few actual hearings and still fewer denials.

29. *Red Lion Broadcasting Co. v. Federal Communications Commission*, 395 U.S. 367 (1969).

30. Fred Friendly has compiled impressive evidence showing that Cook had been part of a campaign by the Democrats to harass stations that sold time for the airing of ultraconservative political programs. See Friendly, *The Good Guys*, pp. 32–77.

31. Quoted in *Illinois Citizens Committee for Broadcasting v. Federal Communications Commission* 515 F. (2d) 397 (1975).

32. *Federal Communications Commission v. Pacifica Foundation* 438 U.S. 726 (1978).

33. Carnegie Commission on Educational Television, *Public Television: A Program for Action* (New York: Harper and Row, 1967). This report, written primarily by Stephen White, who was the television critic for *Horizon*, was the result of eight major meetings and was based on information culled from more than 200 individual specialists and educational organizations. The study was funded by Carnegie Corporation of New York, established in 1911 by robber baron Andrew Carnegie with an original endowment of $135 million.

34. See Network Project, *The Fourth Network* (New York: Network Project, 1971), pp. 17–25.

35. See Michael J. Arlen, *Living-Room War* (New York: Viking Press, 1969), p. 161.

36. Cited in Dave Berkman, "Inner City," *Educational Television* (February 1970): 33.

37. Carnegie Commission on the Future of Public Broadcasting, *A Public Trust* (New York: Bantam, 1979).

38. See Meryl Gordon, "Colossus of Cable," *Channels: The Business of Communications* (October 1986): 26-33 for an informative profile of this company.

39. Section 639 of this legislation does provide for fines of $10,000 or up to two years' imprisonment for anyone who transmits, over any cable system, any matter that is obscene or otherwise unprotected by the U.S. Constitution. Some states and municipalities have attempted to use the "dirty words" decision as a precedent for legislation proscribing—or channeling to the late-night hours—the presentation of indecent material on cable television. Thus far, the lower courts have struck down these laws as unconstitutional. See Howard M. Kleiman, "Indecent Programming on Cable Television: Legal and Social Dimensions," *Journal of Broadcasting & Electronic Media* 30 (Summer 1986): 275-94.

40. "Field Guide '87," *Channels: The Business of Communications* (Fifth Annual Report, 1987): 34.

41. Ben H. Bagdikian, *The Media Monopoly* (Boston: Beacon Press, 1983), pp. 25-26.

42. John J. O'Connor, ''Dramas with Strong Casts Delivered Moving Entertainment,'' New York *Times*, December 28, 1986, Sec. 2, p. 23.

Index

ABC. *See* American Broadcasting Company
A.C. Neilsen Company, 162, 203. *See also* Nielsen ratings
Adams, Samuel, 26
Adult theatres, 124
"Adventures of Sherlock Holmes, The," 158
Adventure shows, 174
Advertising, American Association of Advertising Agencies, 162; abuses of, 124, 177; ad agencies, 151–54; cigarette commercials and, 219; demographic data, 199; FRC and, 146–47; NBC networks and, 135; newscasts and, 209; newspapers and, 18–19; postwar patterns of, 176; promotion methods, 153–54; public TV and, 230; radio, 131–33, 138–39, 142, 151–54; revenue from, 20; serials and, 161; tax on, 18; TV commercials, 186, 188; vaudeville and, 154–57; video recorders and, 205; wartime, 176
Affiliates, TV, 198, 206–07, 219–20
Albee, Edward, 118
Alcoa Corporation, 193–94
"All in the Family", 200
Allen, Fred, 154
America, colonial press in, 24–25
American Association of Advertising Agenicies (AAAA), 162
American Broadcasting Company (ABC), 175; CCC merger and, 233; TV networks, 181
American Civil Liberties Union (ACLU), 111, 192, 221
American Express, 235
American Medical Association, 148
American Revolution, 26

American Society of Composers, Authors, and Publishers (ASCAP), 135–36
American Telephone and Telegraph. *See* AT&T
American Television & Communications, 236
"Amos n' Andy", 155–56, 181
AMPP. *See* Association of Motion Picture Producers
Anchor persons, 208
Anglican Church, 13, 16
Animation, 75, 84
Anthology programs, 187–89
Antitrust regulation, cable systems and, 236; suits, 149
Antonioni, Michelangelo, 119
Arbitron, 204–05
Arbuckle, "Fatty" (Roscoe), 100
Areopagitica (Milton), 16, 24
Aretino, Petro, 10
Arnez, Desi, 91, 182
Art, medieval, 2
Associated Press (AP), 34–35; radio and, 168; Western, 35
Association of Motion Picture Producers (AMPP), 101–03
Association of National Advertisers, 162
Astaire, Fred, 71
Atlanta Constitution, 40
AT&T, 129; line rentals, 134; network monolpoly of, 133–34; Radio Act and, 142; WEAF experiment, 131–33
Aubrey, James T., Jr., 196
Audience Studies, Inc. (ASI), 196–97
Audimeter, 163, 203
Audits of Great Britain Research, 205
Autry, Gene, 184
Aylesworth, Merlin H., 135

Baby Doll, 110
Bagdikian, Ben H., 237
Ball, Lucille, 91, 182
Bands, radio, 146; UHF v. VHF, 181
Bardot, Brigitte, 119
Barnouw, Erik, 188
Barton, Bruce, 151
Bennett, James Gordon, 30–31
Benny, Jack, 154–55, 181, 196
Bergen, Edgar, 163–64
Berle, Milton, 182
Bernhardt, Sarah, 48
Beyond the Horizon, 164
Bible, as first printed book, 5; Luther's
  translation of, 12
Bigotry, on TV, 200–02. *See also* Racism
Biograph film company, 46
Birth of a Nation, 51
Black Entertainment Television, 236
Blacks, advertising and, 163; cable shows
  for, 236; in radio, 155–56; on TV,
  200; WLBT-TV case and, 214–16;
  WWII and, 173–74. *See also* Racism
Blow-Up, 119
Bly, Nelly, 36
Bogart, Humphrey, 66
Books, *Catholic Index* of, 10, 14; censor-
  ship of, 12–15; early manuscripts, 2
  incunabula, 8, 15; literacy rates and,
  3. *See also* Printing
Boorstin, Daniel, 37, 41
Boston *Daily Times,* 30
Boyd, William, 183
Braudel, Fernand, 4
Breen, Joseph, 104, 109
Brinkley, John Romulus, 147–49
British Exchange Telegraph, 168–69
Broadcasting, bands, 146, 181; FCC
  and, 175–76; First Amendment pro-
  tection for, 221; nonprofit, 150; sat-
  ellite, 208. *See* specific type
Brown, Cecil, 171
Burns and Allen, 154

Cabinet of Dr. Caligari, The, 53
Cable Communications Policy Act
  (1984), 237

Cable News Network, 236
Cable television, 205, 230–31; mono-
  polies in, 234–36; pay-per-view chan-
  nels, 235–36; Qube systems, 235–36
Cahier du Cinema, 63
Calvin, John, 12
Calvinist sect, 16
Camera obscura, 43
Cantor, Eddie, 154
Capitalism, free press and, 25; Protes-
  tantism and, 14
Capital Cities Communications, 233
Capra, Frank, 72–73, 86
Carlin, George, 221–22
Carnal Knowledge, 125
Carnegie Commission, 224, 227–29
Cassidy, Hopalong, 183
Catholic Church. *See* Roman Catholic
  Church
CBS. *See* Columbia Broadcasting System
Censorship, 12–13; advisory ratings,
  117–19; curtailment of, 111–13; in
  England, 15–16; FCC and, 220–23;
  of films, 82–83, 95–126; *Green Sheet*
  rating, 117–19; laws, 97; MPPDA
  and, 101; obscenity and, 114–15; of
  radio, 142–43; rating codes, 119–22;
  social value criterion, 115; Supreme
  Court and, 111–13; wartime code,
  171–72. *See also* specific organizations
Chaplin, Charlie, 55, 80–81
Charlemagne, 8
Chicago *Tribune,* 39, 234
Children, obscenity and, 223; public TV
  and, 229; radio and, 159; TV shows
  for, 186; wartime radio shows, 174
Chinese Central News Agency, 169
"Christian Crusade, The", 217
Christian Science Monitor, 39
"Church of the Air", 167
Cigarette commercials, 219
Cinemax, 236
Citizen Kane, 71–72, 105
Civil liberties, ACLU, 111, 192, 221;
  blacks and, 157; TV and, 214–16.
  See also U.S. Constitution, First
  Amendment; Racism

Clark-Hooper, Inc., 162
Cochrane, Elizabeth, 36
Code of Wartime Practices, 172
Code and Rating Administration
    (CARA), 120–22
Cohn, Roy, 192
Colonialism, 23
Columbia Broadcasting System (CBS),
    137; financing of, 138–39; NBC
    rivalry with, 165; networks of, 138,
    161; newscasts of, 168; wartime news
    and, 170
Columbia Phonograph Broadcasting
    System, 137
Columbia Pictures, 72–73; Coca-Cola
    purchase of, 92; Screen Gems and, 186
Columbia Workshop, 164
Comedy, obscenity and, 221–22
Commerce, 18–20; commercial journals,
    29; Dow Jones service, 168; growth
    of cities and, 3; Industrial Revolu-
    tion and, 18; insider information, 34;
    printing and, 5–7; *Wall Street Journal*
    and, 39. *See also* Advertising; Regula-
    tion; specific corporations, types
Commercial(s), 186, 188; cigarette, 219;
    radio, 151–54. *See also* Advertising
Commercial broadcasting, 131–33
Commercial press, 18, 29, 39
Common carriers, 135
Communications Act (1934), 150–51,
    171; censorship and, 220; FCC
    powers and, 211; 1952 amendment,
    214; Sec. 315, 216–17
Communications technology. *See* specific
    media
Communism, 19; House Un-American
    Activities Committee and, 189–90; in
    media, 191; propaganda and, 26
Computer chips, 232
Conrad, Frank, 129–30
Cook, Fred J., 217–18
Cooperative Analysis of Broadcasting
    (CAB), 162
Copyrights, broadcasting and, 135
Corporation for Public Broadcasting,
    224, 227

Correspondents, foreign, newspapers,
    22; radio, 169–70; wartime, 171
Corwin, Norman, 172
"Cosby Show, The", 202
Coughlin, Charles E., 167
Council of Trent, 14
Counterattack, 189–90
Crime, in movies, 64, 66, 102–03; radio
    series, 157–59; TV series, 182
Cromwell, Oliver, 16
Crossley surveys, 161–62
Curtiz, Michael, 65

Dadaism, 54
Daguerre, Louis-Jacques Mande, 44
Dallas *Times Herald,* 234
Darrow, Clarence, 144–45
Davis, Edwin L., 149
Davis, Elmer, 175
Day, Benjamin H., 30
Day of Absence, 226
Daytime serial dramas. *See* Soap operas
De Forest, Lee, 56
DeMille, Cecil B., 68, 99
Dead End Kids, 183–84
Decca Records, 91
Declaration of Independence, 26
Deep Throat, 122–23
Demographics, TV and, 199–200
Denny, Charles R., Jr., 177
Depression, radio and, 158, 167
Detective series, 157–59
Dewey, Thomas, 159
Dickinson, John, 26
Dietrich, Marlene, 67
Dill, Clarence C., 141
Directors, as auteur, 63; foreign, 54;
    task of, 50–52. *See also* specific
    directors
Disc jockeys, 130
Discovery channel, 236
Disney, Walt, 74–75
Disney Studios, TV and, 186; war films
    of, 83–84
Distributors, film, 74, 89, 100
Documentaries, war, 225–26
Doerfer, John C., 211

Don Juan case, 113
Don Lee Network, 139
Dow Jones ticker service, 168
"Dragnet" series, 182
Drugs, films and, 110
Dumont network, 181
Durante, Jimmy, 154

Economics, international, 158
Edison, Thomas, 45, 56
Education, radio and, 150
Educational TV, ETMA sale, 212–13; NET programs, 225–26; public television, 224–27
Educational Television Facilities Act (1962), 213
Educational Television for the Metropolitan Area (ETMA), 212–13
Edwards, Bob, 209
Edwards, Douglas, 206
Eisenstein, Elizabeth, 7, 11
Eisenstein, Segei, 54
Electrical Research Products, Inc., 57–58
Electronic Media Rating Council, 204
England, Anglican Church, 16; censorship in, 15–16; licensing system, 17; newspapers in, 20
Entertainment shows, fairness doctrine and, 218
Erasmus, Desiderius, 10
Ethnic stereotypes, 155
European Sky Channel, 233

Fairness doctrine, 216; First amendment and, 217–19; personal-attack aspect, 217
Fall, Albert, 143
Fan mail, 161
Fanny Hill case, 115, 124
Fantasy movies, 73
FCC. *See* Federal Communications Commission
Federal Bureau of Investigation (FBI), 158
Federal Communications Commission, 150; Blue Book, 176–77; censorship

and, 220–23; conflict of interest in, 211, 213–14; fairness doctrine and, 216–19; investigation of, 211; network probe by, 175; newscasts and, 207; "raised eyebrow" approach, 163–64; TV licenses and, 180. *See also* specific commissioners, decisions
Federal Radio Commission (FRC), 145; conflict of interest on, 149; Great Lakes decision, 146
Federal Trade Commission (FTC), networks and, 134; RCA and, 143
Feudalism, 4
Fiber optics, 232
Films. *See* Motion pictures
First Amendment, U.S. Constitution, 27–28; films and, 98, 111–14; obscenity and, 124–25, 217–19, 221–22
First National Exhibitor's Circuit, 55
Flynn, Earl, 64–65
Ford, Gerald, 227
Ford, John, 69
Ford Foundation, 180, 226
"Ford Theatre", 186
Foreign agencies, newspapers, 21–24; radio news and, 168–69
Foreign policy, TV and, 191–93
Fox, William, 48–49, 59
Fox Broadcasting Company (FBC), 233, 237
Fox Film Corporation, 56; early history, 49; merger of, 69; Movietone, 76
Fox Libel Act, 18, 20
Freedman case, 113, 122
Freedom of expression, 16, 24, 27–28. *See also* First Amendment, U.S. Constitution
Freedom of the press, 16, 24–25
French Line, The, 109
French Revolution, 27
Freund, Karl, 182–83
Friendly, Fred, 190–93
"Front Page Farrell", 172

Gable, Clark, 75
Game shows, 220
Gannett Company, 233

Gargantua (Rabelais), 9
Garroway, Dave, 194
Gaumont system, 56
General Electric Company, 129; NBC-TV
    purchase, 233; RCA and, 134–36;
    Radio Act and, 142
General Motors Corporation, 152
General Teleradio, 185
Gibbons, Cedric, 61–62
Ginsberg case, 120
Gitlin, Todd, 206
Gleason, Jackie, 200
Goldwyn, Samuel, 74
Gone with the Wind, 74
Gorcey, Leo, 184
Gould, Jay, 34
Grady, Henry W., 40
Great Train Robbery, The, 96
Great Dictator, The, 81
Greeley, Horace, 32
Green Sheet, 117
Griffith, D.W., 50–52
Gulf + Western Industries, 91
Gutenberg, Johann, 5–6, 19, 43
Gutenberg Galaxy, The, (McLuhan), 9

Hamilton, Alexander, 24–25
Hargis, Billy James, 217
Harris, Reed, 192
Havas Agency, 22
Hawks, Howard, 65
Hays, Will, 100–01, 110
Hays Office. *See* Motion Picture Pro-
    ducers and Distributors of America
Hearst, William Randolph, 35–38,
    76–77, 105–06
Hearst Corporation, 35–38, 234
Heaven's Gate, 92
"Helen Trent" series, 160–61, 174
Henry VIII, 12–13
Herzog study, 160
Hick, George, 171
High-definition television (HDTV),
    231–32
"Hill Street Blues", 202, 206
Hoaxes, FRC and, 147; newspaper, 31;
    TV quiz shows, 194–95; radio, 165–66

Hobby, Olveta Culp, 225
Hollywood, Depression and, 103; movie
    industry in, 49–52; scandals in,
    98–100; scriptwriters in, 188–89;
    studio system, 61
Home Box Office (HBO), 234, 236
Homosexuality, in films, 116
Hooper, C.E., 162
Hoover, Herbert, 140–41
Hoover, J. Edgar, 158, 217
Horror movies, 73
House Un-American Activities Com-
    mittee, 189–90
Hughes, Howard, 106–07
Hummert, Ann (Mrs. Frank), 160
Hummert, Frank, 160
Huston, John, 66

"I Love Lucy", 182–83
Incunabula, 8, 15
Independents, broadcasters, 136;
    film companies, 47, 74, 89–90; TV,
    195
Index of Prohibited Books, 10, 14
Industrial Revolution, newspapers and,
    28–29; printing and, 1, 18
Innis, Harold, 7
"Inside North Vietnam", 225
Interactive media, 235
International Films Importers and Distri-
    butors of America, Inc., 120
International News Service (INS), 35, 168
Interstate Circuit, Inc. v. Dallas, 119–20
Interstate Commerce Commission (ICC),
    150

Jacobellis case, 114
Jazz Singer, The, 57
Jenkins v. Georgia, 125
Johnson, Lyndon B., 224
Jolson, Al., 57
Journalism, newsreels, 76–79; yellow,
    38, 76. *See also* Correspondents;
    specific media
Journals, commercial, 29
Joy, Colonel Jason, 101
Judson, Arthur, 136

Kaltenborn, H.V., 133, 170
Kansas City Star, 39–40, 148
Kaplan v. California, 124–25
Kennedy, Joseph, 60, 105
Kennedy, Robert F., 193
Kerkorian, Kirk, 92
Kierker, William, 171
Kinetoscope, 45
King Kong, 70–71
Koberger, Anton, 6
Korean War, 191
Ku Klux Klan, 144

Laemmle, Carl, 47, 73
Lamar Life, 214–16
Lasker, Albert, 152
Latin, dominance of, 15
Lear, Norman, 200–01
Legion of Decency, 103, 110–11
LeRoy, Mervyn, 65
Lesbianism, in films, 116
Lewis, William B., 175
Libel, 25; Fox Libel Act, 18, 20; seditious, 16–17
Licensing, renewal of, 214–16; transfers, 212; TV, 180. *See also* Federal Communications Commission
Lighting systems, TV, 183
Lindbergh-Hauptmann case, 78
Lindsay, Vachel, 52
Literacy rates, 3, 15
Long, Huey P., 167–68
Lord, Philips H., 158
Los Angeles *Times,* 233
Lovers, The, 114
Lowe, Marcus, 55
Lubitsch, Ernst, 67
Lumiere brothers, 45
Luther, Martin, 11–12

McCarthy, Joseph R., 191–93
McCormick, Robert, 39
Mack, Richard, 211
MacLeish, Archibald, 164
McLuhan, Marshall, 9–10
McPherson, Aimee Semple, 140
Magazines, 18

Maltese Falcon, The, 66
Mamoulian, Rouben, 68
Man with the Golden Arm, The, 109
Mankiewicz, Welles, 71–72
March of Time, The, 78–79, 85
Marconi, Guglielmo, 127–28
Marx, Karl, 19, 193
Marx Brothers, 68
"Mary Tyler Moore Show, The", 202, 206
"M*A*S*H", 202, 206
"Masterpiece Theatre", 229
Mayer, Louis B., 75, 105
MCA, Inc., 91, 181
Media Monopoly, The (Bagdikian), 237
Medicine, radio and, 147–49
Medieval culture, 2; Carolingian Renaissance, 8; hierarchical order in, 2; world view of, 7–9
Memoirs case. *See Fanny Hill* case
"Mercury Theatre on the Air", 165
Merton study, 174
Metro-Goldwyn-Mayer (MGM), 55; decline of, 92; directors at, 63; independents and, 89; stars, 62; studio complex, 61
Metrotone News, 76–77
"Miami Vice", 203
Miller v. California, 124–25
Milton, John, 16, 24
Minorities, 147, 167; advertising and, 163; name changes by, 155; on radio, 174. *See also* Racism
Minow, Newton, 211–13
Miracle, The case, 112–13
"Mr. District Attorney", 159
Mr. Smith Goes to Washington, 105
Monogram Pictures, 183
Monopolies, mass communication, 235–38; radio and, 149
Montaigne, Michel de, 10–11
Moon is Blue, The, 109
Morality in Media, 222
Moreau, Jeanne, 119
Morgan, J.P., 56
"Morning Edition", 209
Morse, Samuel, 33

Motion picture(s), aesthetics of, 52–55; animation in, 75; antitrust rulings, 88; as art form, 51, 66, 72; attendance decline, 87; Big Five studios, 59; block booking, 48; California-based, 47–49; CARA and, 120–21; censorship laws, 97; communists in, 189–90; constitutional protection for, 111–13; corporate theatre chains, 88–89; costume design in, 62; distribution of, 89; editing of, 63; film techniques, 66, 70–71; financial structures of, 55, 58–60, 89; First Amendment and, 98; flashbacks in, 53; Hollywood and, 49–52; legal problems of, 87–88; length of, 51; Little Three studios, 59, 72–76; *mise-en-scene*, 51; National Board of Review and, 97; national defense and, 83; newsreels, 76–79; Office of Censorship and, 82–83; profits from, 90; rating of, 119–22; scandals and, 100; scripts for, 62; sex in, 96; social control of, 95–126; sound score for, 56–58; star system, 48, 69; techniques of, 50–54; TV and, 183–87; rating of, 119–22; Westerns, 183–84. *See also* specific companies, directors, films, stars

Motion Picture Association of America (MPAA), 107–10, 116–17, 120–21. *See also* Production Code Administration, MPAA

Motion Picture Patents Company, 46–47, 56

Motion Picture Producers and Distributors of America (MMPDA), 100; AMPP and, 101; PCA and, 104

Motion Picture Production Code, 102; changes in, 116–17; classification system, 117–19; Film Board of National Organizations, 117; rating system, 120–22

Motion Picture Rating System, 120

Movie Channel, 236

Movie industry, 44–94. *See also* Motion pictures

Movie theatres, owners of, 120

MPAA. *See* Motion Picture Association of America

MTV Network, 236

Munsterberg, Hugo, 53

Murdock, Rupert, 92, 233–34

Murrow, Edward R., 170–71, 190–92

Mutual case, 98

Mutual Broadcasting System, 139

National Association for the Advancement of Colored People (NAACP), 157

National Association of Broadcasters (NAB), 135–36, 212, 217, 230

National Association of the Motion Picture Industry, 98–99

National Association of Theatre Owners (NATO), 120

National Board of Review of Motion Pictures, 97

National Broadcasting Company (NBC), Blue network sale, 175–76; CBS rivalry, 165; films and, 186; GE purchase of, 233; networks of, 134–36, 181; Radio City complex, 152

NBC. *See* National Broadcasting Company

National Educational Television (NET), 225

National Public Radio, 209

National Telefilm Associates, 212

Nazi Germany, in films, 79, 81; radio and, 165, 170

Networks, daily news and, 168; early history of, 133–39; FRC and, 146; mergers of, 233; TV newscasts, 206–10; TV programming by, 196–206. *See also* specific networks

News agencies, foreign, 21–24

Newscasts, CNN, 236; local, 209; radio, 133, 166–75; TV, 206–10, 236; wartime, 165–75

Newsday, 233

Newspapers, commerce and, 18–19; commercial, 28–29; dailies, 20–21; early American, 24–25; early English,

20; emergence of, 17; foreign correspondents, 21–24; growth in, 20; hoaxes in, 31; national, 233; penny press, 29–32; press associations, 34–35; pseudo-events in, 37; publicity stunts, 36; radio and, 166, 169; satellite systems, 231; sensationalism in, 37–38

Newsreels, 76–79; Lindbergh case and, 78; war topics, 85

New York *Daily News*, 234

New York *Sun*, 30

New York *Times*, 32, 38–39, 238

New York *Tribune*, 32

New York *World*, 36

Nichols, Mike, 125

Nickelodeons, 46–49

Nielsen ratings, 162–63, 203–06; Audimeters, 203; people meters, 205

Niepce, Joseph Nicephore, 44

Nightly news shows. *See* Newscasts

Nixon, Richard, 225, 227

Noble, Edward, 175

Nudity, film, 121

O'Brien, Willis, 70

Obscenity, context and, 222–23; doctrine, 123; FCC and, 163–64; free speech and, 145; laws, 114–15; new guidelines for, 123–26; on TV talk shows, 221. *See also* specific cases, court decisions

Ochs, Adolphs, 38

O'Connor, Carroll, 200

O'Connor, John J., 238

Office of Censorship, 171

Office of Radio Research, Princeton University, 166

Office of War Information (OWI), 82–83, 173, 175

O'Neill, Eugene, 164

Optical fibers, 232

Option time, 138

Outlaw, The, 106–08

Paar, Jack, 194

Pace, Frank, Jr., 224

Pacifica Foundation, 222

Paley, William, 137–38, 175, 181, 233

Panel presentations, 168

Papermaking, 2–4, 20

Paramount Corporation, 55; directors at, 68; dissolution of, 88; European influence on, 67; Kennedy study, 60; news policy, 77; purchase of, 91; stars at, 67; TV sales of, 185; Zukor and, 60

Paramount News, 78

Paris Adult Theatre I v. Slaton, 124–25

Parsons, Louella, 105

Pathe News, 77

PBL project, 226

PCA. *See* Production Code Administration, MMPA

Penny press, 29–32

People meters, 205

Pickford, Mary, 55, 99

Pilots, TV, 196

Politics, media and, 26; films and, 105; franking privilege, 34; Long and, 168; in movies, 79; radio and, 133; Roosevelt chats, 167; sedition laws, 16

Pornographic movies, 121

Power, Tyrone, 69

Preminger, Otto, 109

Prime time access rule, 219–20

Printing, commerce and, 5–7; cultural change and, 1–43; early financing of, 6; freedom of the press and, 24, 28; invention of, 1–3; licensing of, 13, 17; movable type, 6; Protestantism and, 11–13; public-address potential of, 10; spread of, 4–7; technology of, 19–20, 32; unlicensed, 16; vernacular, 10, 12, 15; world view and, 7. *See also* specific types

Printing Press as an Agent of Change (Eisenstein), 7

Producers, AMPP, 101; MPPDA, 100; independent, 74, 90. *See also* Production Code Administration, MMPA

Production code(s), 116–17

Production Code Administration, MMPA, 104, 106; CARA and, 120–21; rulings of, 116–17

Production Code Review Board, 116

Profanity. *See* Obscenity

Programming, TV, 196–206; newscasts, 206–10; prime-time access rule, 219–20. *See also* specific networks, shows

Program Services Endowment, 228

Propaganda, directors and, 86; films and, 51, 79, 83–84; radio and, 172–73; Senate Subcommittee and, 82; war and, 80–83, 85

Protestantism, Calvin and, 12; iconoclasm of, 14; Luther and, 11; printing and, 11–14

Pseudo-events, 37. *See also* Hoaxes

Public Broadcasting Act (1967), 224

Public Broadcasting Laboratory (PBL), 226

Public Broadcasting Service (PBS), 225

Public Financing Act (1975), 227–28

Public interest, court decisions, 146–47; editorial policy and, 216–19; FCC and, 176–77; newscasts and, 207; program diversity and, 219. *See also* Warner-Hatfield amendment

Public Service Responsibility of Broadcasting (FCC), 176–77

Public Telecommunications Trust, 228

Public television, 212–13, 223–30; Carnegie Commission and, 227–29; duplication of efforts in, 228; federal funding for, 227–28; Reagan funding cuts, 230

Pulitzer, Joesph, 35–38

Puritans, 16

Quiz shows, 194–95

Rabelais, Francois, 9

Racism, media and, 155–56; on newscasts, 167; PBL shows of, 226; on radio, 167; on TV, 200; WLBT-TV case and, 214–16; war and, 173–74

Radicals, U.S., 144

Radio, audience measurement, 161–63; channel licensing, 140–57; early history of, 127–31; First Amendment and, 218, 221; government-industry cooperation, 128–29, 140; hoaxes on, 147–49; manufactures of, 129–31; national conferences, 140, 144; networks, 133–39; newscasts on, 133, 168, 170; patent controls, 143; personalities on, 154–57; propaganda uses of, 172–73; public interest decisions, 146–47; rating services, 162–63; regulation of, 139–57; serials, 157–61; shortwave, 170; survey research, 160–63; technology of, 128–29; variety shows, 154–57; war correspondents, 170–71. *See also* specific companies, shows, stars

Radio Act (1912), 139–41

Radio Act (1927), 142–45

Radio Corporation of America (RCA), 58, 129; control of patents, 143; monopoly charges and, 149; network, 134, 142; UIB and, 136. *See also* National Broadcasting Company

Radio-Keith-Orpheum, 58

Ralston, Vera Hruba, 184

Rating board. *See* Production Code Administration, MMPA

Ratings, TV, 203–06

Raymond, H. J., 38

Reagan, Ronald, 230

Regulation, TV, 210–11

Reis, Irving, 164

Religion, films and, 112; printing and, 2, 12. *See also* specific religions, sects

Republic Pictures, 184

Reuters Agency, 22

Revenue Act (1942), 176

RKO, 70–71; financial structure of, 71; Hearst affair and, 105–06; merger of, 90–91; Pathe News, 77; sale of, 185

Robin Hood, 65

Rockefeller Radio City, 152

Rogers, Ginger, 71

Rogers, Roy, 184

Rollo, Charles J., 157
Roman Catholic Church, Erasmus and, 10; film codes, 103–04, 112; *Index*, 10, 14; Legion of Decency, 103, 110–11; medieval, 2
Roosevelt, Franklin D., 82, 166–67
Rorty, James, 153
"Rowan and Martin's Laugh-In", 199
Royalties, ASCAP, 135–36
Russell, Jane, 106–07, 109
Ryan, John Harold, 174–75

San Francisco *Chronicle*, 40
Sarnoff, David, 58, 175
Satellite TV, 208, cable systems and, 234; dishes, 231
"Saturday Night at the Movies", 186
Scandals, FCC bribes, 211; film industry, 98–99; public resources and, 143; quiz shows, 194–95
Schecter, A.A., 168
Schwartz, Bernard, 211
Scientists, in films, 73–74
Scopes trial, 144
Screenwriters, 62
Scripps chain, 35
Scripts, film, 62
Scriptwriters TV, 188–89
Sedition Act (1798), 28
Sedition laws, 16, Fox Libel Act, 18, 20; Sedition Act, 28
"See It Now" programs, 190–91
Selznick, David O., 62, 74–75
Sensationalism, 38
Serials, radio. *See* specific type
"Sesame Street", 229
Sevareid, Eric, 171
Sex, in films, 96, 99, 103–08, 110–11, 116; pornography, 121–23; on radio, 163–64; rating board and, 121; on TV, 199–200, 221
Shakespeare, William, 165
Shirer, William L., 170–71
Silicon chips, 232
Sixth Report and Order on Television Allocations (FCC), 180
"$64,000 Question", 195

"60 Minutes", 219
Skeleton, Red, 200
Smith, Kate, 174
Soap operas, 159–61; cultural roots of, 161; propaganda and, 173–74
Social problems, economics and, 158; racism, 155–56; radio and, 167
Socialism, 19, in films, 56–58, 69–70; McCarthyism and, 191–93
Social value criterion, 115, 121–23
Sound, in films, 56–58
Spanish-American War, 37–38
Spielberg, Steven, 121
St. Louis *Post Dispatch*, 36
Stamp Act (1765), 17, 25
Stamp tax, 17, 20, 25
Stanley, Henry Morton, 23, 171
Station Program Cooperative, 227
Stationers Company, 13, 15
Studios, film. *See* specific studios
Sullivan, Ed, 182
Surrealism, 54
Survey research, radio, 160–63
Susskind, David, 212
Swayze, John Cameron, 206
Sweeps, TV, 204
Syndication, TV, 202, 220

Talk shows, 194, 221
Taxes, on radio profits, 176
Tele-Communications, Inc., 236
Telefilm production, 186–87
Telegraph, development of, 33–34
Telephones, broadcasting and, 135
Television, 179–238; affiliates, 198, 206–07, 219–20; anthology series, 187–89; cable systems, 230–31, 234–37; chip-based technology of, 232; deregulation of, 219–20; early growth of, 87; educational, 212; film libraries, 185; First Amendment and, 217–19; foreign markets for, 188; HDTV systems, 231; interactive systems, 235; license freeze, 180; lighting systems, 183; live, 182, 187; mediocrity of, 194–96; noncommercial, 180–81; optical fibers and, 232;

pilots, 196–97; prime time access rule, 219–20; profits from, 202; programming decisions, 196–206; quiz show scandals, 194–95; ratings in, 203–06; satellite system, 231; share of audience, 203–06; sweeps, 204; syndication, 202; talk shows, 194; telefilms, 186–87; VCRs and, 205, 231. *See also* Federal Communications Commission; specific networks, shows

Temple, Shirley, 68
Thalberg, Irving, 63
Theatres, adult, 124. *See also* Motion pictures
"This is War" series, 172
Thomas, Lowell, 168
Thurber, James, 160
Tighe, Larry, 171
Time, Inc., 234, 236
Times-Mirror Company, 233–34
Tisch, Laurence A., 233
"Today" show, 194
Transradio Press Service, 168
Tri-Ergon, 59
Truman Doctrine, 191–93
Turner, Ted, 92, 233
Twentieth-Century-Fox, 68; Murdock and, 92, 233; TV sales of, 185
"Twenty-One", 195

UHF TV channels, 181
United Artists (UA), 74, 89
United Independent Broadcasters (UIB), 136
United Press (UP) Association, 35
United Press International (UPI), 35, 168
U.S. Supreme Court, fairness doctrine and, 217; FCC and, 175; Fox decision, 59; movie classification and, 119; on movie industry, 88; obscenity and, 114–15, 119, 123–24, 222–23
U.S. v. Orito, 124
United States v. Twelve 200-Foot Reels of Super 8mm Film, 125

U.S. Constitution. *See* First Amendment, U.S. Constitution
UHF TV channels, 181
Universal Pictures, 73–74; Decca purchase, 91; newsreels of, 77; TV sales of, 185
Universum Film Aktiengesellschaft (UFA), 67
USA Network, 236
USA Today, 233

Valenti, Jack, 118, 120–21
Variety, 54
Vaudeville, 154–57, 182
VCRs. *See* Video cassette recorders
VHF-TV channels, 181, 212
Victor Talking Machine, 137
Video cassette recorders, 205, 231
Vietnam War, TV and, 225
Violence, in films, 121
Vitaphone Corporation, 57
von Sternberg, Josef, 67

Wagner-Hatfield Amendment, 150, 168
Wall Street Journal, 39
War, 80; advertising during, 176; censorship and, 171–72; films and, 80–83, 105; Office of Censorship, 171; racism and, 173–74; radio and, 128–29, 169–75; TV documentaries on, 225–26. *See also* Newsreels
War Bond Day, 174
Ward, Douglas Turner, 226
"War of the Worlds", 165–66
Warner Amex Cable Communications, 235–36
Warner Bros., 56–57; films of, 63–67; TV shows of, 186
Warner Brothers-Seven Arts Ltd., 91
Warner Communications, 91–92, 235
Washington Post Company, 234
Wayne, John, 184
Weaver, Pat, 194
Webb, Jack, 182
Welles, Orson, 164–66
Wells, H.G., 165
West, Mae, 103, 163

Western Associated Press, 35
Western Electric, 56
Western Union, 33–34
Westerns, TV, 183
Westinghouse, 129, 134–36
"Wheel of Fortune", 220
White Citizen's Council, 215
Who's Afraid of Virginia Wolf?, 118
WGCB case, 218
Wireless Telegraph and Signal Company, 128
WLBT-TV case, 214–16
Wolff Agency, 22

Wong, Hai-sheng, 77
Wood, Robert D., 201
Wynn, Ed, 154

Yates, Herbert J., 184
Yellow journalism, 76

Zanuck, Darryl, 69
Zenger trial, 24–25
Zenith Radio Corporation, 141
Ziv Television Productions, 187
Zukor, Adolph, 48, 55, 60, 138

About the Author

Robert Henry Stanley has a Ph.D. in Communication and Social Psychology from Ohio University. He taught for several years in the Department of Theatre and Speech Arts at Mount Holyoke College in South Hadley, Massachusetts. He also served as Chair of the Department of Communications at Hunter College of the City University of New York for five years and is currently Professor of Media Studies at that College. His publications include three books: *The Broadcast Industry, The Media Environment* (coauthored with Charles S. Steinberg), and *The Celluloid Empire*. His professional activities have included coordinating faculty/industry seminars for the International Radio and Television Society, and serving on the board of directors of the New York World Television Festival. He has also served for many years as a judge for the Edward R. Murrow Brotherhood Awards and the International Emmy Awards of the National Academy of Television Arts and Sciences.